CHASING CHANCES

How Smart People
Lose Money Investing

ADAM DAWSON, CFP®

ISBN 979-8-9887114-0-7 (hardcover)
ISBN 979-8-218-17478-1 (paperback)

Printed in the United States of America

CHASING CHANCES

To Ron Leavitt and Jeff Burr,
for granting me the career opportunity of a lifetime
and for being the best partners anyone could ever hope for.

ACKNOWLEDGMENTS

My favorite song from the Broadway musical *Wicked*, "For Good," starts with the words, "I've heard it said that people come into our lives for a reason, bringing something we must learn, and we are led to those who help us most to grow if we let them, and we help them in return." I get emotional whenever I hear it because countless people have changed my life for good.

I owe everything I know and everything I am to others who have touched my life. This book includes vital lessons I've learned from a myriad of financial analysts and successful investors who generously shared the knowledge and experience they acquired over a lifetime of investing and studying how markets work.

Although the influences that shaped this book are too many to count, I would especially like to acknowledge the founders and thought leaders of Dimensional Fund Advisors. The pioneering works of Eugene Fama, Kenneth French, David Booth, Dave Butler, Gerard O'Reilly, Weston Wellington, Apollo Lupescu, Jake DeKinder, Savina Rizova, Wes Crill, and many others have profoundly impacted my approach to managing wealth and coaching investors to improve their chances of success.

Thanks also to my fabulous team and wonderful clients for everything you have taught me and for making my work so fulfilling. I am humbled by and grateful for the honor of serving you.

Most importantly, I appreciate my dear wife, Andrea, for being my best support and most frequent sounding board throughout this project. She is a wise and patient counselor, without whom I could not have completed it. If you're considering marrying an author, talk to her first so you'll know how much time you might have to spend discussing book title ideas.

CONTENTS

INTRODUCTION   1

The Tragic Tale of an Ill-Fated Investor   2

The Elusive Easy Street   6

Learning the Right Lessons   9

The Road to Success   12

CHAPTER 1: TIMING THE MARKET   15

The Pipe Dream of Perfect Timing   15

Waiting for the Skies to Clear   18

What Goes Up Must Come Down   21

The Santa Claus Rally   24

Barbers, Bartenders, and Brothers-In-Law   27

It's on TV, So It Must Be True   30

The World Is Coming to an End…Again   37

Yeah, But This Time It's Different   38

Heaven Help Us if _____ Wins the Election   43

Time In the Market, Not Timing the Market   45

Key Points of Chapter 1   47

CHAPTER 2: PICKING STOCKS   49

Nothing but the Best for My Peeps   49

What Goes Up Must Keep Going Up   51

FAANG FOMO   53

Kings of the Hill   55

I Shop There All the Time   58

I Knew That Stock Was Gonna Explode   60

The Illusion of Control   63

Day Trading Disasters 66

Playing with the Big Boys 68

Moneyball and the Vanishing Edge 70

One Egg, One Basket 71

Key Points of Chapter 2 77

CHAPTER 3: CHASING WHAT'S HOT 79

Tantalizing Track Records 79

Tech Fever 84

IPO Hype 87

The Rise and Fall of GameStop 88

Margin Calls & the Crash of 1929 91

They're Called Junk Bonds for a Reason 98

Gold, Gas, and Ground Beef 102

They're Not Making Any More Land 109

Cryptocurrency: The Final Frontier? 120

If It Sounds Too Good to Be True… 125

Key Points of Chapter 3 134

CHAPTER 4: GOING BROKE SAFELY 137

Getting Out of Bed Is Risky 137

Taming the Beast 139

The Risks of Not Investing 142

Your Bank Is Laughing All the Way to the Bank 145

The Promise of High Returns with "No Risk" 146

Key Points of Chapter 4 154

CHAPTER 5: IGNORING COSTS 155

The House Always Wins 155

The True Cost of Free Trading   158

Poisonous Free Lunches   160

The Termites in Your Portfolio   165

Everyone Can Win   171

Stacking the Deck in Your Favor   174

Key Points of Chapter 5   177

CHAPTER 6: DISREGARDING DISCLOSURES   **179**

Who Reads All That Gibberish?   179

Trust, But Verify   182

What You Don't Know Can Hurt You   186

So Sorry I Forgot to Tell You That Part   191

Learning to Love Worst-Case Scenarios   196

Owner's Manuals Are Underrated   201

Key Points of Chapter 6   204

CHAPTER 7: HARNESSING THE POWER OF THE MARKET   **205**

Discover What Drives Investment Returns   205

Embrace Uncertainty   210

Improve Your Investing Experience   213

DIY if You Dare   229

Hire a Coach, Not a Salesperson   236

Optimism Is the Only Realism   241

Key Points of Chapter 7   249

ABOUT THE AUTHOR   **251**

GLOSSARY   **253**

NOTES   **273**

INTRODUCTION

Have you ever felt frustrated or confused when you lost a lot of money on an investment you were convinced would perform well? Would you like to learn why that may have happened and how you can improve your chances of success?

If so, this book is for you. The first six chapters reveal the true reasons why many investors fail. The last chapter illustrates the antidote.

Life is like a race against time. We are all chasing a better life for ourselves and our loved ones, and we only have so many years to accomplish our goals.

While everyone's ambitions are unique, most people want to enjoy a prosperous lifestyle for the rest of their lives without having to work forever. They also hope to leave a meaningful legacy for others. Simple, right?

As I'm sure you know all too well, it's not as simple as it sounds. Very few people can accomplish these objectives without growing their money through investments, but the world of investing can be treacherous.

Many ventures that promise to shortcut the process send us back to start instead, like an infuriating game of Chutes and Ladders. When we fall behind because we didn't get going early enough or lost a fortune on failed bets, we feel even more pressure to catch up by chasing higher and higher returns.

For over two decades, I have been helping hundreds of people manage their investments. During that time, I have observed that many investors take more risk than necessary, attempting to achieve their financial goals as quickly as possible. They have no idea they are playing with fire until it's too late. After suffering significant losses, some assume that if they were smarter, spent more time learning about investing, or followed the market more closely, they could have prevented such regretful outcomes.

They don't realize that many really smart people who study the market for a living regularly lose large sums, too. If even the pros get it wrong so often, how can anyone find reliable success?

Conventional investing practices have failed us. Many popular strategies are based on false notions of predictability that underestimate risk and exaggerate potential rewards. They are also designed to take money out of your pocket and put it in the pockets of financial institutions.

What's the impact? In 2022, 40 percent of Americans feared they might never be able to retire, and the average retirement savings per household was only $65,000.[1] With inflation skyrocketing to the highest levels in decades and almost every type of investment having lost significant value in 2022, many investors became more mystified than ever about how to make their money grow fast enough to have some hope of a decent retirement.

A lot of people simply haven't been saving enough, but millions of responsible, hard-working people who *have* consistently invested substantial sums throughout their careers are still not on track to reach their retirement goals. The closer they get to retirement age, the more pressure they feel to earn big money quickly to make up for lost ground.

They thought they did everything they were supposed to—what went wrong? Let's travel back in time to evaluate why many people have not had as much investing success as they hoped.

As we revisit the impact of a series of disastrous events on investors over the past several decades, reflect on how you or someone you love felt when going through similar experiences. If you haven't been in any of these situations, consider what you would do if you were in a comparable position.

THE TRAGIC TALE OF AN ILL-FATED INVESTOR

Imagine you are starting your first job out of grad school in the early 1990s, excited to finally make money after what felt like an eternity of education. Throughout your life, you have heard that you should "make your money work for you so you don't always have to work for money."

After many years of grueling schooling, getting to the point of not having to work can't come quickly enough, so you want your money to start working for you right away. Although you have been waiting patiently to buy that house and brand new Mercedes you've had your eye on for years, you decide to put these off just a little longer.

Not knowing where to start, you subscribe to *The Wall Street Journal* and begin listening to financial talk radio. Many experts seem to agree that a 401(k) is the best place to start, so you begin contributing as much as possible to your employer's retirement plan. You continue depositing the maximum amount allowed every year, even when you feel you can't afford it.

Throughout most of the 1990s, you can't believe how well this plan is working. The stock market keeps climbing and an exciting new sensation called the World Wide Web appears destined to change the world.

Your latest 401(k) account statement says that your average annual rate of return has been 15 percent per year so far. Not sure whether that's good, you plug that percentage into a retirement planning calculator to see where you stand.

Sure enough, it shows that if you keep earning 15 percent per year, you should easily be able to retire by age 65, if not sooner. You're elated that it looks like you won't have to work forever and glad you made the sacrifice to start saving early in your career.

But your friend bursts your bubble. She boasts that she made over 300 percent last year in a mutual fund filled with "dot-com" startup company stocks. Suddenly you're frustrated that you only earned 15 percent and you move all your money to that fund immediately. Then something unexpected happens.

In 2000, the dot-com bubble bursts, and your 401(k) loses over 70 percent of its value. Shortly after, the stock market's response to 9/11 drives your account values even lower. You grieve over the years of hard work and sacrifice lost. How will you ever be able to recover from this?

Everyone on the news and your colleagues at work are advising you to cash out, proclaiming that internet stocks are dead and that the market will never recover from a loss this big. Adding insult to injury, you are laid off and have no idea what to do next.

After months of looking for a new job, no one seems to be hiring in your field. Since you have no other savings besides your 401(k), you cash out what's left, pay the taxes and penalties, and start your own business.

The business requires much more cash to get going than you expected, so you don't pay yourself much for the first several years. You wonder, "Maybe this is what they meant by making my money work for me, but it sure is taking a while." If only you could get your business to a point where you wouldn't have to work so hard, maybe you could enjoy life a little more.

Several years later your sense of hope and excitement returns. Your company becomes quite profitable, so you can finally buy that Mercedes and build that beautiful custom home you and your spouse have always dreamed of.

Calls from competitors start rolling in regularly, offering astonishing amounts to buy your business. You're surprised and flattered by how much they're willing to pay, but you turn down every offer. You're making more than ever and you're not ready to hand over your cash cow that easily, especially after working so hard to get to this point. Besides, you're hopeful that one of your kids will want to take over the business someday.

Despite the growth of your company, the counsel you always heard to make your money work for you lingers in the back of your mind. Now that your business doesn't require every penny of your earnings to keep it afloat, you decide to invest in something besides your company again.

Although the stock market is showing signs of recovery, you vowed never to touch stocks again. Real estate values are skyrocketing, so you decide to look into that.

Throughout 2006 it seems like your neighbor is buying another rental property every few months, bragging that he has doubled his money in the past three years. You think to yourself, "That looks pretty good. Houses and land can't disappear into thin air like my internet stocks did, so I'm sure that's a lot safer."

You're reluctant to buy rental properties because you've heard horror stories about being a landlord. Besides, you have recently taken a large loan from the bank to buy a building for your business and don't want to take on any more debt. You wonder how you might be able to participate in the incredible real estate growth surrounding you without borrowing anything.

In 2007 you attend a seminar where they guarantee a 14 percent annual return in real estate without having to do any work or requiring loans from the bank. Instead, you would be loaning money to real estate developers through trust deeds, and the value of the land would secure your principal and interest payments.

This is precisely what you were looking for. Stocks certainly couldn't provide a guarantee like that, and worst-case scenario, the land would always be there, so you could simply sell your portion if things went south.

Since your savings account at the bank only pays 2 percent, you decide to pull out $500,000—almost all your savings—and put it in trust deeds. When you hand them the check, they explain that if you let them hold the interest payments and pay you in full when the projects are completed, instead of paying interest to you monthly, you will earn 16 percent per year instead of 14 percent.

Even better! You don't need the income anyway, so you accept their generous offer.

Things hum along well for the first six months. You receive monthly statements showing your account growing by 16 percent, just as promised, so you send them another $50,000. You may finally be able to earn back everything you lost in those cursed dot-com stocks and revive your hope of being able to retire after all!

Then the unimaginable happens. Real estate prices tumble. Construction grinds to a halt on the projects you helped fund.

The developers are in continual litigation, eating up much of the fund's cash reserves in attorneys' fees, with no sign of resolution. Although the value of the land backs your investment, the land is now worth only a fifth of what it was before, and your deposits are pooled with at least 100 other investors.

Needless to say, you never see the $550,000 again. In fact, you never even receive a single interest payment since you chose to have it all paid out when the project was completed.

As if you're not already discouraged enough, the dramatic downturn of the economy in 2008 causes your business profits to fall by 30 percent. You're getting burned out and growing more and more frustrated. You're working harder than ever but can never seem to get ahead.

You lament, "Why won't my money ever work for me so I can stop working so hard? I've tried desperately to invest in what I thought would give me the best chances of getting there, and no matter what I try, it never works!"

You were hoping by this point that at least one of your children would want to work in your business so you could slow down and let them run it, but none of them are interested. Although you have excellent employees who are very loyal, none of them have the ability or desire to run the company.

You decide, "Maybe it's time to sell to one of those competitors who kept knocking on my door. I don't know how much longer I can do this. I don't have the energy or drive I used to, and I want to spend more time with my family doing the fun things we've always wanted to do."

So you reach out to those who were anxious to buy you out, but no one is interested. You have the business appraised and are disheartened to discover it's only worth half as much as you had been offered just a couple of years earlier.

How could this be? You feel more pressure than ever to earn high returns so you don't have to work for the rest of your life, but you can't bear the thought of losing another penny. You resolve to keep all your money at the bank earning less than 1 percent, where at least you know it's safe.

You start to wonder whether you will ever be able to retire. What should you do now?

THE ELUSIVE EASY STREET

Can you relate to any of this tragic tale? I wish it were just a fairy tale. Unfortunately, various versions of those events have really happened to many people I know.

Why is it often so hard to make money investing? The answer is much simpler than it seems, but it isn't easy to implement in real life. Too many people chase a more leisurely life by taking big chances on investments that promise to quickly solve all their financial woes, only to be repeatedly disappointed.

We're all looking for the easy way out. It's human nature. We constantly demand that everything be faster, cheaper, and easier than ever. Amazon Prime still isn't fast enough for my kids. "What? I have to wait two whole days?"

Unfortunately, most of the best things in life don't work like that. Successful careers, meaningful relationships, and abs like Ryan Reynolds' all require effort, patience, and sacrifice.

They also require a certain amount of risk. We want to see the end from the beginning, but that's not usually possible. How many things in your life have turned out exactly as you expected?

There are no guarantees in life. If we're not willing to take any chances, we will never accomplish anything great. Hockey Hall of Famer Wayne Gretzky said it best: "You miss 100 percent of the shots you don't take."[2]

We often think of uncertainty as bad, but it can work in our favor. Growing up in a broken family that struggled a lot financially, I worried about whether I could have a good marriage and successful career.

Despite this uncertainty, I pressed forward in faith and tried my best to do everything within my power to succeed. I've had my share of challenges along the way, just like everyone, but I'm humbled and grateful that my life has generally turned out much better than I ever dreamed it would.

Marrying my wife, Andrea, required a leap of faith, but now, more than 20 years later, she's still the best thing that has ever happened to me, and I'm more in love with her than ever before. Our marriage has not been perfect, especially because of my shortcomings, but it has brought me more joy than I imagined possible.

Becoming a partner at Capstone Capital Wealth Advisors with Ron Leavitt and Jeff Burr in 2016 also required a leap of faith because I was happy at another firm where I had been working for over 10 years. Now I can't believe it ever felt like a risk to make the move because we have had way more success and fun together than I could have predicted. Thank goodness I took that chance, because being a partner at Capstone Capital Wealth

Advisors has been the highlight of my career and one of the greatest highlights of my life.

Yes, uncertainty can bring us great joy, but it can also result in severe disappointment. Not all risks are worth taking. Although we seldom see the end from the beginning, we can improve our chances of success by taking prudent risks. This means we study options, weigh pros and cons, and seek counsel from trusted guides before deciding.

For example, I didn't marry Andrea until after I got to know her well over a long time in a variety of situations, got to know her family, and talked with her at length about who she really was and what she really wanted from life. I didn't leave my great job at another firm to take a chance on Capstone Capital Wealth Advisors before meeting with Ron and Jeff several times, studying the numbers, writing lists of pros and cons, and discussing it at length with my wife and trusted mentors.

I've met people who got engaged after knowing each other only a few weeks, people who jumped into a career simply because someone told them they could make a lot of money at it, and people who poured hundreds of thousands of dollars into investments they knew nothing about simply because they sounded good on the surface. Of course, these scenarios could work out if you're lucky, but why not take your time and do a little homework to increase your chances of success before making such potentially life-changing decisions?

When it comes to investing, anyone can promise huge returns with little to no risk, but what are the real risks? (There are always risks, don't let anyone fool you.) Here are some examples of questions that can help you take prudent risks rather than jumping in simply because an investment looks good at first glance:

- What are the best-case and worst-case scenarios?
- What are the costs?
- How much experience do they have with this type of investment and how well has it performed in the past?
- How does it fit with your goals and other assets?

It saddens me to see so many hard-working, honest people suffer huge losses unnecessarily. Too many people take bold, unnecessary chances because they feel like they have to catch up. Most of the time it puts them even further behind and they don't realize they could probably accomplish their goals faster without taking so much risk.

I am passionate about helping people avoid the devastating consequences of poor financial decisions because I know how it feels not to have any money. As the oldest of 10 children with divorced parents and living on welfare throughout much of my childhood, I learned the value of money at a young age.

We were grateful to have enough to eat most of the time, but we dreamed that one day we might enjoy luxuries like new clothes, Christmas presents, a couch without rips and stains, and a car that didn't need to be refilled with oil every other week. My mom and stepdad perpetually convinced us that our situation was temporary and that success was just around the corner, but a quick, easy solution never came.

Maybe we're all born with the tendency to search for effortless solutions to our financial dilemmas, but we must resist the urge because it usually ends in heartache. Easy street eludes us for a reason: life is not meant to be easy, and few things are truly free.

LEARNING THE RIGHT LESSONS

You know the frustration of losing money if you have invested long enough. It doesn't take much effort to go from making a lot to losing a lot.

Ideally, over time we would all become better investors by learning from our mistakes. However, too many people learn the wrong lessons from their losses.

Some people who lose money in stocks, mutual funds, exchange-traded funds (also known as ETFs, which are tax-efficient funds that trade like stocks), real estate, and other assets conclude they must be poor investments. (See the Glossary at the end for definitions of these and other investing terms found throughout this book.)

In reality, these can all be excellent investments, but those people may not have invested properly or given it enough time. Giving up on investing in general due to a bad experience is like saying you'll never date again because your last boyfriend was a jerk.

Most major investment failures stem from common misconceptions that appeal to human nature. Our natural emotions of fear and greed lead us to try to predict the perfect times to enter and exit the market, pick the best stocks, and chase the hottest new trends.

These strategies might work at times. However, decades of academic research performed by a number of analysts with PhDs in finance and Nobel Prizes in economics show that they are not reliable methods for achieving positive investment outcomes. They tend to result in large losses and lost hope.

Much of the financial media and many big brokerage firms capitalize on our emotions and encourage us to invest in these ways because it makes them more money, even when it's not good for us. Michael Jackson even wrote a song about brokerage firms: "All I wanna say is that they don't really care about us."[3]

When I speak of the harmful effects of fear, I refer to our universal fear of losing money and concern about what other people think of us. Sometimes our investment decisions are influenced too much by unfounded anxiety over potential losses, peer pressure, or our desire to keep up with the Joneses.

When I describe the impact of greed, I allude to our innate desire to acquire wealth as quickly and easily as possible. Greed is often defined as a selfish, insatiable appetite for more and more of the things we don't really need, but that's not what I'm talking about. Most of my clients are generous, gracious people whom I would not call greedy, but they still want to make as much money as possible with the least amount of time and effort required. There is nothing wrong with that type of greed, as long as we don't seek it at others' expense or allow it to supersede good judgment.

The instincts of fear and greed are not inherently bad—at a fundamental level, they are essential for survival. However, if we don't keep them in check, they can lead us to make irrational, imprudent choices that harm our financial and emotional well-being.

Most investors have no idea how much their susceptibility to these powerful instincts are hurting their wealth-building efforts.

My objective throughout this book is to open your eyes to the futility of many popular practices that ruin returns. The lessons we will discuss are based on decades of research and my observation of many people who have failed by following these practices.

The first six chapters include a lot of doom and gloom, so at times you might feel like this is just a depressing book about a bunch of investment strategies that don't work. After all, the subtitle is "How Smart People Lose Money Investing," and most people already feel like they're pros at that!

Don't worry, we won't stop there. In Chapter 7, you will learn proven investment solutions that have consistently worked for many who have built *and kept* substantial wealth. But first you need to know the main reasons why so many people fail.

Since the stories throughout this book are real-life examples, I have omitted any potentially identifiable information to protect anonymity. I share them in humility and deep gratitude for the lessons I learned from these people. I also do so with respect for everyone willing to take risks to grow their money and sympathy for those who have suffered devastating losses. If any of these examples can help others avoid similar frustration, perhaps their losses will not have been entirely in vain.

Some of these accounts might make you laugh; others might make your heart sink. If you see glimpses of yourself in any of them, don't worry—we've all been there, and we're laughing and crying with you. Remember, I share them to expose common investing myths that distort most people's mindsets, so you're not alone.

If you are frustrated that you have already lost a fortune investing when you were trying to be smart about it, don't lose hope. Investing can be a powerful tool to help you achieve your goals when utilized appropriately. It doesn't have to be complicated, and you don't have to be an expert to succeed.

You just need to learn the basics about where returns come from, build a prudent plan based on your goals, set realistic expectations for the inevitable ups and downs, and avoid the common pitfalls we will discuss throughout this book.

THE ROAD TO SUCCESS

Contrast the fear and frustration of the ill-fated investor we discussed earlier to the experience of one of my successful business owner clients who learned the proper lessons from his investment mishaps. Despite all the ups and downs, he has continually invested in the stock market throughout his career. He also bought several rental properties over time, aggressively paying off all debts as quickly as possible, so he is now debt-free.

Although he believed in the power of the stock market, he couldn't understand why he never seemed to be able to make much money in it. He worked with a few different financial advisors over the years. No matter whom he worked with, he always felt like they were the only ones making any real money, even when the market was doing well.

When I first met him, he was frustrated by his perpetually dismal returns and that his current advisor made him do so much of the work. Whenever he was concerned about a specific investment in his account, the advisor would typically respond with something like, "Good point. Yes, we should probably get rid of that."

Periodically, the advisor would call to recommend changing a particular stock or mutual fund or suggest it was time to exit a specific market sector. Then the advisor would send him a ton of reading material, asking him to study the options and let him know what he thought would be best.

This client would then spend many sleepless nights at the end of each long workday trying to make sense of it all, overwhelmed with having to decide on something he didn't completely understand. He felt obligated to constantly stay on top of the latest financial news and research how all his investments were performing because clearly, he couldn't trust his advisor to do so.

Why did everything have to be on his shoulders? What was he paying his advisor for?

He began to worry that he might never be able to retire. His business is very labor-intensive and he was starting to develop aches and pains, wondering how much longer he could work. He also wanted to spend more time with his wife and grandkids.

I was honored that he was willing to give my team and me an opportunity to serve him, especially since he didn't have the best experience with other advisors. First, we helped him and his wife clarify their goals so we could understand what kind of lifestyle they wanted in retirement. Then we helped them develop a solid financial plan so they could see what they needed to do to accomplish those goals.

After discussing various options to determine how much fluctuation they could tolerate, we evaluated their investment portfolio to see why they might have been so disappointed with their returns. We helped them see where they had been taking more risk than necessary and how excessive hidden fees were eating into their performance.

We built a new set of investments for them with much lower fees and a more organized structure. Since then, my team and I have met with them many times over the years to update their plan as needed, review their investment performance, advise them on current market conditions, and continue educating them on a variety of financial topics. We have never called them with hot new tips or asked them to research how they think we should manage their investments. We simply handle it all for them because we know their objectives.

In one of our recent meetings, I was touched when his wife exclaimed with emotion, "We can't tell you how much we appreciate everything you have done for us. My husband is much happier than before we started working with you. He doesn't watch the financial news anymore or stress about every down day in the market. He hardly even looks at our investment accounts. He has full confidence in your team and your approach and has been very happy with the results. Most importantly, he has hope that he will be able to retire in a few years, and he spends more time with me and our grandkids than he had in a long time."

This made my day because I respect both of them a lot. They have worked really hard and sacrificed much throughout their careers to save substantial amounts of money and invest it wisely, so they deserve to be at peace about their financial future. No one who works that hard should have to worry so much about their investments or whether they will ever be able to retire.

I don't share this story to disparage their former advisors. I'm sure they were doing the best they could with the tools they had.

Neither do I share this story to brag. Quite the opposite: these clients deserve the credit for having the courage and patience to try yet another approach to achieving their goals, despite former disappointments. I am humbled and grateful that we were able to help them simplify their life, enhance their peace of mind, and find real hope for a better future.

I wish I could promise the same outcome for you. Unfortunately, there are no guarantees in life. Your level of success will depend on a variety of factors. However, applying the principles we will discuss in this book can boost your likelihood of attaining a similar result.

Buckle your seat belt because much of what I'm about to say may fly in the face of what you think investing is all about. Some of the stories might seem like extreme examples that are unlikely to happen to you, but remember that every account is authentic. Of course, not everyone's results would be as dramatic, but the unfortunate outcomes I share are more common than you might think. I include them to expose lesser-known risks of less-effective tactics because salespeople tend to emphasize best-case scenarios and downplay the downsides.

To be clear, you *could* make a lot of money with any of the strategies I am criticizing. However, as I mentioned earlier, based on decades of research by many well-respected analysts, they are more likely to make you lose a lot of money over time. I'm tired of seeing so many intelligent, responsible people lose their money and their minds following the advice of incompetent or devious guides who make promises they can't keep.

Hang in there for the first six chapters because they get a bit dismal. After learning why many things you have been taught about investing might not have worked as well as you expected, the solutions in Chapter 7 will be more meaningful. That's where we'll discuss how to increase your probability of success through a more prudent, disciplined approach.

What financial dreams are you chasing, and how can I help improve your chances of attaining them? Read on.

CHAPTER 1

TIMING THE MARKET

THE PIPE DREAM OF PERFECT TIMING

When is the best time to invest? I'll tell you as soon as you tell me who will be the next president of the United States or when it will rain again in Las Vegas.

This is probably the most common question investors ask me. Believe me, I wish I knew! Many experts pretend to know, and occasionally some get lucky. However, no one can consistently predict the best time to invest.

It is a perfectly rational question, though. Everyone knows that the secret to making money in any investment is to buy low and sell high. So why not just invest at the lowest point, just in time for the next big spike in the market?

It sounds so obvious and simple, but it's almost impossible to implement in the real world. The market goes up and down all day every day with no consistent patterns, so the bottom usually cannot be identified until months after the fact.

Strangely, the market often has a huge run-up while the economic picture still looks very bleak. Why? Because those who invest are seeking an expectation of future growth. Many investors don't realize that the market is forward-looking, so it tends to recover long before the rest of the economy.

In two-thirds of the recessions that have occurred since 1980, the stock market already bottomed out well before the National Bureau of Economic Research even announced that we were in a recession. In the COVID-related recession of 2020, the market reached its lowest point in March, a full three months before the official recession announcement in June 2020.

As of the time of this writing, the best-performing month in the U.S. stock market for the past 25 years was March 22-April 22, 2020. Do you remember how you felt right after most of the world was shut down for the first time in history due to COVID-19? Were you excited to invest, confident that the market would soon recover? Few could have predicted that would be the market's best-performing month in 25 years. Sometimes the greatest gains immediately follow the largest losses, when most people least expect a market surge, as you can see in Figure 1.

Figure 1: S&P 500 Historical Prices, Jan-Dec 2020[1]

Any guesses as to when the best-performing week in the market was during the past 25 years? You may be just as surprised to learn it was the week ending on November 28, 2008, at the height of the Great Recession. At the time, were you thinking that would be a great time to invest? If you cashed out during that week in response to all the turmoil, or during March and April of 2020 as mentioned above, you would have ended up with lower returns over the past 25 years than if you had simply stayed invested through the ups and downs.[2]

Every year Dalbar Research performs a study comparing actual stock market returns to the average returns that all investors collectively earn in the market. The results consistently show that over rolling 20-year periods, investors as a whole tend to earn 3 percent to 5 percent *less* per year on average than the market.

This is largely due to investors' efforts to get in and out of the market at the right times rather than staying the course through the ups and downs. After a big market decline, many investors sell their stocks to wait for things to get better, locking in their losses. After substantial market increases, they finally feel comfortable getting back in, perhaps just in time for another drop, missing out on the chance to recover their losses.

Even if you were able to find someone who had timed the market successfully in the past, how would you measure whether they did it by skill or by sheer luck? How would you know whether they could do it again?

Above all, why would they share their secret with you? Wouldn't they make a lot more money investing only their own funds with their magical methods?

Many so-called experts know they can make more money selling their supposed market timing mojo than they can make in their own investments. Investors so desperately want to know the "right time" to enter and exit the market that they'll listen to practically anyone who claims with conviction that they can predict what's going to happen, whether it's true or not. The fact that they're willing to tell you what's going to happen should be enough of a clue that they have no clue.

Perfect market timing is merely a pipe dream. The secret to successful investing is *time in* the market, not *timing* the market. I'll demonstrate why throughout this chapter.

Right now you may be thinking, "I know that no one can time the market—I would never do that." Still, you unknowingly may be falling prey to other myths that sound logical but are clever disguises for timing the market. As we explore these common misconceptions throughout the rest of this chapter, take note of which ones might be impacting you the most.

WAITING FOR THE SKIES TO CLEAR

The seemingly bottomless market free-fall from October 2007 to March 2009 due to the sub-prime mortgage crisis resulted in the greatest losses in the market since the Great Depression. You remember those days. Most people's 401(k) melted down to a "201(k)" and many who were planning to retire had to work several years longer.

In March of 2009, when the market finally hit bottom, many people were afraid to invest because financial newscasters were sounding alarms like, "Get out now before it's too late! If you thought the first 50 percent drop was bad, you ain't seen nothin' yet—another 50 percent drop is right around the corner."

Unemployment persisted at record highs. Not a single ray of hope would peak through the storm clouds to grant a glimpse of recovery.

Many felt they could no longer endure the beatings and sold all their investments at the bottom. It was already too painful to watch half of their hard-earned money vanish and they couldn't bear the thought of losing more. They jumped out of the boat in the middle of the storm to wait for the sailing to look smooth again.

But the stock market didn't seem to care about the state of the economy. It brazenly ignored all warnings and almost doubled in value over the next year. Everyone who jumped out at the height of the storm missed out on that extraordinary recovery.

Thankfully, most of my firm's clients stuck to their investment strategy through it all. Everyone who stayed in the boat eventually recovered their losses and earned a healthy return in the end.

Sadly, a small handful couldn't hang on long enough. One in particular stands out who invested $1 million close to the peak of the market and rode it all the way down to about $500,000. She was an accounting professor at a prestigious university and was certain things would get worse before they got better.

Despite our best efforts to convince her otherwise, she finally pulled the plug a few days before the market hit bottom in March 2009. She never invested again, so she never recovered from her losses. Her extremely unfortunate outcome was a classic example of Dave Ramsey's famous admonition, "The only people who get hurt on a roller coaster are the ones who jump off."

What was this poor professor's biggest mistake—investing at the peak just in time to feel the full wrath of the crash? If all her knowledge of finance had enabled her to predict the drop so she could have avoided the losses, would she have been better off?

In 2017 I met a man who did accurately predict this market plunge. He was an IT expert who studied the stock market every day and enjoyed doing his own investing. In July 2007, he pulled all his money out of the market. This was impeccable timing because just a few months later the market began its roughly 50 percent decline over the course of the next 17 months.

I had met a lot of people who tried to exit the market at the right time during that horrific period, but most of them didn't get out until *after* they had already lost 50 percent, like our accounting professor client. I had never met anyone who timed it as well as this IT expert, so I was impressed.

I was curious, "How did you know when to get out?"

He boasted, "I watch the market every day and spend a lot of time reading the financial news. I felt like things were getting really overpriced and I could tell that a recession was coming, so I sold everything and put it in cash until I could determine the right time to get back in."

Now I was even more curious, "How did you figure out the right time to get back in?"

My heart sank as he responded, "Oh, it's still not the right time to get back in. I have been watching it every day since 2007, and I'm waiting for the right opportunity."

Still not the right time to invest after 10 years of waiting? Did he realize that if he had just stayed in the market those full 10 years, riding the 50 percent plunge all the way down and patiently holding onto his stocks throughout the long recovery, his investments would likely have grown to about two-and-a-half times the value they were when I met him?[3]

He knew he had missed out on some growth, but I didn't have the heart to tell him the true cost of his nearly perfect prediction. He still thinks he's the smartest guy in the world and will probably never fully recognize his lost opportunity. I don't know if he ever reinvested, but I certainly hope he did because market values have grown substantially higher since 2017, even after suffering significant losses in 2020 and 2022.

It's tragic enough that this highly educated, hard-working investor missed out on such a major wealth creation opportunity. Add to that the enormous loss of his time, energy, and emotional anguish trying to figure out the right time to get back in the market every day for at least 10 years.

People don't often think about the value of their time, but it can really add up. Even if he only spent an hour a day studying the market and made $100 an hour at his job, that would have cost him at least $300,000 in lost time over those 10 years. Even worse, all that time was wasted because he never took action on anything he learned. The aggregate costs of trying to time the market can be astounding even if you make an accurate guess.

This story illustrates an even bigger challenge with timing the market effectively: you must be right twice in a row. It's hard enough to be right once like my IT expert friend, but to be right twice is next to impossible. It's simply too unpredictable.

I always chuckle when newscasters say things like, "There is uncertainty in the market today." Really? Show me a single day there *wasn't* uncertainty in the market. The only thing certain about the market is that it is always uncertain, so it should be expected. That's why it can produce such high returns.

Some people think they can reduce their anxiety by selling their investments after a big loss, but this is often replaced with a new anxiety my teens call FOMO (Fear of Missing Out). It can be just as frustrating to sit on the sidelines while the market climbs, especially if you recently experienced heavy losses and got out to avoid losing more.

Then you are faced with an even more difficult question: when do you get back in? After a rally, do you invest because the market is showing signs of recovery, or will you get on the roller coaster just in time for it to fall again?

Waiting for the skies to clear may sound like a sound strategy. No one wants to invest right before the market takes a deep plunge, and sometimes things really do get worse before they get better. The problem is that it's impossible to predict. The market often recovers well before the skies clear, so if you wait until the sailing looks smooth, that ship probably will have already sailed.

Even if the sea and sky appear calm when you first board the ship, they are not likely to remain calm for the entire journey. Storms often arise without much warning. If you're waiting for a promise of perfect weather throughout your voyage, you might never go aboard.

You don't need to determine the perfect time to get on board. The key is to enter a ship with the best chance of arriving at your destination as quickly, safely, and comfortably as possible. On a long journey you should expect to hit a few storms along the way. When the storms rage, you are more likely to reach your target if you stick to the plan and stay on the ship.

WHAT GOES UP MUST COME DOWN

Gravity affects everything we do more than we realize. Much like a fish doesn't notice it's in water until you pull it out, we are scarcely aware of gravity's profound impact on everything around us.

Obviously, without gravity things would not fall when you dropped them. However, did you ever think about the fact that you would not be able to write with a normal pen because the ink would not flow down to the tip? If you tried pouring milk on your cereal it would float around in little spheres, never giving you the satisfaction of soggy Cheerios again. It would be equally as difficult to stay on the free throw line as it would be to shoot a basketball through the hoop from there. These concepts are foreign to most of us because we have never experienced life without gravity.

Prolonged exposure to zero gravity could result in serious health consequences, too. According to the Weizmann Institute of Science, without gravity it would be harder for us to balance and fluids would be redistributed throughout our body in unhealthy ways. We would lose bone and muscle mass since they would no longer have to work to support the weight of our body, making us more prone to injury.[4]

A friend of mine whose sister is an astronaut said that whenever she returns to Earth, everything hurts for a while—standing, sitting, even lying down—because she's more acutely aware of the power of gravity pulling down on every part of her body. One more thing for the rest of us who are stuck on Earth to be grateful for. Next time you're struggling to fall asleep and developing a cramp on one side, just think to yourself, "Sweet, gravity is building my muscles and bones."

Since gravity has such a predictable, perpetual effect on everything in our world, it's natural for us to assume that all things that go up must eventually come down, including the stock market. Believe it or not, Earth's gravitational pull has zero effect on stock market values, and the market has no fear of heights. We can scarcely imagine how something could possibly soar to the sky and never come back down to where it started, but in the market's case, the sky truly is the limit.

Of course, the market cannot go straight up without suffering any losses ever again. The point is that just because the market reaches an all-time high does not mean that it's due for a downturn.

The media likes to make a huge announcement every time we reach a new high-water mark, but when you look at the big picture it's not that big of a deal. Since stocks are priced to provide positive returns over time, we should expect all-time highs to happen on a fairly regular basis. In fact, throughout the history of the market, about 30 percent of the months have ended at new highs. It is much more likely to double in value again over the next 10 years than to simply maintain its current value.

So why all the fuss? The media's job is to entice you to keep watching because better ratings translate into more advertising revenue for them. Anything they can sensationalize and turn into a reason for you to pay attention is a win for them, even if it's meaningless to your financial well-being.

The media often asserts that when the market reaches a new high, stocks have hit a ceiling or are over-valued and are due for a drop, but it's not necessarily true. If you believe them, I understand why you would be hesitant to invest at an all-time high. No one wants to enter the market just in time to watch the value of their investments fall.

This is why some investors are tempted to wait until the market pulls back before investing again. If that's your strategy, you could be waiting for a while and miss out on some big opportunities. You might be surprised to discover how often the market keeps trucking along, even after all-time highs.

A few years ago, a long-time client of mine received a sizeable windfall and sent me a large amount of cash to hold in his account. Despite my reminders of the futility of market timing, he asked me to wait for at least a 10 percent drop in the market before investing it, because the market had recently reached an all-time high.

Then he watched the market closely, poised to pounce on the 10 percent drop he believed was right around the corner. Instead, the market steadily climbed about 20 percent over the course of the next year. In exasperation he finally asked me to go ahead to invest the full amount.

Luckily, the market continued climbing after he invested, so it's worth more now even though he didn't get the 10 percent pullback he was looking for. Even if a 10 percent drop had come, he would have been better off investing it right away rather than waiting for a 10 percent drop after a 20 percent increase.

Of course this would not be the outcome every time. The market could have dropped 20 percent when he decided to wait, and then he would have been really glad he waited. But if he had invested when it dropped 10 percent like he planned, it would have dropped another 10 percent after that, and he would have been frustrated he didn't wait even longer.

If you plan to invest after a certain percentage decline in the market, it's really hard to follow through on your plan when that day comes. A few other clients of mine have tried to avoid losses by waiting for a 10 percent to 20 percent drop before investing a large additional chunk. Ironically, when the decline finally happens, they are reluctant to invest because they think it might fall even further. Usually the market recovers substantially before they jump in, and they're back to wondering whether they should wait for another decline.

Can you see how this can be a no-win vicious cycle? You'll drive yourself crazy trying to figure out the right timing, whether the market is at an all-time high or at its lowest point in years.

The key to making money in the market is to "play the game" in a way that increases your chances of success. What are the odds of earning a positive return over time if you invest when the market is at its highest point in history? Let's look at what the real numbers say.

Dimensional Fund Advisors conducted a fascinating study from January 1926 to December 2021 to measure how many months the S&P 500 (U.S. large stocks) ended higher than any previous month in history. As I mentioned earlier, they discovered that 30 percent of the months ended at all-time highs.

They also measured whether the market tends to underperform after reaching a new high. Surprisingly, the one-year returns after all-time highs were 14.1 percent on average, even higher than the 12.5 percent average one-year returns for all sample periods, regardless of whether they ended on a new high or not.

What about for longer periods? Five years after new highs, the average annual return was 10.1 percent, astonishingly similar to the 10.2 percent average annual return five years after all month ends.[5]

In other words, based on this study there is virtually no disadvantage to investing right after the market reaches an all-time high. In fact, one-year returns after all-time highs tend to have a slight advantage, so why wait for a drop before investing?

THE SANTA CLAUS RALLY

Timing the market, in all of its forms, is big business. A lot of really smart people spend a massive amount of time, money, and energy trying to make sense of the chaos. They pour over millions of data points attempting to discover any inkling of predictability.

Finding any sort of advantage, however slight it may be, could result in millions, even billions of dollars of additional gains. When you look at all the resources spent on this endeavor, you realize why they are so anxious to claim at least some new discovery to hang their hat on.

One such popular notion among market timers is what they call the Santa Claus Rally, first observed by Yale Hirsch in the 1972 version of the *Stock Trader's Almanac*. There is little consensus among its proponents as to whether it occurs during the week before Christmas, the week after Christmas, or the whole month of December. Don't ask me how they gauge its predictability when they can't even agree on what they're measuring, but their general claim is that stocks tend to perform well around Christmas time, however you want to define it.

A variety of theories have been posed as to why this might happen. Some believe it's because people tend to be in a more optimistic mood during the holidays, which could make them more likely to invest their year-end bonuses. Others assert that strong retail spending around Christmas time leads to better expectations for corporate earnings, which could increase stock prices. Another contributing factor could be tax-loss harvesting strategies at year-end. Also, pessimistic institutional investors tend to be on vacation, leaving room for the little people to make a bigger impact on market prices with their bullish cheery holiday spirit.

This all sounds logical, right? Besides, who doesn't love the idea of the holidays lifting everyone and everything around us, including our stocks!

Is the Santa Claus Rally predictable or is it just like any other week or month in the market? An interesting article on *Investopedia* addresses this question:

> To see if there is any validity to the proposition of a regularly occurring Santa Claus effect, we looked back at the last 20 years of performance of the Standard & Poor's 500 (S&P 500) in the week leading up to Dec. 25. Based on our review of the data, we can state that there is minimal evidence of any discernible Santa Claus rally. The average return over the time period was +0.385 percent, or effectively flat.
>
> Of the 20 weeks we analyzed, there were 13 weeks with a positive return, five with a negative return and two weeks with no change. The range spanned +5.4 percent in 2021 to -10.7

percent in 2018. Of the winning days, the average win was +1.58 percent, while the average losing day was -3.28 percent. We think the numbers bear out the conclusion that there is no reliably meaningful Santa Claus rally.

Given such a small historical return, and a marginally positive frequency of occurrences, traders should be extremely cautious about buying or selling based on the supposed Santa Claus rally. While Santa Claus can be counted on to deliver the presents on Christmas, the stock market cannot be relied upon to always deliver gifts. That said, any positive gain in the stock market around Christmas is virtually guaranteed to lead financial market observers to refer to the Santa Claus rally.[6]

A recent article on SeekingAlpha.com is perhaps even more interesting because this website is a popular resource for market timers. The author arrived at a similar conclusion that the historical numbers "illustrate the risk of investing based on calendar theories like the Santa Claus Rally. There is no way to predict if one will occur and sometimes the impact is relatively minor or can even be negative. Also, because it is unclear exactly why the Santa Claus Rally occurs, it is impossible to predict whether those influences will recur in any given year."[7]

What about other "calendar theories" this author referenced? Here is a mere sampling of the numerous theories out there, and some of them are quite comical: the January Effect, the September Effect, the October Effect, the Halloween Effect, the Monday Effect, the Congressional Effect, the Lunar Effect, and my personal favorite, the Super Bowl Indicator.

No, I didn't make that up. Some people really believe if an American Football Conference team wins the Super Bowl, it's an indication that the market will decline the following year, and if a National Football Conference team wins, the market will rise in the following year.

The funny thing is that this actually happened 74 percent of the time through 2021. But there is a big difference between correlation and causation. We cannot reasonably conclude that the Super Bowl has any meaningful impact on stock market performance. Even though a correlation was there 74 percent of the time, it failed to predict some major market declines, including the crash of 2008.[8]

Some of these calendar theories predict positive outperformance during the targeted periods, like the Santa Claus Rally. Others predict negative outcomes. While these notions may be fun to entertain, they are not very useful because none of them have proven to be reliable predictors of how markets will behave. They are more anecdotal than scientific, so making investment decisions based on them can be risky.

Even if any of these calendar effects had indeed been predictable at some point, wouldn't they lose their effectiveness after everyone found out about them? Stock market prices are driven by supply and demand, and everyone is trying to get an edge, so you would think that any advantage, if there ever was one, would disappear as soon as it became public knowledge.

If you recently learned that Santa Claus isn't real, I hate to disappoint you again, but neither is the Santa Claus Rally, nor any other calendar theory. Don't lose hope, though—maybe you can be the first to discover an Easter Bunny Rally. If you do, let me know in 50 years how consistently predictable it is. Then I might be interested. Better yet, keep it to yourself and become a gazillionaire if you really believe it works.

BARBERS, BARTENDERS, AND BROTHERS-IN-LAW

I'm sure your brother-in-law is a legitimate expert in basketball, brain tumors, and smoking brisket. But do you really want his advice to cause your investments to go up in smoke?

Why do we often seek counsel from family and friends who may be least qualified to give it? We trust them because we know they love us, have our best interests at heart, and would do anything to help us. However, they may not always have the training or tools to provide real solutions to our most complex problems.

One of my favorite books is *The Speed of Trust* by Stephen M. R. Covey. Most of us think of trust as a character issue. We trust those who have proven their integrity and good intentions consistently over time. However, Mr. Covey teaches that an equally important element of trust is competence, which requires the knowledge, skills, and experience to deliver the results we need.

For example, he has a wonderful relationship with his wife and trusts her more than anyone in the world because of her impeccable character and unconditional care for him. However, if he had a brain tumor, he would not allow her to perform brain surgery on him because she has no competence in that area.

While investing is not brain surgery, it does require expertise. Too many people have been badly burned following the investing advice of well-intentioned friends and family members who didn't know what they were doing.

You would be amazed at how many people ask their coworkers when they should invest or how they should allocate their 401(k) funds. I have met people who lost as much as 70 percent of their retirement savings because they followed the advice of a coworker who told them to put it all in the company stock or last year's best performing fund, then recommended they cash out after a market crash.

It's easy to get caught in the trap of going with the flow. If many of your colleagues at work cash out during a market drop to wait for things to settle down and strongly recommend that you do the same, what are you most likely to do?

We are all vulnerable to a common fallacy called *argumentum ad populum* (Latin for "appeal to the people). This means we tend to believe something is true or good if most of the people around us believe it.

This is obviously not always the case. Was the world flat thousands of years ago simply because most people believed it was flat? Some things are what they are, even if most people believe otherwise.

When everyone around us behaves a certain way or believes a certain idea, it can be really hard to do the opposite, even when we are right and everyone else is wrong. We tend to follow the crowd because it feels safe. We like our thoughts and actions to be confirmed and approved by like-minded people.

Increasing your awareness of how this natural inclination may impact your propensity to time the market could dramatically improve your investing experience. Learning to follow through on what you know to be right and ignoring what others are doing is very empowering and liberating.

Have you noticed when a certain type of investment is really booming, suddenly everyone thinks they're an expert and wants to spew their vast knowledge all over you? At the height of the real estate bubble in 2006, even barbers and bartenders claimed to be real estate geniuses because they didn't have to know anything to succeed. Many of these self-proclaimed "experts" got in deep just in time to lose everything, bringing their friends and family members down with them. If you're a seasoned real estate investor, the best time to sell your rental properties might be when your barber thinks he knows more about real estate than you.

Another reason taking investing advice from friends and associates can be risky is that they might not be telling you the whole story. People love to brag about their wins, but no one likes to admit their losses. Everyone wants to look smart, even if it means making something up to save face. They might not have made as much overall as it sounds.

Right after the sudden market decline in 2020 due to COVID-19, many investors flocked to battered airline and cruise line stocks and bragged about how much money they made. It seemed so easy because most stock values soared during that rocket-ship recovery. However, airline and cruise line stocks in general took another hefty beating in 2021 and 2022. You'd never know it unless you followed the market, though, because everyone stopped talking about it.

Be careful about following what your friends are doing too closely because their situation could be very different from yours. Since personal finance tends to be a personal, taboo topic, chances are they don't know enough about your situation to know if what they are doing would be good for you.

One of my friends who owns a small business hangs out a lot with the owner of a much larger business. He tries desperately to keep up with this guy whose annual income is probably at least 20 times higher than his.

The owner of the larger business regularly shares investing tips with my friend, who feels pressure to act on them because this guy is so successful. Unfortunately, most of what he has told him to invest in has failed. The other business owner makes many risky bets because he can afford the losses, but my friend can't afford them. It's killing him, but he can't seem to break the cycle because the pressure to keep up is too great.

I'm not saying we should never seek advice from family members or friends. They can be valuable, trusted sounding boards. Admittedly, I even discussed ideas for this book with my barber *and* my brother-in-law. But I have never asked them for investing advice, even if they did make a killing in airline stocks in 2020.

IT'S ON TV, SO IT MUST BE TRUE

If we can't rely on our closest associates for sound investment advice, who can we trust? Naturally, we need to find someone who really knows what they're talking about.

Why not turn to some of the most well-known financial experts on TV, the internet, podcasts, books, or other mainstream media? They must know what they're talking about or they wouldn't be so famous, right?

Harry S. Dent, Jr. is a widely publicized author and media personality known for his bold predictions of the market. According to his website, he has appeared on *Good Morning America*, PBS, CNBC, CNN, Fox News, and is a regular guest on Fox Business. He has also been featured in *Barron's*, *Investor's Business Daily*, *Fortune*, *U.S. News & World Report*, *Businessweek*, *The Wall Street Journal*, and many other publications.

He has written at least 11 books (impressive—this is only my second book), and his 2009 book, *The Great Depression Ahead*, appeared on the *New York Times* Best Seller List (even more impressive—neither of my books have even appeared on the Pahrump Valley Times Best Seller List).

How much did all those books help investors? I'll just state the facts and you be the judge. Don't worry, I won't review all of them, but after a few examples you'll get the picture.

In his book entitled *The Roaring 2000s*, published in October 1999, Mr. Dent predicted, "The Dow will reach at least 21,500 and possibly 35,000 by the year 2008." Did that happen? Quite the opposite—the Dow peaked just above 14,000 in October 2007, then fell just below 8,800 by the end of 2008. Whoops.

He must have learned his lesson about being overly optimistic because in January 2009 he published a new book with a very gloomy forecast entitled *The Great Depression Ahead*. This was right in the middle of the Great Recession after the Dow had already lost nearly 40 percent, so his message was definitely in sync with how everyone was feeling at the time.

What did he say would happen next? "The economy is moving toward a major depression, with the deflation of bubbles in stocks, real estate, and commodities between 2009 and 2012, and it could last for a decade or more."

How accurate was this prediction? Just two months after the book was published, the Dow bottomed out around 6,500 and doubled to over 13,000 by the end of 2012. Not exactly the 10-year slump he was expecting.

In January 2014 he published yet another book called *The Demographic Cliff*. This time he warned, "Investors should sell stocks by mid-January 2014 and look to buy them back in 2015 or later at a Dow as low as 5,800."

What did the Dow do instead? It ranged from around 15,600 to 18,300 throughout 2015 and has never closed below 15,000 since then. In fact, it has grown to soar well above 30,000. If he's still preaching to wait for the opportunity to buy at 5,800, I certainly hope his readers get the chance before he dies.

I figured at least his potential for future book sales would have died by 2015 after so many miserably failed predictions. But this time I was the one who predicted erroneously.

In 2017 I was browsing through Barnes & Noble with my daughter when I was horrified by the sight of a new book staring at me defiantly on the bookshelf. "Oh no!" I exclaimed. My daughter was concerned, "Are you okay, Dad?" "Of course I'm not okay—Harry Dent has published another book!"

I grabbed it and flipped straight to the inside front cover, outraged by the boldness of his deception: "There's no better guide to financial cycles than Harry S. Dent, Jr. For more than 30 years he has earned a reputation for eerily accurate predictions about the world economy and financial markets. For anyone who heeds the signs and follows Dent's advice, the looming correction is a once-in-a-century opportunity to gather immense wealth. Your globally diversified portfolio won't protect you from the coming crash. But there are other investment strategies that *will* work."

Yep, you guessed it, he was wrong again, but people keep buying his books. I'm starting to think Harry Dent might be the true father of the stock market. It seems to do the exact opposite of everything he says, just like my kids.

Since his predictions are so persistently pathetic, how does he sell so many books, and why is he regularly featured on such famous financial news outlets? The truth is, he *was* lucky with a few forecasts a long time ago, which he has bragged about ever since.

But does that really mean he can foretell the future? Obviously not. What is the cost of following his advice when he is wrong?

Contemplate how well your investments would have performed if you made big changes based on Harry Dent's prognostications over the past 20 years. Probably just as poorly as the investment funds he used to manage.

Although he claimed his strategies would work much better than a globally diversified portfolio, they all had to be shut down because the performance was so bad. Larry Swedroe wrote an interesting article on CBS News MoneyWatch that sums it up well:

> Why do people listen to Harry Dent in light of his obvious inability to accurately predict the future? I believe it is because most of us want certainty, even when we know, logically, that it doesn't exist. With investing it is a desire to believe that there's someone who can protect us from bear markets and the devastating losses that can result. That leads to what we can call the "Wizard of Oz" effect. We come under the spell of wizards, authoritative voices [whose words] we are "trained" to take…as truths. We want to believe that we can control things because as Woody Allen put it, otherwise "life is scarier."

A fitting denouement to this story is the tale of the AIM Dent Demographic Trends Fund, which was launched on June 7, 1999. Dent was a consultant to the fund. The fund was up 54 percent for the remainder of that year. Unfortunately, the fund's results were miserable afterwards. From 2000 through 2004 the fund lost over 11 percent per annum and underperformed the S&P 500 Index by almost 9 percent per annum. In 2005 its sponsor put investors out of their misery by merging it into the AIM Weingarten Fund.

Undaunted, at least in his belief that investors would entrust their assets to him, in September 2009, the AdvisorShares Dent Tactical ETF (DENT) was launched, with Dent himself as the co-manager. The fund's track record was so poor that in August 2012 the fund was liquidated and sent to where it belonged—the mutual fund graveyard."[9]

Anyone who makes enough predictions will eventually be right about something, but that doesn't mean they'll be right again. Famous forecasters typically brag about a lucky call or two for years while sweeping all other inaccurate projections under the rug, hoping no one remembers them. Even a broken clock is right twice a day, but it's not a very reliable indicator of when you need to leave work so you're not late for dinner with your in-laws. That might result in even worse consequences than losing money in the market.

Maybe Harry Dent is just telling people what they want to hear. He must know he's wrong most of the time, but maybe he doesn't care as long as he continues selling books and they keep calling him back on Fox Business.

I don't begrudge his success. I'm just angry that he's preying on the gullibility of thousands if not millions of investors without taking any responsibility for how remarkably false his predictions have been. Instead, he continues to misrepresent how accurate his track record is because he knows it will keep people coming back for more. Our society just can't get enough of it.

It devastates me to consider how many people might have been badly hurt by following Harry Dent's advice. I doubt very many of his readers have measured how inaccurate most of his forecasts are, and he is never going to tell them. They just want to know what's going to happen so badly that they'll listen to anyone who is famous, successful, and sounds like they know what they're talking about.

I'm also angry that none of the news outlets seem to care how bad his advice is, either. They're just looking for someone to talk about the market in a way that will make people listen, even when it's clearly false. Please don't follow the advice of Mr. Dent unless you want a huge dent in your investments.

But this isn't just about Harry Dent. Another well-known example is Jim Cramer, who is probably even more influential than Harry Dent. Cramer is the host of *Mad Money* on CNBC, a very popular, energetic investing show that has been running every weekday since 2005.

During his show, Cramer typically discusses big market news and a handful of stock tips. Each day he covers different stocks to keep things interesting.

It's very in-your-face and very urgent. CNBC would never hire me for that job because I would be way too boring, even if I had access to his soundboard of machine guns, electric shocks, train wrecks, bowling pins, and another two dozen obnoxious sound effects he uses for punctuation.

I must admit I could only stand to watch a few episodes, but his advice seemed to be fairly inconsistent from one show to the next. Once I heard him say you should own at least five stocks, but no more than 10, but an article on his website listed the 34 stocks in his Charitable Trust Portfolio.[10]

While his delivery may be entertaining, do his recommendations actually help investors? I couldn't find any recently completed academic studies measuring his performance, but a very comprehensive analysis was conducted by the University of Pennsylvania's Wharton School from 2001 to 2017. In this study, the researchers determined that "at the end of the 17-year period, the annualized performance of Cramer's recommendations clocked in at just 4.08 percent. During the same period, the S&P 500 produced annualized gains of 7.07 percent."[11]

Underperformance by 3 percent might not sound like much, but that would make a huge difference in the growth of your investments over 17 years. Based on this data, if you had invested $1 million in the S&P 500 over that time period, it would have grown to about $3.2 million, whereas Cramer's picks would have only grown to less than $2 million.

The study also determined that Cramer's picks had a higher standard deviation and a lower Sharpe ratio than the S&P 500 over the same period. This means he was taking more risk and picking stocks with lower potential returns than the general stock market—the opposite of what any prudent investor should do.

Part of the reason his returns were so much lower than the S&P 500 over the period studied is that he likes to hold a lot of cash as protection against market downturns and to seize "buying opportunities" when they arise. He held up to 50 percent in cash during the recovery pulling out of the Great Recession while the S&P 500 grew substantially. This highlights yet again the cost of trying to time the market, even for the pros.

According to *Kiplinger*, Cramer doesn't dispute the findings of the Wharton School study. He responded, "We have never promised outperformance," and called his subscription service "largely an educational product."[12] Yet who would follow his advice and not expect to outperform the market?

The other issue with following Cramer is that even if he did outperform the market, you would have to watch every show and act on every piece of advice immediately to reap the rewards. One of my friends used to loosely follow Cramer. He bought many shares of one stock Cramer recommended on the show, then lost a lot of money on it over the next few months. Later he found out that Cramer recommended selling it a few weeks later, but my friend missed that episode.

Why spend so much time watching shows like this and doing all the work to continually buy and sell individual stocks when you could get higher returns with less risk by simply investing in a broadly diversified portfolio? That approach would also lower your taxes, trading costs, and stress level, but I'm getting ahead of myself—we'll discuss this more in Chapter 7.

Please watch *Mad Money* with Jim Cramer if you're looking for a good laugh. He really is a masterful entertainer with boundless energy and he's obviously a very smart guy. Just remember to take his advice with a grain of salt because that's probably about as much as it's worth.

In their defense, Harry Dent, Jim Cramer, and everyone else who profits from providing entertaining, ineffective advice is simply giving society what it wants. I guess we could argue it's not really their problem. As long as millions of Americans crave the type of recommendations they give, why shouldn't they make millions of dollars providing it? The joke's on us if we don't see it for what it is.

I'm sure not all financial experts on TV and other mainstream media are as bad as these guys. However, I haven't found any who provide consistent, sound advice that would really help people in a meaningful way.

Why are the good ones so hard to find? They're too boring. As I mentioned earlier, the media desperately needs us to tune in every day and hang onto every word because they are paid with advertising revenue driven by ratings of how many people are watching. Getting our attention requires bold predictions and bold personality, not accuracy or usefulness.

Also keep in mind that the media must ensure the advice they broadcast is in the best interests of those who pay their bills. Most advertising revenue typically comes from big brokerage firms that derive huge profits from convincing people they should be trading in and out of their investments on a regular basis. Always consider the motivations of those from whom you receive advice.

I'm not saying we should never watch the news. Of course we need to be well-informed. Just remember that news outlets and big media personalities are in the entertainment business and have no fiduciary duty to you, relationship with you, or care for your financial well-being. They are not paid to help you grow your wealth or enhance your peace of mind. That's why they have those disclaimers at the end of every show: "This program is for entertainment purposes only and should not be construed as investment advice."

The problem is that most people don't just view it as entertainment. Millions of investors turn to these "trusted sources" regularly for critical information about what they should do with their life savings. Due to the frequency of their forecasting failures, it may be the most expensive kind of entertainment they could possibly watch.

THE WORLD IS COMING TO AN END...AGAIN

"And, lo, there was a great earthquake; and the sun became black as sackcloth of hair, and the moon became as blood; And the stars of heaven fell unto the earth...and every mountain and island were moved out of their places. And the kings of the earth, and the great men, and the rich men...said to the mountains and rocks, Fall on us, and hide us from the face of him that sitteth on the throne, and from the wrath of the Lamb: For the great day of his wrath is come; and who shall be able to stand?" (Revelation 6:12-17)

These verses from the Holy Bible are enough to make anyone want to sell all their investments, hide the proceeds under the mattress, and crawl in bed with the covers over their head. However, prophets have been foretelling the end of the world for thousands of years, so if you do that you might be waiting under the covers for a while.

I'm not making light of the prophecies—I believe that the world as we know it today will eventually come to an end as the Bible says. Still, I see no value in making investment decisions based on predictions about when it will happen.

Jesus himself made the ambiguity of its timing very clear: "But of that day and hour knoweth no man, no, not the angels of heaven, but my Father only" (Matthew 24:36).

How many times have you feared it might actually be the end of the world for real this time? Hundreds of failed predictions have come and gone, including Y2K in 2000, multiple warnings of asteroids colliding with the earth, the Mayan calendar's end in 2012, the blood moon prophecy of 2014-2015, and Jean Dixon's predictions of Armageddon in 1962 and again in 2020, only to name a few.

If we have learned anything from these examples, hopefully we have learned that overreacting to end-of-the-world propaganda doesn't help us at all, no matter how many people might believe it. In fact, it can cause significant financial harm if it drives us to sell our investments after a market dip or keep all our money in cash for years.

Although not quite as dramatic in its approach, the financial media seems determined to continually convince us it's the end of the world for our investments. Why do they do that? Because fear sells.

In 1979 Psychologists Daniel Kahneman and Amos Tversky published a study in *Econometra* entitled "Prospect Theory: An Analysis of Decision Under Risk." They observed that people are far more motivated by the avoidance of a potential loss than by the prospect of gaining something. In fact, through their research they determined that the pain of losing is about twice as powerful as the pleasure of gaining.[13]

Many financial "experts" use this psychological phenomenon against us by capitalizing on our emotions after large market declines. They love to make people believe it will never recover so they can sell some supposedly safer alternative such as insurance products, gold, commodities, or cryptocurrencies.

Yes, we should be prepared for unexpected catastrophes by keeping plenty of cash, food storage, water storage, and medical supplies on hand. We never know when we might have to deal with a sudden job loss, medical emergency, food shortage, utility failure, or natural disaster.

These and other scenarios might feel like the end of the world for us personally and are far more likely to occur during our lifetime. However, perpetual irrational fear of the end of the world can result in huge unnecessary emotional and financial costs, so stop worrying about it!

YEAH, BUT THIS TIME IT'S DIFFERENT

If the media can't convince us that it's the end of the world, maybe they can at least get us to believe that whatever may have happened in the past, this time it's different. One of the most alarming terms they love to use is "unprecedented." The underlying message is, "You have never seen anything like this before. Stay tuned for our updates because this will be the scariest ride of your life."

A level-headed financial host on CNBC would put everyone to sleep. No one wants to turn on the news and hear, "Well, it's just another day in the market. It goes up and it goes down, but none of what happens today will matter in the long run. Just stick to your strategy and everything will work out fine." CNBC would be out of business in a heartbeat if they told investors the types of things that would help them most.

Once you recognize their tactics for trying to convince you that every story is a big deal, many headlines sound comical because they're not usually of much consequence at all:

- "Worst Tuesday for the S&P 500 in three weeks."
- "Tesla stock plummets, erasing four straight days of gains."
- "The Dow tumbles 497 points on news that Kanye and Kim Kardashian finally settled their divorce, the largest decrease on a celebrity divorce settlement day in history."

As a side note, their attempt to pin each day's market movement to a single cause also makes me chuckle because hundreds if not thousands of distinct variables impact the outcome. If you pay attention, you'll notice that sometimes they even use the same story to explain the market's reaction regardless of whether it went up or down.

For example, I took a screenshot of these two different articles shown on the next page that popped up on my phone on January 7, 2019, both by the same columnist. In the morning he said the Dow dropped because the U.S. started trade talks with China. But by the end of the day the Dow closed up, so he changed it to say the Dow gained 94 points because the U.S. started trade talks with China. So did the market like the idea of trade talks with China or not?

Of course this time it's always a little different somehow, but that doesn't necessarily mean we have to do anything about it. Millions of first-time events happen every day all over the world, but what does that have to do with us personally?

Think of the market as a giant basketball tournament with a different lineup of players and teams every day. In every game, at least one player is bound to hit some kind of record high or low number of points, rebounds, assists, turnovers, blocks, steals, or three-point shots for the week, month, season, their career, or even in all of basketball history.

The media could make a big deal out about any of these new records every day. To an observer who knows nothing about basketball, it would just look like another basketball game. And so it would be, with no real impact on your life.

If you look hard enough, you can always find some new statistic in the market that has never happened before, but it usually doesn't mean much. Check out this excerpt from a *USA Today* article on February 5, 2018, the first time in history the Dow dropped by more than 1,000 points:

> The Dow Jones industrial average suffered its biggest one-day point drop in history, plunging 1,175 points on Monday

and giving back all its 2018 gains as a flash-crash-style drop intensified a free fall in stocks that began last week.

Fears of spiking inflation and borrowing costs caused investors to rethink their bullish views on stocks, which until just last week had fueled huge gains in the blue-chip Dow.[14]

Yes, a 1,175-point drop is big, but not as alarming as this article made it sound. It was only a 4.6 percent loss, closing at 24,345. If you had sold your stocks in response to this article, you would have missed out on sizeable gains over the next few years.

To put this in context, the largest one-day percentage drop in history was 22.6 percent on October 19, 1987, now dubbed Black Monday. Although this was only a 508-point drop, which doesn't sound like much today, it was a big deal back then because the Dow was only at 1,738 after the decline.[15]

Even though that was a much bigger deal, the market eventually recovered very nicely from that unprecedented event, too. Now the Dow is over 30,000, making the 1987 crash look like a minor blip on the timeline of market history.

It can be dangerous to make rash investing decisions based on the notion that old rules no longer apply because "nothing like this has ever happened before." Since the year 2000 alone, consider how many colossal, unprecedented events have shaken us to the core:

- Do you remember the unsettling uncertainty of whether our technology-based society could survive Y2K?
- Were you at all affected when dot-com stocks dropped by 75 percent in 2000, erasing $1.7 trillion in value?[16]
- Did you feel as vulnerable as I did on 9/11 when the market was closed immediately and all airplanes were grounded for days in response to an unprecedented terrorist attack on American soil?
- Were you excited to invest and did you expect a bright future ahead during the Great Recession, when market values were chopped in half and unemployment rates soared to 10 percent, more than double the norm?[17]

- Were you certain there would be little to no long-term impact on the market when the whole world was shut down in 2020 due to an unprecedented global pandemic that we feared might wipe out half the population?

Not to mention the countless other first-time major challenges since 2000 that nobody talks about anymore, such as the U.S. credit rating downgrade, record deficit spending, the fiscal cliff, sovereign debt problems in Europe, negative interest rates, flattening yield curves, the "lost decade" for U.S. stocks, the Brexit vote, trade wars, and geopolitical turmoil in the Middle East, just to name a few.

Do you recall any of these big headlines that sent many people into a panic at the time? Our memories are surprisingly short. This is a good reminder of how insignificant even very impactful issues can become over time.

During each of these extremely unnerving first-time events since 2000, many people said, "This time it really is different. Things have never been this bad before. The market is never going to recover. I'm selling everything and putting it in the bank or burying it in my backyard."

They were right. Nothing quite like those difficult periods had ever happened before, but look how well we came out of them. We have survived them all and thrived beyond what most thought possible, given how dismal things appeared at the time. If you had invested $1 million in the S&P 500 on January 1, 2000, staying disciplined through all the ups and downs and reinvesting all dividends, you would have ended up with $4.3 million by December 31, 2022.[18]

Although we have suffered many serious challenges since 2000, something tells me it might have been even more difficult and frightening to endure certain unprecedented events in former generations. Consider the struggles and disappointments associated with World War I, World War II, and the market crash of 1929, which plunged 89 percent and led to the Great Depression with a 25 percent unemployment rate.[19] While the COVID-19 pandemic was very challenging, can you imagine what it must have been like to live through the Black Death, which killed between 30 percent and 60 percent of all Europeans?[20]

Somehow humanity survived all these devastating tragedies and more. Through it all, wealth continues to be created and our standard of living worldwide continues to improve.

Yes, this time it's different, but what are you going to do about it? There will always be some new unexpected event and challenge to face. In that sense, this time it really isn't different, and life goes on.

Paul Harvey said it best: "In times like these, it helps to recall that there have always been times like these."

HEAVEN HELP US IF _____ WINS THE ELECTION

As you can see, trying to time the market in all its forms is more likely to hurt you than help you. Could election season be an exception to this rule? Surely if your pick for the next president doesn't win, the world is going straight to hell in a handbasket. How could so many seemingly intelligent people vote for the devil incarnate?

Many people ask me this question every election season. Some candidates' proposed platforms and policies might be expected to improve the economy more than others. Still, no one can predict their ability to put these proposals in place, much less how the market will respond.

The president of the United States wields a lot of power and might occasionally have a limited short-term effect on the market. However, the impact is not always what the president intended, nor does it tend to be very meaningful or enduring.

If you have always thought the president has a large influence on the market, I don't blame you because that's what we've been trained to think. Whenever the market does well, the president is quick to take credit for it. When the market struggles, the opposing party places full blame on the president.

In reality, the market is influenced by hundreds, if not thousands of other factors every day, as I mentioned earlier. Stock prices are continually determined by the buying and selling decisions of millions of people across the planet. It is way too vast and unwieldy for any one person or organization to control.

Individual candidates aside, does the market tend to perform better when a Republican or a Democrat holds the presidency? Based on another illuminating study by Dimensional Fund Advisors, for the past nearly 100 years no apparent correlation has existed between market performance and which party controls the White House.

This study also found that "data for the stock market going back to 1926 shows that returns in months when presidential elections took place have not tended to be that different from returns in any other month." In other words, contrary to popular belief, election month does not perform any better or any worse on average than any other month.

If this surprises you, remember that you're investing in companies, not political parties. Businesses focus on earning a profit by providing valuable products and services to their customers regardless of who is in the White House. They will always strive to do so, even if it means finding creative ways to adapt to new laws and government policies.

The chart in Figure 2 demonstrates that since 1926 the market has generally trended upward, rewarding people who stayed invested regardless of who was in the presidency. The dark shaded periods represent Republican presidential terms, and the lighter shaded periods represent Democratic presidential terms.[21]

What about party control of U.S. Congress? In a similar study, Dimensional Fund Advisors found no correlation between stock market returns and party control of Congress, regardless of whether Democrats controlled both the House and the Senate, Republicans controlled both, or whether control was mixed.[22] Making investment decisions based on predictions of how the market will respond to elections is a recipe for disappointment.

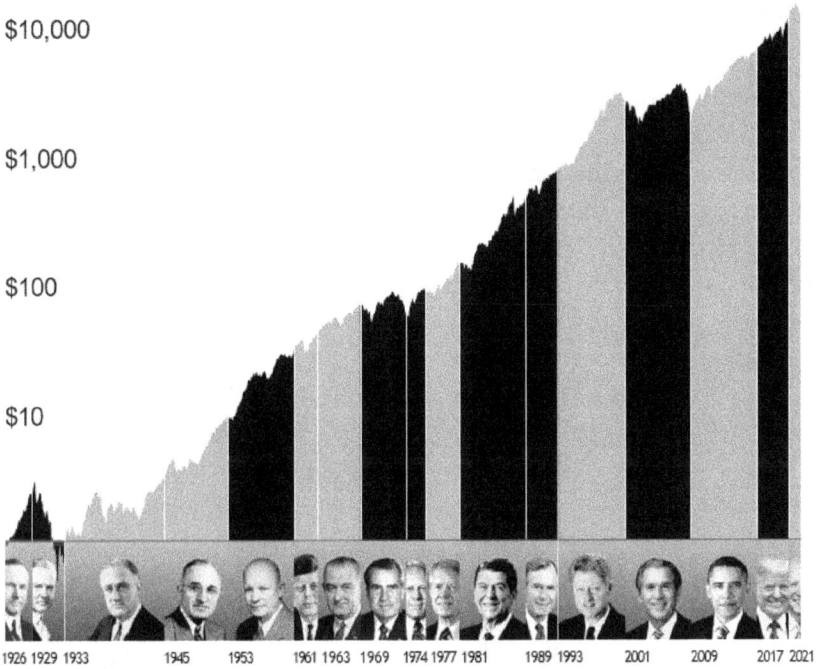

Figure 2: U.S. Presidential Elections & Market Returns Hypothetical Growth of $1 Invested in S&P 500 Index January 1, 1926-June 30, 2022

TIME IN THE MARKET, NOT TIMING THE MARKET

All these forms of timing the market might seem prudent and logical on the surface. Unfortunately, none of them work consistently enough to be useful because the market is too unpredictable. They are more likely to hinder your ability to build and retain wealth.

The good news is that you don't have to time the market to be a successful investor. Even if you occasionally get lucky with good timing, it doesn't usually have much of a long-term impact anyway.

For example, my wife and I bought a new home in March 2011. A few months after we bought it, Zillow said it was already worth 10 percent less than our purchase price. I was frustrated at the time, but now it's worth two-and-a-half times the amount we paid for it. At this point does it really matter that the value dropped right after we bought it?

One of the keys to successful investing is *time in* the market, not *timing* the market. Investors who stay in the market through the ups and downs tend to earn more over time than those who try to figure out the best times to get in and out of the market.

I have seen the power of this phenomenon help countless investors succeed throughout my career. One particularly poignant example is a long-term client of mine who is a retired corporate executive.

He has been very patient and disciplined through the market fluctuations over the past 20 years of investing with my firm. Like most people, his account value dropped substantially in 2008. It even sank below the amount he had originally entrusted to us five years earlier, but he stayed the course and was well-rewarded for his perseverance in the long run.

He invested a little less than $2 million with us in 2003 and has gradually spent about $1.3 million of it since then. Amazingly, his account is worth $3.4 million at the time of this writing (beginning of 2023), even after those painful losses in 2008 and many others along the way.

Of course, not everyone would have the same outcome as him. Each individual's experience depends on a myriad of variables, including the type of investments, the amount and timing of deposits and withdrawals, and other factors. Past performance is no guarantee of future results.

The point of this example is to illustrate that you don't need to time the market to produce successful long-term results. Although this client was impacted by the same market fluctuations most investors endured over the past 20 years, he never attempted to time the market. He simply stayed in his seat for the whole roller coaster ride despite a number of frightening drops along the way.

If he had bailed in 2008 and never got back in, like the accounting professor we discussed earlier, he probably would only have about $700,000 left instead of the $3.4 million he has today. While everyone's circumstances are unique, those of our clients who have stayed invested through the ups and downs and followed the principles we will discuss in Chapter 7 have typically enjoyed much better long-term outcomes than those who tried to figure out the "right times" to get in and out of the market. You may also improve your investing experience if you resist the temptation to time the market—the choice is yours.

KEY POINTS OF CHAPTER 1

1. No one can consistently time the market.
2. You can lose a lot of money and miss out on huge growth opportunities trying to do so.
3. Many popular investing practices called by other names are market timing in disguise.
4. The market can grow significantly even after reaching all-time highs.
5. Taking financial advice from family and friends who are not experts can be risky.
6. Just because someone is famous and found on mainstream media does not mean you can trust their recommendations.
7. The media doesn't care about your financial well-being and has no accountability for giving bad guidance.
8. No reliable patterns related to seasons, major historical events, or presidential elections have been found.
9. Fear-based investment decisions based on forecasts of the end of the world or other catastrophes can be dangerous.
10. You don't need to time the market to be successful. The key is *time in* the market, not *timing* the market.

CHAPTER 2

PICKING STOCKS

NOTHING BUT THE BEST FOR MY PEEPS

If timing the market doesn't work, what other tools can we use to ensure great returns? Shouldn't we invest in only the highest-quality stocks that are bound to outperform all others?

On a brisk fall day in 2000, I was excited to start as a new financial advisor at a large, well-known investment firm. I heard many investors had recently lost their shirts in technology stocks, so I was determined to protect my clients from such injustice and give them only the best.

I had one simple question for my all-knowing sage supervisor who had a whole six years' experience in the investment business: "What is the best investment that will give my clients the highest rate of return with the lowest amount of risk?" I'll never forget the smirk on his face as he responded to my naiveté, "Let me know when you figure it out—that's the biggest challenge in our business because there is no 'best' investment." I was crushed.

Our firm had many resources to help each advisor figure out what we thought would work best for our clients, but who was I to determine that on my own? I spent years trying to figure it out but grew more and more frustrated because most of the tools were backwards looking, evaluating past performance to determine future expected return.

As luck would have it, many of the best-performing investments the year before would mysteriously morph into the worst-performing investments the next year. Sure, my clients made money, but I wanted them to have only the very best, and I felt like I was driving down the freeway looking only at the rear-view mirror.

I poured over the research, figuring if only I had more training or spent more time studying the options, I could figure it out. Over time I learned I was not alone. Since the history of the investment advisory business, this dilemma has been a huge source of frustration for advisors and investors alike. Even the smartest, most successful money managers get it wrong all the time.

After years of running on that hamster wheel, I finally discovered a better way to invest that has significantly improved my clients' chances of success, which we will discuss in Chapter 7. Sadly, many advisors never embrace this method for a variety of reasons.

Some who learn about this approach don't implement it because they're afraid their clients would leave them. If they admitted their inability to predict which stocks, mutual funds, exchange-traded funds (ETFs), or other investments will perform best in the future, they would feel irrelevant. They have no idea how to be of service without relying on the vicious cycle of all that unproductive research.

The longer I work in the investment advisory business, the more convinced I am that the main reason this research-heavy, prediction-based approach is so popular among advisors and clients alike is that most large financial institutions profit greatly from it. We'll discuss how in Chapter 5. They don't want advisors or investors to realize how much it costs them in hidden fees and lost opportunity.

The other reason these "traditional" methods are so popular is that they appeal to the natural human emotions of fear and greed. These emotions drive us to try to make as much money as possible as quickly as possible, regardless of the potential costs.

Picking the "best" stocks consistently is even harder than timing the market, so it is not a reliable investment strategy. The temptation to place big bets on a specific stock can be hard to resist when its value has recently skyrocketed or when you think you understand its potential better than anyone else.

However, this practice can lead to devastating consequences. In this chapter we will explore common myths about picking stocks so you can better resist urges that could burn you big time.

WHAT GOES UP MUST KEEP GOING UP

Am I the only person who finds it ironic that when the market soars to new heights many investors expect it to fall, but when a specific stock skyrockets they expect it to keep climbing? Stocks in general tend to continue rising in value over time, but that phenomenon does not automatically apply to any particular stock.

The stock market is somewhat like a school of fish. The school may travel many miles across the ocean, but it will not go in a straight line. The movements of each individual fish appear somewhat random and they don't all swim at exactly the same speed. But when you look at the whole school, you can sense the general direction. You can't predict which fish will lead the pack at any given moment. Many will linger towards the back and some may die along the way.

Just as stocks don't obey the laws of gravity, they don't obey Newton's first law of motion, either. A stock that has recently increased in value will not necessarily continue growing. One reason we assume it will is that analysts often use misleading language. "Google continues to climb" and "Meta is in a downward spiral" imply that inertia will keep them moving in that direction. The following would be more accurate performance descriptions: "Google has climbed" or "Meta has declined." What has already happened is fact. What they say will happen in the future is fiction.

As a side note, recent studies suggest that momentum might have limited impact on stock performance in some cases. However, it tends to burn out very quickly so it is not a reliable indicator of outperformance. When it does occur, momentum is so short-lived that in order to capitalize on any advantage it may provide, investors would have to trade in and out of momentum-affected stocks at such frequency that the costs would normally outweigh the benefits.[1]

Our inclination to believe that a stock that has recently performed well will continue to do so stems from a cognitive bias that affects all of us. It is called "recency bias." We tend to place greater emphasis on recent events because they are freshest in our minds, even if they are not relevant in the long run. An interesting article on *Investopedia* highlights how this bias leads to irrational choices:

> One example of recency bias is in the case of the "hot hand," or the sense that following a string of successes, an individual is likely to continue being successful. This was first identified in the sport of basketball (hence the hot hand), whereby players who have scored a number of baskets in a row are thought to keep scoring. As a result, players may pass that person the ball more often, even though their actual performance may not actually be above average.
>
> In the markets, investors are similarly tempted to invest with fund managers who have recently outperformed the market over the course of several years, feeling that they, too, have the hot hand. In reality, portfolio managers who have had an unusually long winning streak often underperform their peers in future years.
>
> For investors, [recency] bias affects the trading decisions that people make based on recent events or headlines, expecting such events to be more frequent than they actually are...
>
> Recency bias can be difficult to counteract because it plays on human emotions of fear and greed, which are powerful forces. Moreover, our brains are wired to put the most emphasis on recent events that are fresh in our memories as older events fade out of mind.[2]

An article from *The Evidence-Based Investor* sheds additional light on the negative effects of this bias:

> It is the tendency to overweight recent events or trends and ignore long-term evidence. That leads investors to buy after periods of strong performance—when valuations are higher and expected returns are now lower— and sell after periods of poor performance—when prices are lower and expected returns are now higher. Buying high and selling low is not exactly a prescription for successful investing. Yet, it is the way many individuals invest.
>
> The research demonstrates that companies with comparably low recent returns and high distant ones

significantly outperform their counterparts….Investors should be particularly careful to avoid getting euphoric because when something is highly popular, it runs the risk of being bid up in price and thus is prone to disappointment. The bottom line is that adhering to your plan by rebalancing your portfolio will help you avoid the mistakes caused by recency bias and overconfidence.[3]

FAANG FOMO

A classic example of recency bias is what I like to call FAANG FOMO. If you have no idea what this means, here is your algebra lesson for the day:

FAANG = Facebook, Apple, Amazon, Netflix, and Google
FOMO = Fear of Missing Out
FAANG x FOMO = FRUSTRATION

The growth of these five "FAANG" stocks has been astronomical over the past 10 years. From 2012 to 2021, they collectively produced a 28 percent average annual return, leaving most other U.S. stocks in the dust. The Russell 3000, a benchmark representing all U.S. stocks, only earned a 16 percent average annual return over the same period.[4]

After realizing how much FAANG stocks were outperforming the rest of the market, some people decided they didn't need to invest in anything else. Why not keep it simple and just own those five stocks?

That would be a no-brainer if it were really that predictable. Unfortunately, determining which stocks are going to outperform in the future is even more difficult than forecasting the future performance of the whole market.

One reason FAANG stock values grew so rapidly during that period is that their earnings growth far exceeded investors' expectations. Since everyone knows how successful they've been, current stock prices include an anticipation of future success.

Now they face a new challenge: how can they keep up with these expectations, let alone exceed them again? Once they reach a certain size and level of public awareness, it is extremely difficult for any company to do so, as evidenced by the struggles of Facebook (now Meta) and Netflix in 2022.

From January 1, 2022, to May 31, 2022, all five of the FAANG stocks underperformed the general U.S. stock market by almost 11 percent. This is a classic example of the risks of buying individual stocks based on recent outperformance, even if they outperform as long as 10 years.

As strong as all five of these companies are, no one can predict how new competition, government regulation, or public scandal could quickly derail them regardless of their track record. Now some analysts are saying Netflix should be dropped from FAANG and Microsoft should be added, renaming the group MAMAA for Meta, Apple, Microsoft, Amazon, and Alphabet (Google's parent company name).

Other analysts suggest that Facebook (Meta) should also be dropped and the acronym should be changed to MATANA for Microsoft, Apple, Tesla, Alphabet, Nvidia, and Amazon. Great idea—encourage everyone to dump two large holdings right after they drop substantially and replace them with three others that have already grown a ton. Sounds like a great strategy for buying high and selling low, the opposite of what successful investors do.

Personally, I'd like to know why no one is talking about the BLANT stocks: Blaze, Lululemon, Amazon, Nordstrom, and Target. Those are bound to have a bright future because that's where my wife loves shopping the most!

If you start paying attention to the performance of the FAANG, MAMAA, MATANA or BLANT stocks and notice you're missing out on huge returns, don't give in to your FOMO. If you do, you might be jumping on the bandwagon just in time for a bumpy ride down a very steep hill.

KINGS OF THE HILL

Speaking of steep hills, as a seven-year-old I loved playing king of the hill with the neighborhood kids. One day we were playing on a large dirt mound on a nearby vacant lot. I started as king of the hill and the other kids threw dirt clods at me to get me to come down. One of the clods felt extra hard as it slammed into my forehead just above my hairline.

That was no ordinary dirt clod. It turned out to be a sharp rock lightly covered with dirt. Blood was streaming down my face, and everyone was freaking out. That was a very effective method to get me to come down from the top of the hill. I was rushed to the emergency room for stitches, and still have the scar as a reminder of how difficult it can be to stay on top when everyone is taking shots at you.

As ruthless as seven-year-olds can be, that's nothing compared to cutthroat corporate America. The struggle to say on top isn't just a problem for tech giants like Facebook (Meta) and Netflix. Market leaders in all industries have come and gone over time for many different reasons. In Figure 3, check out the list of the 10 largest companies in the U.S. by market cap (company size measured by total value of all stock shares) 20 years ago verses today.[5]

2002	2022
1. General Electric	1. Apple
2. Microsoft	2. Microsoft
3. Walmart	3. Alphabet (Google)
4. Pfizer	4. Amazon
5. Citigroup	5. Berkshire Hathaway
6. Intel	6. UnitedHealth Group
7. Johnson & Johnson	7. Tesla
8. AIG	8. Johnson & Johnson
9. IBM	9. Visa
10. Merck	10. Exxon Mobil

Figure 3: Ten Largest U.S. Companies Then & Now

What stands out to you in this comparison? I was amazed to discover that only two of the top 10 stocks from 2002 are still in the top 10 today. I also noticed that technology companies are much more dominant now. Poor Microsoft, still in second place.

In 2002, Tesla didn't even exist, Amazon and Google were very new, and Apple almost went bankrupt just a few years earlier. Who could have predicted back then that they would be in the top 10 today? Which companies have we not even heard of yet that will be market leaders 20 years from now?

Some giants eventually fall out of the top 10 simply because other up-and-coming companies surpass their growth. Others suffer large declines due to a variety of factors, such as changing market conditions, ineffective management, and new competition.

For example, General Electric's market cap sank from $400 billion in 2002 to $80 billion in 2022. Conversely, Apple's market cap climbed from $8 billion in 2002 to over $2 trillion in 2022.[6]

We tend to feel safer investing in the largest, most well-known companies that have a track record of outsized returns, but is that a reliable indicator of future performance? Let's look at the historical performance of each of the largest U.S. companies since 1927, before and after their first year of joining the top 10 list.

For 10 years before making the top 10, these companies outperformed the general market by 10 percent per year on average. For the three years immediately before making top 10, they outperformed by an astounding 24 percent average annual return.

You might think such strong market leaders would continue producing exceptional returns, but their growth tends to slow down substantially after reaching that size. The first three years after making top 10, they only outperformed the market by less than 1 percent per year on average. Ten years later, they did 1.5 percent *worse* than the general market.[7]

This shows that once you're king of the hill, it's really hard to stay on top. Once companies reach a certain level of growth and maturity, apparently it's almost impossible for them to keep growing at the same pace. Chances are they will lag the rest of the market, so we should be wary of concentrating too heavily on the winners of the past.

Sadly, many of yesterday's market leaders have gone bankrupt or are hanging on for dear life, unsure of how much longer they can survive. How many of the 20 companies shown in Figure 4 that were icons 20 years ago could you have predicted would fall so far so fast?

Most of these brands are nostalgic to me and had a positive impact on my life, so it makes me sad to remember how great they once were. I hope you didn't invest too much in any of them as they were on their way out. Many investors assumed they couldn't possibly fail since they had been successful for so long.

Figure 4: Twenty Major Company Failures Since 2002

On the flip side, the future is bright for companies that continually innovate to respond to evolving consumer demands. How many of the 20 companies in Figure 5 that didn't even exist 20 years ago have become an indispensable part of your life today?

Many of today's small companies will become the large leaders of tomorrow. Hopefully most of the current top 10 will continue to grow and thrive for a long time, but most of them are not likely to outperform the rest of the market, and some of them will eventually fade away. No one can predict who will fail and who will rise to the top, so investing too heavily in yesterday's winners can be a dangerous game to play.

Figure 5: Twenty Iconic Companies Born Since 2002

I SHOP THERE ALL THE TIME

Some people invest in a particular stock simply because they're familiar with the company. One of my friends admitted, "Every time I shop at Target it looks busy, so I figured it would be a good stock to buy." That's about as sophisticated as stock analysis can get. Too bad Target's stock price is based on a lot more than how many people you happen to see when you shop at the store closest to your house.

What else can impact a stock's price? The leadership team, marketing strategy, public image, pricing strategy, cost of goods sold, labor costs, benefits costs, utility costs, technology, legal issues, competition, government regulation, taxes, consumer demand, supply chain issues, forecasted future cash flows, expected performance of similar companies, general market and economic conditions, and a whole host of other issues all play into the current stock price and its future potential growth. Even if you had a handle on how all these issues would impact the stock price, could you have predicted the massive data breach in 2013 that compromised info on up to 110 million Target customers and caused a 46 percent drop in sales during the holiday season?[8]

In behavioral finance, we call this blind spot "familiarity bias." We often develop unwarranted confidence in the growth potential of a particular stock because we feel like we know the company.

Familiarity bias comes in many forms. We might be inclined to buy the stock because we shop there all the time, as in the Target example above, or simply because we love the brand. This is a big reason many people I know have bought Disney stock.

We might also feel confident buying a stock because we have done a lot of research on it. However, we couldn't possibly outsmart the research teams of large institutional investors, and they get it wrong all the time, too.

One of my friends decided to invest a lot of money in a local manufacturing company because he drove by their headquarters every day. It was a massive, beautiful building, and the parking lot always looked full, so he figured they must be doing something right. Out of the blue, something bad happened to the company. He's not even sure what happened, but he lost almost everything he invested with them.

Another friend received a sizeable amount of General Electric stock from her grandfather when he passed away many years ago. He had worked there for most of his career and was a big fan of the company. She knew he had made a lot of money on the stock over time and heard him always bragging about how great the company was while she was growing up, so she felt it would be a dishonor to him to sell it. Unfortunately, as we already discussed, General Electric has not fared so well in the past 20 years.

The scandal that led to the collapse of Enron in December 2001 was a particularly heart-breaking example of the risks of familiarity bias. Almost 60 percent of all Enron employees' retirement assets were held in Enron stock.

Most employees were very proud to work there. The CEO frequently proclaimed how well they were doing and how bright the future of the company was, so they were happy to own so much Enron stock in their retirement accounts.

Tragically, it was all a lie. When the truth finally came out, about 4,000 employees lost their jobs overnight. To make matters worse, no one could sell any Enron stock held in their 401(k) while its value was dropping because the plan had been frozen.

During this time, executives who held massive amounts of Enron stock outside their 401(k) were able to unload their shares at close to peak prices before the stock basically became worthless.[9]

This was an unfair, devastating blow to these hard-working, loyal employees. They probably figured they knew the health and potential of the company better than anyone since they worked there, so they loved owning large amounts of its stock.

Thankfully, most employees will never experience this level of betrayal. Yet, it is a stark reminder of the importance of not investing too much of our hard-earned savings in one company, no matter how well we think we might know it.

I KNEW THAT STOCK WAS GONNA EXPLODE

If you have ever owned Tesla stock, you have likely experienced quite a roller coaster ride. Several people I know have been caught in a vicious cycle with Tesla due to another insidious psychological phenomenon called "hindsight bias." Here is a typical scenario of how this has played out:

Let's say you buy a large amount of Tesla stock in January 2019 around $300 per share because you love the company and think it's poised for explosive growth. It seems like a great time to acquire it because earlier in the month it was trading around $375 per share. Over the next several months, right after you buy, it continues to sink all the way down to about $180 per share in May.

A 40 percent loss over four months is not quite what you had in mind. You're kicking yourself because you had a hunch it was going to drop right after you bought it. "All the signs were there and I ignored them," you complain. "I knew I should have waited a little longer. Why didn't I listen to the warnings of those analysts?"

Despite your disappointment, you're determined to earn your money back. You still believe in the company so you decide to hold on a little longer.

Thankfully, the stock price starts climbing again and by the end of January 2020 it soars to $650 per share. You're very pleased with how smart you are and think, "I knew it was going to come back. I more than doubled my money in a year and now is the perfect time to sell before it drops again like the analysts are predicting."

Just a month later, the stock price rises to over $900 per share, and now you're kicking yourself again: "I knew I should have held it just a little longer!" Suddenly everything shuts down due to COVID-19 and the stock price plunges to about $360 per share in March 2020. This makes you feel much better about the timing of your sale.

You still like Tesla as a company and believe they have room to grow, so you're tempted to buy it again. However, everyone on the news is saying the economy won't recover for a long time, and you're determined not to make the mistake of buying too soon again. Tesla already sank 60 percent in one short month, and you're not about to jump in while it's on that steep of a downward trend.

Then in an unbelievable recovery few could have predicted, Tesla stock skyrockets to over $2,200 by the end of August 2020, just before its first split.[10] You exclaim, "I *knew* it was undervalued and I should have bought it when it dropped 60 percent!"

But did you *really* know? Be honest with yourself and give yourself some credit. No intelligent person who really knew what was going to happen would have waited to jump on that amazing of an opportunity.

I hope you're happy that you doubled your money in a year because of how brilliant you were at "predicting" what the stock would do. If you had held onto your Tesla stock just seven months longer, you could have earned more than *seven times* your original investment.

These are real numbers demonstrating how devastating the impact of hindsight bias can be. In this scenario, it would have caused you to miss out on a lot more potential growth, but at least you would have doubled your money. Usually hindsight bias causes much bigger problems and can lead to very large losses.

As they say, hindsight is always 20/20. However, foresight is not. Most of us have no idea how hindsight bias skews our ability to make rational decisions.

We all like to think we can predict what's going to happen because it helps us feel smarter and makes our chaotic, unpredictable world seem safer. After an unexpected event occurs, we try to make sense of what happened by identifying signals which at the time seemed innocuous, inaccurate, or irrelevant.

This psychological phenomenon often leads to frustration or regret. We feel like we should have trusted our gut because "all the signs were there," even if we didn't act on them.

The truth is, maybe some indications of what was about to happen were there, but the end result was only one of many possibilities. Other observable signals were present suggesting drastically different outcomes, but afterwards we tend to place greater emphasis on the signals leading to what happened.

Why does this matter? If we trick ourselves into believing we predicted outcomes more accurately than we did, we might be too confident in our ability to predict future events. If we're not careful, our overconfidence can lead us to taking more risk than we should.

I can't tell you how many people have told me, "I knew I should have bought tons of Apple stock in the early 2000s!" Or Amazon. Or Google. Or Tesla. Or…fill in the blank.

Since they are convinced they saw it coming and are determined not to miss out on the next big thing, they overload on some hot new stock that claims to be the next Apple. Unfortunately, it seldom if ever ends up performing as they expected.

The fact is, they didn't *know* those stocks were going to explode. Otherwise, they would have cashed out all the equity in their house, maxed out every credit card they could get their hands on, borrowed as much as they could from every family member and friend, sold all their other investments, and put it all in that company.

"Confirmation bias" is another insidious deterrent to rational decision-making. We tend to seek out and emphasize information that confirms our preconceived notions because it makes us feel smarter, makes decision-making more efficient, and avoids the discomfort of having to reconcile information that conflicts with our views. Like hindsight bias, it can cause us to make foolish investment decisions that could cause us to take on more risk than we should or miss out on big opportunities.

Experts recommend keeping a record to detail the steps of your investment decision-making processes. This can help reduce your vulnerability to hindsight bias and confirmation bias. If you write down the reasons for your choices, later on you can more accurately reflect on how you arrived at your conclusions without placing undue bias on issues that became more obvious after the fact.

After each event, the practice of brainstorming other outcomes that could have happened is healthy. This can help you acknowledge that the outcome was not as inevitable as it may seem on the surface. Seeking a wide range of info, including views that challenge your perspective, also leads to wiser decisions because it ensures you're considering all angles rather than looking for confirmation that you were right. [11]

Don't be fooled by your own hindsight bias or confirmation bias. Remember that foresight is never 20/20 and that your vision can be greatly clarified by considering other perspectives besides your own.

THE ILLUSION OF CONTROL

Several years ago I attended a professional conference with hundreds of people. One of the speakers asked, "How many of you think you're an above-average driver?" Almost every hand in the audience shot up. We all laughed, realizing we couldn't *all* be above-average drivers. Statistically speaking about half of us should not have raised our hands, but not very many people think of themselves as below-average drivers.

If you really are an above-average driver, in which of the following scenarios would you feel the safest?

1. You drive a car across the country.
2. You ride in the passenger's seat while your friend drives across the country (assuming your friend is also an excellent driver).
3. You fly in a commercial airline across the country.

Most people say they would feel safest being in the driver's seat, even though they would be just as safe with their friend driving and flying would be the safest by far. In fact, one study points out that "a sold-out 727 jet would have to crash every day of the week, with no survivors, to equal the highway deaths per year in this country."[12]

We all love being in control of our own destiny. It makes us feel safe and empowered, but we don't always have as much control as we think. Some outcomes are simply uncontrollable. I can barely control myself, let alone my kids or anyone outside my family.

Driving is one of those areas where we tend to think we are always in control. Yet we cannot control or perfectly predict what the hundreds of drivers around us are going to do.

One of my friends insists he is a way better driver than I am despite the fact that he has paid thousands of dollars in speeding tickets, has been in multiple accidents, and had his driver's license suspended twice. How could he think of himself as a better driver while I have an almost flawless driving record?

Finally I realized he was talking about his perception of his technical driving "skills," such as his ability to take sharp corners really fast and to weave in and out of traffic at high speeds. How silly of me—I always thought the definition of a good driver was someone who obeys the law, is courteous to other drivers, and drives defensively to minimize potential accidents.

Despite his "superior" driving skills, how much control does he really have? What are his chances of maintaining control if someone were to change lanes right in front of him because they didn't expect anyone to approach at over 100 miles per hour? How would he react if he hit a patch of loose gravel or black ice just as he was trying to swerve between two cars? What would he do if a pedestrian stepped into the crosswalk just as he was attempting to take a sharp turn at record speeds?

Many people also think of themselves as above-average investors even though their performance has been pathetic. They are so confident in their investing prowess that they believe they can weave in and out of stocks at breakneck speeds without getting hurt. They exaggerate their wins and don't measure the cost of their losses because their ego is at stake.

The illusion of control often tempts investors to take inordinate amounts of risk. When people have done a lot of research about a specific company, they often feel they can accurately predict what will happen to its stock price. This gives them a feeling of control over the outcome, convincing themselves they will be able to get in and out of the stock at the right time because of their superior knowledge.

Many years ago, a friend of mine was really good friends with the CEO of a large publicly traded company. He didn't work at the same company, but they had long conversations at least monthly. The CEO would often slip him little hints concerning somewhat meaningful non-public information about what was happening at the company. This guy admitted that several times he bought or sold shares in that company's stock based on what the CEO told him.

I tried to warn him that what he was doing could be considered insider trading, which is totally illegal. (Remember when Martha Stewart went to prison for covering up her sale of stocks due to non-public information?) He responded, "Not that it did me any good anyway! I'm never going to listen to what the CEO says anymore. Every time I have bought or sold his company's stock based on what he shared, it did the exact opposite of what I expected, and I have lost a ton of money investing in it." I found it comical that not even the CEO's insider information could give my friend an edge on predicting what the stock would do.

In reality, as we have discussed with other investing fallacies, the outcome of every stock's price is far more subject to chance than you might expect. Even if you make reasonable assumptions about what the stock should do based on your research, and even if your info came firsthand from the CEO, too many other factors cannot be controlled or predicted.

Public sentiment, changing market conditions, and a host of other factors can have a huge impact on stock prices, regardless of the company's fundamentals. The market is not rational and doesn't care how much homework you did.

Some investors feel they must take control of their investments by constantly analyzing and tweaking their portfolio. They consider a more passive approach to be too lazy to yield a healthy return. Since most other things in life require effort to produce results, they mistakenly believe they need to regularly put a lot of work into their investments to increase their chances of a positive outcome.

Stocks are not like gardens that need to be constantly watered, weeded, fertilized, and pruned to thrive. They are more like bars of soap. The more you handle them, the smaller they become.

If you're craving control over something, get your own TV with a remote that no one else can touch, and learn to control your temper. Whatever you do, don't fool yourself into thinking you can control the outcome of your investments through your "above average" knowledge and skill, or you will get hurt.

DAY TRADING DISASTERS

Day traders are extreme examples of investors who actively strive to take control of the outcome of their investments on a daily or hourly basis. They employ a very risky style of investing that involves trading in and out of individual stocks very frequently based on predictions of short-term movements in stock prices. They may buy a stock in the morning and sell it only a few hours later in hopes for a quick short-term gain.

Some day traders have made hundreds of thousands of dollars in a very short amount of time. So have a handful of people playing baccarat at the Bellagio. Both groups tend to brag more about their wins than their losses, so you can never really get the full scoop on how much money they made overall. Both are games of pure chance, and both can be very dangerous.

Based on a study of 450,000 day traders from 1992 to 2006, less than 1 percent of them were able to consistently profit from it after fees over time. Of the 99 percent that lost money attempting to day trade, the overwhelming majority lost up to a fourth of one percent per day, a gigantic annualized loss.[13]

Part of the reason it is very difficult to make money day trading is that frequent stock trades can be expensive. Even with commission-free trading platforms, there is always a difference between the buy price and the sell price. This is called the "spread." It is a built-in fee you pay every time you buy or sell a stock, and it can reduce your returns.

Taxes are also higher when you buy and sell stocks so frequently. Any stocks sold within a year of buying them are subject to short-term capital gains tax rates, which are typically the same as ordinary income tax rates. If you hold a stock for more than a year, the tax rate is much lower.

Day traders also tend to focus more on small stocks and penny stocks because they tend to be much more volatile, meaning their prices fluctuate a lot throughout each day. This gives them a greater opportunity to capture big gains over a short period, but it also means they can wipe out all their gains very quickly. The fees for trading these types of stocks tend to be much larger as well, making it even harder to make money after fees.

Besides the high trading costs and unlikelihood of success, day trading can take a lot of time and a huge emotional toll. Based on the same study quoted earlier, more than 75 percent of day traders quit within the first two years. I know many people who have tried it, and most of them didn't even last that long. It's simply too risky and too stressful.

Many free online trading platforms and phone apps make it easier than ever to trade individual stocks on your own. I am bombarded regularly by my online savings bank to buy stocks through them, and they're not even an investment company! The allure can be strong, but smart investors recognize that just because it's easy and free doesn't mean it's a good idea. Besides, as we will discuss in Chapter 5, "free" trading platforms are never really free.

Some of our clients like to maintain a separate account to trade individual stocks on their own just for fun, but they never put much money in this type of account. We affectionately call it their "casino account" to remind them it's essentially a form of gambling. If you decide you want to dabble in trading individual stocks, please don't put too much time, energy, or money into it, or it could ruin your life.

PLAYING WITH THE BIG BOYS

Let's assume for a moment that you don't believe anything I've said up to this point and you think you really can consistently determine the right times to get in and out of the market. You're also certain that you can pinpoint which are the best stocks to invest in and when they should be sold based on your analysis. Maybe you even think you can predict and profit from short-term movements in the market from day to day.

If you do believe all these things and feel confident in your ability to pick stocks yourself, you have another dilemma to face. How are you going to outsmart the thousands of full-time institutional investment analysts with advanced degrees, certifications in financial analysis, and decades of professional experience? On top of that, they have an astronomical research budget and access to mountains of data you will never be able to access, including the ability to interview the executives of publicly traded companies.

Between $10 and 20 billion is spent on investment research each year worldwide by asset managers of large financial institutions seeking information to help them get an edge on other investors.[14] This type of research requires a lot of people and a lot of money because there is a lot of data to process. The following is just a sample of the types of info they study in an effort to make informed investment recommendations:

1. **Industry research** – Measures the potential impact of politics, social trends, technological innovation, competition, and many other factors. This type of information must be gathered and accurately interpreted on a regular basis to understand how general industry trends could affect each stock price within the industry. This information should be gathered for every industry an investor would like to participate in.

2. **Management assessment** – Research analysts from large institutions often have access to speak directly with top executives from the companies they analyze in order to assess their competence and their assessment of the direction of the business. Individual investors don't have as

much access to this data or the ability to ask questions of top management.

3. **Historical financial results** – Analysts pour over years of data to determine how closely a company's forecasted results matched their actual performance over time. The financial results measured typically include revenue, net income, earnings per share, price-earnings ratios, return on equity, return on assets, and many other factors.

4. **Forecasting** – Predictions of future earnings estimates and stock price movement based on both top-down analysis (starting with the industry), and bottom-up analysis (starting with the revenue drivers of a specific company).

5. **Valuation** – Estimates of how much analysts believe the company should be worth based on the synthesis of all other information obtained. It is normally based on some form of discounted future expected cash flows or a valuation multiple consistent with industry peers.[15]

6. **Technical analysis** – Some analysts believe stock prices move in patterns according to trends, so they focus on studying trading volume, price movement, charts, trends, and other issues to try to forecast future stock prices.

7. **News Updates** – Analysts constantly stay on top of breaking news that could affect the companies they monitor, the industries those companies are in, the general market, and the global economy. They immediately relay any relevant information to the investment managers to make necessary adjustments as quickly as possible.

Do you have the knowledge, experience, tools, and access to be able to gather all that information on your own and compete with these professional analysts? If so, do you have the time and desire to do it?

By the way, despite the billions of dollars and millions of hours spent on all this research, the "big boys" still strike out most of the time, so what's the point of even playing their game? Studies show that the vast majority of active managers who try to outperform the market tend to significantly underperform the market over time. We'll discuss specific examples of this in Chapter 3.

Sure, they might get lucky from time to time, but then again, so do roulette players, and roulette doesn't require nearly as much time or effort to lose the game.

MONEYBALL AND THE VANISHING EDGE

Even if a genius analyst were to come up with a legitimate new tool or strategy to beat the market through their innovation, any advantage would likely be very short-lived. As soon as others figured out what they were doing, the advantage would disappear.

Have you read the book *Moneyball* by Michael Lewis or seen the movie starring Brad Pitt? It's an intriguing story about how Billy Beane, general manager of the Oakland A's, revolutionized baseball. Since he had to work with one of the lowest payrolls in all of Major League Baseball, he was determined to find creative ways to compete.

Traditional recruiting methods focused on ranking players based on a specific set of stats such as batting average, stolen bases, and runs batted in. Billy Beane believed he could radically improve his team's chances of winning despite his meager budget by focusing on undervalued players with overlooked skills.

He discovered an underappreciated set of stats that he calculated would have a much bigger impact on the team's ability to win, such as on-base percentage and slugging percentage. He was able to acquire players who excelled in these areas for a lot less money because none of the other teams recognized their value. His theory was proven correct, and he took the A's all the way to the playoffs in 2002 and 2003 for the first time in years, competing head-to-head with much richer teams like the New York Yankees.

A friend of mine was a pitcher for the A's during this period. He said it was a very exciting time for his team. However, it didn't take long for the other teams to catch on to what they were doing.

My friend observed that as soon as word got out, many other teams began to employ a similar strategy, and the A's didn't perform nearly as well from that point forward. Unfortunately, their unique advantage had disappeared after only a few short years of exceptional performance.

This same phenomenon affects competition in the stock market. The market is very efficient, especially in today's high-tech world where information travels instantaneously. Any edge or hidden inefficiency an investor or group of investors may find in the market is usually swallowed up as soon as others start to recognize what is happening. It's almost impossible to profit long-term from any type of major advantage a unique strategy may provide.

ONE EGG, ONE BASKET

The timeless adage "don't put all your eggs in one basket" is commonly attributed to Miguel de Cervantes, who wrote a similar expression in his novel *Don Quixote* in 1605. Although this counsel applies to many aspects of life, we use it in the investing world to highlight the importance of diversification.

As a side note, I just realized I never gave my children more than one basket for any of their Easter egg hunts. Hopefully they will teach their children to be more prudent Easter egg collectors.

Diversification means investing in many different things so you can capture the potential for high returns while significantly reducing your likelihood of losing a lot of money. It is widely recognized as one of the best ways to control investment risk since you have no control over the outcome of most investments.

Many investors who brag about how much they made on brilliant stock picks don't realize their success may have had more to do with the growth of the general market than the specific stocks they chose. Since rising tides lift all boats, investors often can make just as much with a lot less risk by employing a more diversified strategy.

Several investors told me they saw a stock buying opportunity shortly after the steep market drop in March 2020 related to COVID-19 fears. They thought they were geniuses because the handful of stocks they picked increased by 50 to 60 percent by the end of the year. They didn't realize that the S&P 500 also surged 66 percent by the end of 2020 from it's low on March 23. Would you rather earn 50 to 60 percent in a few risky stock picks or 66 percent in 500 of the largest U.S. companies?

Obviously, sometimes you might make a lot more than the market by concentrating on a small selection of stocks, but I don't recommend it because you can also lose a lot more, as we have discussed. The prices of individual stocks fluctuate way too much, and you have no control over their outcome.

There is one possible exception to this rule: your own business. If you own a business, you have a lot of control over many of the risks your business might face, so diversification may seem less critical. You are free to adjust products and services to meet changing demands. You can cut expenses to weather the storms of falling revenue. You can revamp your marketing strategies, change suppliers, and create fresh solutions to circumvent unexpected challenges or take advantage of exciting opportunities as the economy constantly evolves.

Most of my clients are successful business owners or self-employed professionals. Due to their ability to control these and other risks, I tell them all the time that I probably will never find an investment opportunity that would give them a higher potential return for a comparable level of risk than they are likely to earn in their own business.

Some businesses owners are so confident in their abilities that they figuratively hold all their wealth in one egg and one basket: their business. However, most of my clients prefer to regularly invest some of their profits in more traditional assets such as stocks, bonds, mutual funds, and real estate, even if the potential returns might be lower than what they expect to earn in their business.

Why would they do that? They understand that while great wealth may be created through asset concentration, wealth is best preserved through diversification. They also want to have a backup plan because they recognize their vulnerability to the following realities:

1. Business owners cannot fully predict or control all risks that may threaten their business.
2. Most businesses do not survive long-term.
3. Most business owners overestimate how much their business is worth and how much they can earn from the proceeds after selling it.

4. With no other assets, they may face too much pressure to sell at an unreasonable price or unfavorable terms, forcing them to work longer.
5. If they have no experience owning other types of assets, it might be too difficult for them to trust in passive investments after selling their business.

Let's break each of these down a bit. First of all, business owners cannot fully predict or control all risks that may threaten their business. Changes in consumer demand, competition, technological advances, costs of goods sold, labor markets, supply chains, demographics, government regulations, theft, and the state of the general economy are only some of the uncontrollable factors that could take a business down.

Second, most businesses do not survive long-term. According to the U.S. Bureau of Labor Statistics, about 20 percent of new businesses fail within the first two years of opening, 45 percent fail within the first five years, and 65 percent fail within the first 10 years. Only 25 percent of new businesses survive 15 years or longer—not great odds for those seeking a prudent long-term investment strategy.[16]

Third, most business owners overestimate how much their business is worth. They might get excited when they see an article or hear another business owner talk about some crazy multiple of revenue they could sell their business for. However, these figures may not be relevant if they're in a different industry or don't take into account their particular operating costs, growth patterns, or unique risk factors.

They also tend to overestimate how much passive income they will be able to derive from the net proceeds after selling their business. For example, assume you own a business with $5 million annual revenue and $1 million net income. Your friend tells you he sold his business for three times his gross revenue, so you assume your business is worth $15 million. You decide to sell your business and start listing all the cool stuff you're going to buy with the proceeds.

After a year of enormous effort trying to get your business ready to sell, evaluating various offers, and going through the due diligence process with the buyer you think will be best, you are only able to sell for $7.5 million. After taxes and fees, you end up with $5 million in your pocket.

Since this is your only asset and you don't have the time or energy to start another business, you can't afford to take much risk with this money. As you begin researching reasonably safe investment options, you discover you should probably only take about $150,000 to $200,000 per year from your new investment accounts so you don't risk spending all your money too quickly. You want to ensure you and your spouse don't outlive your money and hope to leave something to your children and grandchildren.

So much for all that cool stuff you were going to buy with $15 million. Now you have to figure out how to maintain your lifestyle with only $150,000 to $200,000 of income when you were used to making over $1 million per year. If you had built other investments outside your business along the way, you wouldn't be so dependent on your business sale proceeds for retirement income.

This leads us to the fourth issue: many business owners with no other assets have to work longer than expected because they can't sell their businesses for a high enough price to maintain their lifestyle. Alternatively, they may be forced to sell to a less than ideal buyer with unfavorable terms because they are so desperate to get out.

A friend of mine owns a business that provides a highly specialized service to several of the largest companies in Nevada. He was very involved in the day-to-day operations of the business for over 30 years. Since very few businesses provide this type of service and his company was one of the best, he was well respected and valued by his customers.

The business provided a great lifestyle for him. Due to the seemingly endless capital needs of his company and family, he never invested much outside his business, so he didn't acquire very many other assets.

He employed a great team, but no one had the desire or ability to purchase the business from him, much less run it after his departure. Finally, he convinced one of his sons to join the team and eventually buy him out.

After three years of learning the ropes and getting to know all the clients, he figured his son was ready to run the company on his own. He couldn't wait another day to retire, especially since he was dealing with some relatively significant health problems. His son didn't have any assets of his own and he didn't want to put too big of a cash flow crunch on the business, so they agreed to a 20-year buyout with no down payment.

Relieved that after a long, hard career his working days were finally over, he sold his house and rode off into the sunset. He and his wife moved to a much better climate over 1,000 miles away from the business and built their dream home.

Everything was going as planned until two years later when most of the world was shut down due to the COVID-19 pandemic. His son became overwhelmed and didn't know what to do. He had an emotional meltdown, ran up a big debt with vendors, wouldn't answer the phone at the office, and was afraid to call people back. In my friend's words, he was like an "armchair quarterback," not willing to really dig in and do what needed to be done to help the business survive.

The company stopped receiving income, so my friend stopped receiving his buyout payments. Finally his son called and admitted he couldn't hold it together anymore. He told my friend he could have the business back, but that was the last thing he wanted. He just wanted his payments so he could enjoy his newfound freedom!

This was financially devastating to my friend and his wife and was hard on their relationship with their son. It caused their other children to harbor hard feelings toward this son, too. He has lost all motivation in his career. Now he earns just above minimum wage polishing floors at night for a janitorial company.

Since then, my friend has been commuting over 1,000 miles each week to salvage the business, returning home each weekend to see his wife. He's very frustrated but hopeful that he'll be able to turn it around and sell it to a more qualified buyer. Then he can go back to enjoying the retirement he thought he had already locked in.

If my friend had gathered sufficient additional assets such as stocks, bonds, mutual funds and real estate, I'm confident he would not have been so dependent on selling the business to his son under such risky, unfavorable terms. Additionally, when the business began to struggle, he would not have been so dependent on the payments from the business sale to meet his income needs.

The financial and emotional costs of being 100 percent dependent on the sale of your business for retirement income can be massive. This is a perfect example of why so many of my clients regularly invest in other assets besides their business.

The fifth and final issue with business owners not having any assets outside their company is that they might have trouble trusting in passive investments after the sale. Due to their success in business, many take on more risk than they should after selling their company. They falsely assume that their business acumen will easily translate to any type of business in any industry. This attitude has caused some business owners to lose everything they have worked a lifetime to build.

Ironically, they may feel they can trust other small businesses more than they can trust the stock or bond markets, simply because they have no experience investing in them. However, even with the volatility of the market, a well-diversified mix of stocks, bonds, or both, tends to be much safer than investing in a small business—especially if you don't have full control over that business.

Don't forget that investing in a small business is just another form of stock ownership, but it's not as safe or as liquid as investing in publicly traded companies. With small business ownership, you can't get your money out whenever you want, if ever, and they are much more likely to fail than larger companies.

Business owners who have experience investing in more traditional assets like publicly traded stocks, bonds, mutual funds, and real estate throughout their career become familiar with the ups and downs of normal market cycles. This helps them gain confidence in the market's ability to generate healthy, sustainable income for the remainder of their life after they sell their company. They are less likely to overreact to every morsel of market movement, improving their chances of long-term passive investing success.

Most people need time and experience to determine which investment strategies will meet their goals after selling their company. I strongly recommend that business owners also build other assets throughout their career.

If you haven't done so yet, get started now by opening a retirement or brokerage account and investing some of your profits every month. I call this "paying yourself first" to ensure you're not left penniless if you lose your business.

If you don't own a business, you don't need to start one to be successful. Many people have accomplished their financial goals and enjoyed a great retirement by saving a healthy portion of their income and investing in a diversified assortment of traditional assets throughout their career.

Small business is the backbone of America. It is vital to our economy, yet very difficult to succeed at it. That's why I believe those who are able to successfully grow a small business deserve to be paid very well for what they do.

Survival isn't just a challenge for small businesses, though. According to *Harvard Business Review*, 37 percent of publicly traded companies fail within five years after they go public.[17] As we discussed earlier, giant corporations that have been around for a long time can fail, too.

These are some of the reasons most people who have amassed enough wealth to meet their financial goals eventually get to the point where they value stability and low stress more than future growth potential. That's where diversification shines, and that's why you might want to invest in more than one basket.

KEY POINTS OF CHAPTER 2

1. No one can consistently predict which stocks will perform best in the future, and trying to do so can be dangerous.
2. Just because a stock has performed well in the past doesn't mean it will continue to outperform.
3. The largest companies of the world may have outperformed the market in the past, but then they tend to underperform and can even go out of business.

4. Beware of investing in companies simply because you're familiar with them.
5. Record the steps of your decision-making processes to reduce your vulnerability to hindsight and confirmation bias.
6. You can't control the outcome of your investments regardless of your knowledge, skill, and time spent on it.
7. Even if it were possible to pick the "best" stocks, you are unlikely to be able to compete with professional analysts.
8. The predictions of professional analysts usually fail, too.
9. The market is very efficient, so any advantage discovered tends to be short-lived.
10. Although your business will probably give you the highest potential returns for the risk, you would be wise to diversify by also investing in other assets.

CHAPTER 3

CHASING WHAT'S HOT

TANTALIZING TRACK RECORDS

Imagine your investment strategy was to bet all your money on the team that won last year's Super Bowl. After all, wouldn't that be the best indication of who will win the next Super Bowl?

As of this writing, in the 57 Super Bowls since 1967 the same team has won two years in a row only eight times, and only one team has done it twice: the Pittsburgh Steelers. That's only a 14 percent chance that your strategy would work.

You may argue that some teams are more likely to win than others because of their past success or the advantage certain star athletes provide. True, the New England Patriots and Pittsburgh Steelers have won more Super Bowls than any other team (six each), but these teams have won less than 11 percent of the total Super Bowls so far—not very good odds for an investment strategy.[1]

Most people would never say that this year's Super Bowl champion is destined to win again next year. However, many people believe that this year's best-performing investment will win again next year.

We already talked about the dangers of relying too heavily on the past performance of a specific stock. The same principles apply to relying on the past performance of specific mutual funds, exchange-traded funds (ETFs), types of investments, regions of the world, or market sectors, a fancy word for distinct areas of the market like technology, health care, and so on.

At the beginning of Chapter 2, I talked about how frustrating the process of chasing last year's winners can be. In our training as new wealth advisors they told us that was our job. Now I know why—the more you move stuff around, the more financial institutions (and some advisors) make. But that approach typically does not result in superior returns.

At the end of 2020, Citywire named the Morgan Stanley Inst Discovery fund (MPEGX) the best-performing fund of the year, which ended 2020 with an astounding 143 percent one-year return. How did this fund do in 2021? It lost 12 percent while the average return of all funds in the same category that year was a positive 13 percent.[2]

The worst-performing fund in 2020 according to Citywire was the Highland Small-Cap Equity fund (HSZYX), which lost 50 percent in 2020.[3] Apparently it is now known as the NexPoint Climate Tech Y fund. (You'll never guess why they changed the name.) How did this fund do in 2021? It earned a positive 38 percent, way outperforming the other funds in its category.[4] See how hard it is to win this game?

Granted, these are extreme short-term examples. Some people · say if you look at a longer time horizon, say five or 10 years, you will get a much better indication of who will outperform going forward. Let's test that theory.

Of the 2,813 U.S. stock mutual funds and ETFs that existed 20 years ago, only 44 percent have survived. Even worse, only 18 percent have outperformed their benchmarks, not much better odds than predicting next year's Super Bowl champion.

No problem, why not invest only in the top 18 percent winning funds? Just one catch: you don't get to know ahead of time which 18 percent will win in the future, and the 82 percent remaining will likely be losers.

Few could have predicted 20 years ago which funds would survive, let alone outperform their benchmarks. The ones who did outperform over the past 20 years on average did not outperform every year. Of the funds that made the top 25 percent five years in a row, only about a fifth appeared in the top 25 percent the following five years. Good luck predicting which ones.[5]

Among other reasons, I primarily use mutual funds and ETFs from Dimensional Fund Advisors because they are very disciplined in sticking to their strategy through all the ups and downs of the market. This helps them produce more consistent results over time. They don't outperform their benchmarks every year, but *all* of their funds that were open 20 years ago are still open today, and 79 percent of them have outperformed their benchmarks over the last 20 years (as of the end of 2022).[6]

What about focusing on certain sectors of the market that have done well and avoiding those that have not? The S&P 500, which contains 500 of the largest U.S. stocks, has performed so well in recent years that most people don't remember how poorly it performed from January 2000 through December 2009. Now dubbed the "lost decade," the S&P 500 *lost* an average of 1 percent per year during that time.

That decade was quite a roller coaster with the bursting of the dot-com tech bubble, 9/11, the Great Recession, and a whole host of other challenges. After all these ups and downs, many S&P 500 index investors were furious that they had lost money over 10 painful years of trying to stay patient and disciplined, vowing to never invest in stocks again.

Who can blame them? They would have made more in a guaranteed bank account over that 10-year period with far fewer headaches. At the time many experts even said U.S. stocks were dead and would never again see the 10 percent-plus average annual returns they had enjoyed before the lost decade.

But that doesn't tell the whole story. While it may have been a rough decade for U.S. large stocks, many other types of stocks made a lot of money over that same period, including value stocks, U.S. small stocks, international stocks, and emerging markets. International small value stocks earned an astonishing 13.7 percent average annual return over those 10 agonizing years.

In other words, if you had invested $1 million in the S&P 500 at the beginning of the decade, you would have ended with about $900,000. If you had invested $1 million in international small value stocks, it would have grown to about $3.6 million.

Does this mean you should have moved all your money to international small value stocks at the beginning of 2010 since its performance was clearly superior to U.S. large stocks over the previous decade? Isn't that a long enough track record to determine who the winner will be for the next decade? Absolutely not!

Let's examine what happened for the next decade. From January 2010 to December 2019, the S&P 500 index came roaring back with a 13.6 percent average annual rate of return. All the other indexes mentioned above made money, too, but none of them performed as well as the S&P 500. International small value stocks only earned an average of 7.5 percent per year.

What was the total outcome after combining both decades? International small value stocks clocked in at a 10.5 percent average annual return from January 2000 to December 2019, almost double the S&P 500 average annual return of 6.1 percent[7] (see Figure 6).

	Average Annual Returns for Each Period		
	2000-2009	2010-2019	2000-2019
S&P 500	-1.0%	13.6%	6.1%
Int'l Small Val Stocks	13.7%	7.5%	10.5%

Figure 6: Diversification Lessons from the "Lost Decade"

Who will be the winner for the next 10 years? Can U.S. large stocks continue their remarkable track record of the past decade? Or will international small value stocks beat out U.S. large stocks again for the next 20 years?

Nobody knows. The best way to improve your chances of success is to own a wide variety of asset classes and stick to your plan. The best way to lose money or to miss out on big opportunities is to chase the winners of the past.

Just for fun, in Figure 7 check out the best-performing and worst-performing developed countries throughout the world in the past 20 years.[8] Can you find a pattern? How many years has the U.S. been the top performer?

In case you can't tell, there is no pattern—the returns are totally random and unpredictable. Note that Austria was the best-performing developed country in 2017 with a 58 percent gain, then the worst-performing country the very next year with a 27 percent loss. Ireland was the worst performer two years in a row, losing almost all its value, then hit the top of the list three years later.

Surprisingly, the U.S. only had the highest returns one year in the past 20 years. Also note that some countries were more volatile than others. Finland is the only country that was the best performer three times *and* the worst performer three times. Several countries stayed in the middle of the pack for the full 20 years, so they don't even show up on this chart: Australia, France, Hong Kong, Italy, Netherlands, and Switzerland.

Year	Highest Return		Lowest Return	
2002	24%	New Zealand	-33%	Germany
2003	65%	Sweden	19%	Finland
2004	72%	Austria	6%	Finland
2005	28%	Canada	-2%	Ireland
2006	49%	Spain	6%	Japan
2007	49%	Finland	-20%	Ireland
2008	-29%	Japan	-72%	Ireland
2009	87%	Norway	6%	Japan
2010	34%	Sweden	-22%	Spain
2011	14%	Ireland	-36%	Austria
2012	40%	Belgium	3%	Spain
2013	46%	Finland	2%	Singapore
2014	13%	U.S.	-38%	Portugal
2015	23%	Denmark	-24%	Canada
2016	25%	Canada	-16%	Denmark
2017	58%	Austria	12%	New Zealand
2018	-3%	Finland	-27%	Austria
2019	38%	New Zealand	10%	Finland
2020	44%	Denmark	-11%	United Kingdom
2021	42%	Austria	-17%	New Zealand

Figure 7: Stock Returns of Developed Markets

Chasing tantalizing track records can be quite a wild ride and is often a recipe for disaster. Thankfully, you don't have to predict where future returns will come from in order to have a good investment experience.

Maintaining a globally diversified portfolio can help improve your chances of a more reliable outcome over time. Throughout the rest of this chapter, we will explore other ways many people have been burned by chasing what's hot.

TECH FEVER

If no one can consistently predict the best stock, mutual fund, ETF, asset class, or country to invest in, surely someone could at least figure out which sector of the market will outperform going forward, right? In the 1990s, the most sensational sector was clearly technology.

If you were investing in the 1990s, you remember how exciting that time was. Stocks consistently boasted some of their best returns ever, year after year, with no end in sight. On top of that, the proliferation of the internet promised to change the world, and it did.

In the wake of this exhilarating new economy, the old rules of business valuation were thrown out the window. Any company with "dot-com" on the end of its name appeared destined to make a killing even if it didn't earn any profits.

Many new mutual funds focused on dot-com start-up companies and some of the returns were astronomical. According to *Pensions & Investments*, 168 mutual funds gained more than a 100 percent return in 1999 at the peak of the tech boom.

While the average U.S. stock mutual fund earned "only" 27 percent in 1999 (its third best-performing year in history), the average internet-based fund earned 131 percent. The top-performing fund that year, the Nicholas-Applegate Global Technology Fund, earned an unfathomable 496 percent.[9]

No wonder so many people wanted to move all their investments to technology stocks in 1999 and 2000. Who can be happy with a 27 percent return when you find out you could have earned 496 percent in one year?

Alas, it was not sustainable. The world finally realized that not every company with dot-com on the end of its name was automatically going to be a winner.

In 2000 tech stocks began their colossal downfall like a house of cards. The Nicholas-Applegate Global Technology Fund lost 36 percent in 2000, plunged another 49 percent in 2001, and continued its steep decline by another 49 percent in 2002. Then the fund managers decided to close the fund at the ripe old age of four years.[10]

Many investors shied away from tech stocks for years because they were still licking their wounds. But tech was here to stay and eventually came roaring back to dominate the U.S. stock market. In 2022, information technology stocks represented the highest percentage of all sectors in the S&P 500.

In 2020, when many companies struggled to survive because the world was shut down due to the COVID-19 pandemic, tech stocks enjoyed another glorious day in the sun because no one could shop at "real" stores or even attend meetings in person.

Hence the explosive growth of new companies like Zoom, which gained 396 percent in 2020. Big tech fared exceptionally well in 2020, too. Apple surged 82 percent and Amazon increased 76 percent, while the S&P 500 returned only 18 percent.

Obviously, as we learned in 2000, this run-up in tech couldn't last forever, either. In 2021 Zoom lost 45 percent, then fell another 62 percent the following year. In 2022, even Apple dropped 26 percent and Amazon shed almost 50 percent.[11]

The unpredictability of performance is not just a challenge for the technology sector. Many people have lost a lot of money adjusting their portfolio regularly to try to capture which sectors seem to be outperforming, just in time for those sectors to significantly underperform. Last year's winners often mysteriously morph into this year's biggest losers, and vice versa.

Can you find any patterns in Figure 8 showing the best-performing and worst-performing sectors of the S&P 500 each year for the past 15 years?[12]

As you may have guessed, no predictable patterns can be found in specific sectors of the market, either. Trying to chase winning sectors can be just as devastating to your returns as the other strategies we have already explored.

For example, after being the worst-performing sector for two years in a row (2014-2015), energy came roaring back in 2016 as the best-performing sector, earning 27 percent. If you had moved all your investments to energy in 2017 to try to capture those superior returns, you would have lost 1 percent the following year (not shown on this chart because it was the second-worst performer). Then if you decided to stay the course, expecting it to come back, you would have been stuck in the worst-performing sector for the next three years in a row. By 2021, surely you would be sick of losing so much and would get completely out of energy, just in time to miss out on its fabulous 55 percent recovery in 2021.

Chasing the best-performing sectors doesn't work. As you can see, each sector takes its turn and balances out the others, but not in any regular fashion. A well-diversified portfolio gives you the best chance for success, reducing risk while capturing the opportunity for significant gains.

Year	Highest Return		Lowest Return	
2007	34%	Energy	-19%	Financials
2008	-15%	Consumer Staples	-55%	Financials
2009	62%	Info Technology	9%	Communication
2010	32%	Real Estate	3%	Health Care
2011	20%	Utilities	-17%	Financials
2012	29%	Financials	1%	Utilities
2013	43%	Consumer Discret	2%	Real Estate
2014	30%	Real Estate	-8%	Energy
2015	10%	Consumer Discret	-21%	Energy
2016	27%	Energy	-3%	Health Care
2017	39%	Info Technology	-1%	Communication
2018	6%	Health Care	-18%	Energy
2019	50%	Info Technology	12%	Energy
2020	44%	Info Technology	-34%	Energy
2021	55%	Energy	18%	Utilities

Figure 8: S&P 500 Sector Performance

IPO HYPE

Few investment opportunities are as exciting as when one of your favorite brands first goes public. The IPO (initial public offering) of a high-profile, fast-growing company often creates quite a stir. This is by design because the more an IPO is hyped up, the more the company founders and banks underwriting the deal are paid.

But how well do IPOs work out for common investors? Typically, early trading drives the stock price higher than the initial offering price within its first day, but most investors are not able to participate in this opening surge because they are not eligible to obtain shares directly from the underwriting bank. Those shares are often reserved for select clients of the bank.

More importantly, after that initial one-day surge, IPOs tend to substantially underperform the general market for the first year. Many of them don't even survive very long after going public.

From 1992 to 2018 the average first-year return of IPOs was 6.9 percent while the Russell 3000 average annual return was 9.1 percent.[13] Why would you risk losing all your money in a single stock with a 6.9 percent average potential return when you could earn an average of 9.1 percent by investing in a much safer, more diversified portfolio of 3,000 U.S. stocks?

Let's revisit the IPOs of a few famous companies. In May 2012, the highly anticipated Facebook IPO was way over-subscribed—as much as 25 times in Asia, meaning 25 times more shares were ordered for purchase than were available to purchase. Originally, the initial share price range was set at $28 to $35, but in response to excessive demand, Facebook increased its opening price to $38 per share. This resulted in a market capitalization of over $100 billion, one of the largest IPOs in history. (Market capitalization is the price per share multiplied by the total number of shares outstanding, a measurement of a company's total value.)

Critics observed that this valuation was outrageous, representing almost 100 times the previous year's profits—much higher than Apple and Google, which boasted significantly higher revenues. Shortly before the IPO, Facebook expanded the number of shares available by an additional 25 percent to further capitalize on the excess demand, but this move backfired. Many investors ended up receiving more shares than they anticipated, essentially forcing them to sell the unwanted shares right away.

On top of that, an unusually high 57 percent of shares sold came from Facebook insiders. Typically, IPO insider sales are less than 10 percent, so this sparked additional fears that Facebook was overvalued.[14]

Due to these and other reasons, Facebook's stock price struggled to stay above its $38 opening price on the first day and dropped 15 percent within the first week. A few months later, it had fallen more than 50 percent and took more than a year to climb back to its $38 listing price.[15] Despite its rocky start, Facebook grew to be one of the best-performing stocks of the decade, but you would have been a lot better off waiting to buy it after the drama of its first year as a public company.

More recently Snap Inc., which owns Snapchat, went public in March 2017. It opened at $24 a share and closed at less than $15 a share by the end of the first year, almost a 40 percent loss.[16] It lost another 62 percent the following year, but then came roaring back, earning 196 percent in 2019 and 206 percent in 2020. Unfortunately, after its 2021 and 2022 losses, at the end of 2022 it was trading at only about a third of its 2017 IPO listing price.[17]

Spotify was the largest IPO of 2018 and performed well for the first four months. Then it collapsed by 45 percent over the next four months and took close to a year-and-a-half to get back to its IPO price. Despite its astounding growth in 2020, at the end of 2022 it was trading at about half its initial opening price.[18]

No doubt some of today's IPOs will be the backbone of tomorrow's future. However, chances are you will do much better waiting to invest in them after the frenzy has subsided, ideally at least a year after they go public.

THE RISE AND FALL OF GAMESTOP

GameStop's breathtaking spike and crash in 2021 is a particularly striking example of the unpredictability of the market and the dangers of chasing highfliers. GameStop is a brick-and-mortar video game and electronics store that went public in 2002. Struggling to compete with online retailers, it steadily declined from about $50 a share in early 2014 to $3 a share in March 2020.

A group of do-it-yourself investors communicated by way of a social media forum called WallStreetBets on Reddit. They saw GameStop as a buying opportunity, which propped up the stock's share price to almost $20 by the end of 2020.

This caught the attention of many large hedge fund managers, who felt the stock was significantly overvalued, so they "short sold" it. Short selling stock is a risky strategy where you sell stock that you borrowed, hoping to buy it at a lower price later to pay off the loan. You can make money if the stock price falls, but you can lose a lot if the price increases.

When the investors on WallStreetBets learned that these hedge funds shorted GameStop, they decided to ignite a "short squeeze." They rallied thousands of investors to buy and hold the stock to drive up the price, forcing the hedge funds to buy the stock at much higher prices to cover their loans.

At the beginning of January 2021, about 10,000 individual accounts were trading GameStop per day, many of them on a new do-it-yourself trading app called Robinhood. By the end of January, the trading volume had soared to 900,000 accounts per day.

By January 20, GameStop's stock price doubled to almost $40 per share. Just five days later, it practically doubled again to $76. Three days after that, on the morning of January 28, it exploded to an outrageous $483. This caused hedge funds to lose billions of dollars, forcing several of them into bankruptcy. WallStreetBets and other groups were thrilled that the "little people" had taken down Wall Street giants, like David defeating Goliath.

Granted, a lot of stocks are volatile, but this was a new level of insanity driven by the power of the masses. Even though it peaked the morning of January 28 at $483, it closed at $194 at the end of the day. By February 4 it fell to about $50 a share.

Over the course of a week, GameStop had skyrocketed to more than 12 times its value, then lost almost all of it by the end of the following week. Measuring from its $3 low in March 2020 to its short-lived peak, it multiplied by 161 times in less than a year.

Many investors made a killing on this unexpected windfall, but their timing had to be impeccable. Needless to say, thousands of investors got caught in the frenzy just in time to lose a fortune within a few days. If you bought it at the peak and sold it at $50 per share a week later, you would have lost almost 90 percent of your investment.

Figure 9: GameStop closing Prices, Jan 1-Feb 15, 2021[19]

Alexander Jones from *International Banker* observed the following:

What was especially intriguing about the event was just how much it imbued several inexperienced traders with a false sense of mastery in trading and financial markets. "I thought I could make a lot more money by continuing to trade. A few YouTube videos and Reddit forums convinced me that I was a professional," recalled Thomas Zheng, who initially pocketed around $60,000 in profit as GameStop surged and quit his part-time job to devote more time to day trading. But things didn't go as well as Zheng had planned. "I had $60,000 burning a hole in my brokerage account and the adrenaline of an 18-year-old at [a] high school prom. I spent the better part of the next year turning that $60,000 into nothing," he was quoted as saying by Fidelity Investments on the fund-management giant's website.[20]

GameStop wasn't the only stock affected so dramatically by WallStreetBets and other social media investing groups, but it was the first successful instance of what is now commonly referred to as "meme stocks." AMC Entertainment, Blackberry Limited, and Bed Bath & Beyond are other examples of struggling retailers these "Robinhood" investment groups have attempted to short squeeze to drive up the price, with varying degrees of success.[21]

Meme stocks are typically labeled as such when they quickly capture the attention of a large group of small individual investors, often driving their price "to the moon" for no explicable reason other than a sudden viral interest in them. Although a lot of money can be made, as we observed with GameStop, these stocks tend to be extraordinarily volatile. Interest is often short-lived and can drop like a rock as quickly as it was picked up, making them especially risky.

MARGIN CALLS & THE CRASH OF 1929

If you think investing in GameStop and other meme stocks sounds risky, you ain't seen nothin' yet. A whole new world of opportunity for exponential gains—and losses—awaits you. It's called *leverage*.

Currently many brokerage firms allow you to borrow 50 to 75 percent of the value of your investment account "on margin." A margin loan is a lot like a home equity line of credit, with the value of your account serving as collateral. You only have to pay interest when you carry a balance and it can be used for anything.

Margin can be a useful tool in the right situation but it can also create a lot of unnecessary risk if used unwisely. I recommend using margin only as a last resort and only if you know you will be able to pay off the loan from other sources quickly. Hoping to pay it off from stock gains is a dangerous game.

As a prudent example of using margin, let's say you need to make a large down payment to purchase a building for your business. You don't currently have enough cash to cover it, and you are selling another property soon, but it will not close until after you need the funds for the new building.

You have two options. The first is to sell a large portion of your stocks and bonds, pay the transaction costs and taxes on any gains, then repurchase the same stocks and bonds in a few months when your other property closes. A less costly option might be to borrow the down payment from a margin loan, then repay the loan when the other property closes. This strategy can be especially helpful when market prices are low since it gives your stocks a chance to recover.

I also recommend limiting your borrowing to much less than the maximum loan amount available. If you max out your margin loan, even a small drop in the value of your investments could cause the brokerage firm to send you a "margin call."

A margin call requires you to immediately pay down enough of the loan to bring it back to the maximum percentage limit. For example, if the value of your account is $1,000,000 and your margin limit is 50 percent, then the most you can borrow is $500,000. If the value of your investment account drops to $800,000, your limit reduces to $400,000.

If you borrowed $500,000, you must pay off $100,000 of your loan balance right away to bring it down to the new $400,000 limit. If you don't, they will force sell $100,000 of your holdings. This means they will automatically sell $100,000 of the investments in your account without your consent, and you won't be able to choose which ones they sell. Since your portfolio is their only collateral for the loan, this is how they minimize their risk.

Some people use margin loans in a speculative manner to magnify their potential returns. This works great when stocks perform well, but if they tank, it magnifies your losses because you're still on the hook for the amount you borrowed, like the hedge fund managers that shorted GameStop. With too much leverage, you can get caught in a chain reaction over which you have no control, potentially forcing you to lose everything.

Like many do-it-yourself investors during the pandemic, a friend of mine did exceptionally well in a handful of stocks when the market came roaring back with a vengeance. In May 2020 he invested $25,000 in three individual stocks. In less than a year his account grew to about $200,000, eight times his original investment.

He grew very excited. "Wow, this is easy," he thought. "If I put a lot more money in, I can become a multimillionaire overnight!"

He had owned four rental properties for 10 to 12 years each and was getting tired of managing them. After more than a decade of all that hard work and hassle, they still didn't generate positive cash flow because the rents were barely enough to cover the mortgages and other expenses.

Over time he had accumulated a decent amount of equity in them, but it was nothing compared to the recent explosive growth of his three brilliant stock picks. He decided it was time to sell all his rental properties and buy more stock.

In the summer of 2021, he took the full $400,000 proceeds from the sale of his real estate and added it to the $200,000 he already owned in those three stellar stocks. For the first several months everything was going great, so at the end of 2021 he borrowed the maximum amount available from his margin loan and put it all in those same three stocks.

In January 2022 the market began to drop and in March he started getting margin calls. He had invested everything he owned in those three stocks, so he didn't have any other cash to satisfy the margin calls. The brokerage firm immediately sold enough shares to cover the loan, and the stock values kept sinking.

The margin calls continued to pour in *every day* for about a month, and the brokerage firm force sold more and more shares of his stocks to cover the required balance. By May 2022, what had once been a $1 million stock portfolio dwindled down to less than $10,000.

My friend's first mistake was to invest everything he owned in only a few stocks. He says he was blinded and emboldened by his initial success, overconfident that he could consistently produce a similar outcome. He also ignored warnings from others who were more seasoned investors. Two of the stocks he bought dropped by about 60 percent in value from January to May 2022. One eventually dropped to as low as an 87 percent loss by November 2022.

Those losses would have been devastating enough on their own, but his second mistake was to max out his margin loan to buy even more. Without the margin calls forcing him to sell when they plummeted, at least he could have held onto them in hopes that their value might eventually recover.

He takes responsibility for his choices, but he is frustrated with the brokerage firm for allowing him to borrow so much money on margin. He feels this was the main cause of his severe losses. He complained, "They don't care about us—they just want to make as much as they can, regardless of the consequences to investors. They exploit our human nature and make it easy and exciting to take more risk than we should."

He knew they could require him to pay off parts of the loan if the stock values dropped, but he figured they would give him at least a few days' notice. He had no idea they could sell his shares immediately without his consent.

He recalled that it was really easy to set up the margin loan but the bank never warned him of the downsides. He explained, "It was a really long agreement—who ever reads those? I think they made it long and complicated on purpose to trick people into signing without really understanding it. The bank can't lose—they protect themselves no matter how badly it hurts their customers." They were happy to charge him all that interest on the hundreds of thousands he borrowed, then sell all his assets immediately to get all their money back at the first sign of trouble.

He expressed that the most painful part was realizing that within a few short months he lost 15 years' worth of his investing efforts. Now he has to start over because he was in too big of a hurry to grow his investments. His job is very physically demanding and now he will have to work longer than he expected.

This loss also affected his current lifestyle because he feels a lot of pressure to rebuild his assets. He used to drive a brand new

Tesla Model S and travel the world regularly. Now he drives a 16-year-old Nissan Versa and takes short road trips to nearby states.

When he told me this story, my heart sank to hear that he suffered such a devastating loss. I'm grateful he was willing to disclose the details so openly because this has been a very humbling experience for him. He hopes that by sharing his story through this book, others can learn from his mistakes.

In extreme cases, buying stocks on margin can result in severe ramifications for society at large, too. Most people don't realize that margin calls played a significant role in the infamous stock market crash of 1929, one of the leading causes of the Great Depression.

During the Roaring Twenties, the stock market enjoyed rapid expansion and periods of wild speculation. Newspapers touted tales of chauffeurs and cooks making millions in the market. No one wanted to miss out on the action.

Stock prices soared to such heights that many Americans could not afford to invest much on their own. A lot of people mortgaged their homes to buy stocks. Banks freely extended margin loans requiring only 10 percent down, with the stocks serving as collateral for the loan.

Consequently, 90 percent of the stocks owned by millions of Americans were purchased with borrowed money. Since there were no regulations against it at the time, many banks also bought stocks on margin with their customers' deposits.

The hundreds of millions of shares being carried on margin by the end of the decade inflated stock prices even more, but this was a house of cards that could not remain standing. On October 28, 1929, the Dow dropped almost 13 percent, and margin calls started pouring in. The following day it fell another 12 percent, requiring additional margin calls, and banks changed margin loan terms to require higher percentages down.

Since most investors did not have the means to pay down their loans, a mass forced sale of stocks to cover the margin balances of millions of investors triggered a further reduction in stock prices, igniting a downward spiral. By mid-November, the Dow had fallen almost 50 percent. It continued its descent through the summer of 1932, when it finally bottomed out at an 89 percent loss (see Figure 10).[22] It took 25 years for the Dow to return to its pre-crash peak prices (although some economists argue that investors recovered much sooner than that due to deflation and the payment of large stock dividends throughout the period).[23]

After the crash, many banks were only able to honor as little as 10 percent of the value of their customers' deposits because they had used them to buy stocks without their consent. Thankfully, this is no longer allowed.[24] Now you know why brokerage firms only allow investors to borrow 50 to 75 percent of their account values today, and why I strongly discourage borrowing money to invest.

As a final note about leveraging, many people who would never borrow to invest don't realize that some of the funds they own might be using leverage in an effort to boost performance. A very risky type of fund called a "leveraged ETF" seeks to deliver up to three times the return of a specific index or sector of the market on a daily basis by investing with borrowed money or through derivatives.

Figure 10: Dow Jones Industrial Average, 1925-1933

These are designed to radically enhance potential gains, but they can also severely multiply losses. For example, if the index gains 5 percent in one day, the leveraged ETF gains 15 percent. If the index loses 5 percent, the ETF loses 15 percent.

An "inverse ETF" is just as risky, if not more risky. This type of fund seeks to deliver up to three times the *opposite* of the daily performance of an index by investing in options and other derivatives that use a lot of leverage. Investors typically use these to bet against an index or sector of the market they think is about to decline. You can lose a lot of money if the underlying asset increases in value, much like the hedge funds that shorted GameStop.

If the index loses 5 percent in one day, a triple inverse ETF *gains* 15 percent. If the index gains 5 percent, the inverse ETF *loses* 15 percent. Since the market tends to go up more than it goes down, these could be even more likely to lose money than leveraged ETFs.

Since these types of ETFs triple the gains and losses on a daily basis, they typically produce very different outcomes from the actual returns of the index, often not in a good way. The SEC has warned investors about the excessive risks associated with these types of funds. The SEC stands for Securities and Exchange Commission, a government agency created to regulate the market and protect investors.

They cited a poignant example between December 1, 2008, and April 30, 2009, when a certain index grew by 8 percent. You would think that a triple leveraged ETF tied to that index would have earned 24 percent (three times 8 percent), right? Wrong. Since it tripled the returns on a daily basis, not on an annualized basis, the timing of daily returns for a certain triple leveraged ETF tied to that index resulted in a 53 percent loss over the same period. Its triple inverse ETF counterpart fared even worse, losing 90 percent.[25]

This would be quite a disappointing outcome when you could have earned 8 percent by investing just in the plain index without the leveraging. Needless to say, I never recommend these strategies.

THEY'RE CALLED JUNK BONDS FOR A REASON

After losing money in stocks, some people turn to bonds. They can be safer than stocks because of their guaranteed interest payments and guaranteed return of principal. But some types of bonds can be almost as risky as stocks, so they don't provide much safety.

When you buy a stock you own part of the company. You make money when the company value increases or when it pays dividends to its shareholders, but there are no guarantees. Stocks tend to have a higher expected return than bonds because they are riskier.

When you buy a bond, you loan money to a government entity or a corporation. They promise to pay you a specific interest rate each year until the bond matures. They also promise to return your original deposit, or "par value," on the maturity date. These guarantees are only as good as the municipality or corporation that issues the bonds, so you have to be mindful of their ability to meet their financial obligations.

How can you determine the credit worthiness of a bond? Most bonds are rated by a number of ratings agencies. This is a measure of the issuer's financial stability and history of paying bills on time, much like a credit score for you and me.

If it makes sense for you to own bonds, I only recommend investing in high-quality, investment-grade bonds (BBB or higher ratings) because they have an extremely low default rate. That means they pay all promised interest and principal to their investors on time. Bond issuers love having high ratings because it reduces their cost of borrowing and helps attract investors.

Some bond issuers are rated below investment grade. They are less likely to pay their debts on time and might not even pay them back at all. These are called high-yield bonds, also affectionately known as "junk bonds" due to their low quality.

Why would anyone invest in junk bonds? The promised interest rates can be much higher than high-quality bonds. However, they can also be dangerous because of their much higher default rates.

Of course, we all would love to earn 10 percent "guaranteed" when the safe stuff is only earning 3 percent, but the higher interest rate comes at a steep price. It could mean missing out on the 10 percent promised yield *and* not getting your principal back.

In early 2018, I started working with a new retired client in her late 70s with a very conservative investment objective. All of her investments were in bonds because she didn't want to take a lot of risk.

When we first met, she asked me to review the investments her former advisor had chosen for her. She couldn't understand why her account lost about 10 percent of its value overnight. She thought all of it was safe.

Upon review, I discovered her former advisor had invested about 10 percent of her account in Toys "R" Us bonds. They had recently gone bankrupt, erasing the full value of the bonds she owned.

I'm surprised the other advisor would buy Toys "R" Us bonds when everyone knew the company was struggling so much, but I think I understand why he did it. They were paying 7.4 percent interest while high-quality bonds were only paying 2 to 3 percent interest. A 7.4 percent interest rate might not sound very high to you depending on where interest rates are when you read this, but at the time, interest rates were extremely low and that high of a rate required a lot of risk.

This is a common mistake that investors often make, and even some advisors. My industry calls it the trap of "chasing yield."

Some people were frustrated with high-quality bonds back then because interest rates had been so low for so long. Her advisor was probably trying to help her by chasing a higher interest rate, but he apparently underestimated the potential cost of shooting for such high returns in bonds. She would have been much better off in the long run with a lower interest rate that paid consistently and gave all her money back when the bond matured.

Fortunately, we were able to get her out of the other junk bonds she owned before it was too late, including 8 percent JCPenney bonds that became worthless when they declared bankruptcy in 2020. She had no idea how much risk she was taking. She figured since they were bonds, she was safe.

An even more extreme example occurred during the subprime mortgage crisis in 2008. A friend of mine who is a financial advisor had a client who wanted to buy a Washington Mutual Bank bond that was paying 20 percent interest with only a six-month maturity date. He knew it was somewhat risky because of what was happening in the economy, but he thought, "Come on, it's Washington Mutual, one of the largest banks in the country, and it's only a six-month bond. They couldn't possibly go out of business in the next six months."

As you may have guessed, the impossible did happen. Only a month or two after the client invested several hundred thousand dollars in this bond, Washington Mutual declared bankruptcy and was taken over by the Federal Deposit Insurance Corporation (FDIC).

JPMorgan Chase purchased the assets, meaning that all loans and mortgages people owed to Washington Mutual remained intact and were transferred to JPMorgan Chase. However, the value of all Washington Mutual stocks and bonds vanished.

According to the FDIC, it was "the largest failure of an insured depository institution in the history of the FDIC."[26] My friend's client not only lost the entire amount they invested in the Washington Mutual bond, but never saw a single interest payment.

The right types of bonds can add stability to your portfolio, but chasing high yields can be quite an expensive endeavor. This poor client would have made a lot more with low-interest, high-quality bonds because those fared just fine throughout the financial crisis and the Great Recession that followed.

Another variation of low-quality bonds that can be extremely risky is private debt. This involves loaning your money to a privately held company instead of a publicly traded company or government entity. Some people, when frustrated with fluctuations in value of their publicly traded stocks and bonds, turn to private companies who promise high returns with no volatility. They like the fact that the reported value doesn't change with the regular market, but they fail to understand why it doesn't fluctuate, because it's not possible to sell their interests if they want out early or if things aren't working out as they hoped.

These types of bonds are not rated at all, which makes them even more risky than low-rated junk bonds. Since they are not publicly traded, they are not required to disclose their financials, making it impossible to determine how likely they are to repay you. Many of them are saddled with huge commissions to the brokers who sell them, as well as conflicts of interest and fraud.

The Wall Street Journal cited a disturbing example:

Jeff Temeyer, 64 years old, is a semiretired farmer in Independence, Iowa. In 2016 he invested in private debt and equity in a Texas cancer-treatment facility offered by a local broker, Dana Vietor. Mr. Temeyer, who says he was told he would earn at least 8 percent annually, invested more than $900,000 in all—only to learn that the securities were near-worthless. Mr. Vietor…also was an owner and manager of the cancer facility he got his clients to invest in—even though he lacked extensive experience as a healthcare manager and often didn't fully disclose his interest to clients, according to investors and their lawyers.[27]

I'm not a fan of junk bonds because they can be almost as risky as stocks but don't have as much growth potential. Bonds shine best as ballast to an investment portfolio. Despite rare exceptions like 2022, high-quality bonds can provide significant stability because they don't usually drop in value when the stock market plunges.

Conversely, junk bonds can't provide that type of safety because they tend to lose value when stocks tank. When stocks do well, they have trouble keeping up. Sure, you can find brief periods when junk bonds have outperformed stocks and high-quality bonds, but these are rare occurrences. Over time, they have underperformed stocks without providing the safety and stability of high-quality bonds, making them the worst of both worlds.[28]

Resist the temptation to chase risky high-flying bonds that claim to be for your eyes only. Of course we all want our James Bonds to be as exciting as possible, but if you prefer not to be shaken *or* stirred by your investments, remember the BBB rule: boring bonds are better. Anything below BBB is junk.

GOLD, GAS, AND GROUND BEEF

The realization that some individual stocks and bonds can suddenly vanish into thin air even for established companies can be extremely unnerving. Would it be safer to invest in tangible assets that can't disappear and will always be worth at least something?

For thousands of years, people have considered gold to be one of the most valuable and desirable tangible assets for a variety of reasons. It boasts a rare beauty and luster, does not corrode or tarnish, and is uniquely dense and malleable. It is also relatively scarce yet plentiful enough to be accessible to all cultures throughout the world.

Notwithstanding its obvious benefits and historic appeal, how valuable is it today as an investment? What are its prospects for future growth and wealth creation in our modern global economy compared to other assets?

Warren Buffett, one of the most successful investors of our time, explained his perspective in a speech at Harvard in 1998: "Gold gets dug out of the ground in Africa or someplace. Then we melt it down, dig another hole, bury it again and pay people to stand around guarding it. It has no utility. Anyone watching from Mars would be scratching their head."

When asked by CNBC in 2009 where he thought the price of gold would be in five years, he responded, "I have no views as to where it will be, but the one thing I can tell you is it won't do anything between now and then except look at you…it's a lot better to have a goose that keeps laying eggs than a goose that just sits there and eats insurance and storage…."[29]

In his 2011 Berkshire Hathaway Annual Report to Shareholders, he further expounded on his view of gold:

Today the world's gold stock is about 170,000 metric tons. If all of this gold were melded together, it would form a cube of about 68 feet per side. (Picture it fitting comfortably within a baseball infield.) At $1,750 per ounce—gold's price as I write this—its value would be $9.6 trillion. Call this cube pile A.

Let's now create a pile B costing an equal amount. For that, we could buy all U.S. cropland (400 million acres with output of about $200 billion annually), plus 16 Exxon Mobils (the world's most profitable company, one earning more than $40 billion annually). After these purchases, we would have about $1 trillion left over for walking-around money (no sense feeling strapped after this buying binge). Can you imagine an investor with $9.6 trillion selecting pile A over pile B?

Beyond the staggering valuation given the existing stock of gold, current prices make today's annual production of gold command about $160 billion. Buyers—whether jewelry and industrial users, frightened individuals, or speculators—must continually absorb this additional supply to merely maintain an equilibrium at present prices. A century from now the 400 million acres of farmland will have produced staggering amounts of corn, wheat, cotton, and other crops - and will continue to produce that valuable bounty, whatever the currency may be. Exxon Mobil will probably have delivered trillions of dollars in dividends to its owners and will also hold assets worth many more trillions (and, remember, you get 16 Exxons). The 170,000 tons of gold will be unchanged in size and still incapable of producing anything. You can fondle the cube, but it will not respond.

Admittedly, when people a century from now are fearful, it's likely many will still rush to gold. I'm confident, however, that the $9.6 trillion current valuation of pile A will compound over the century at a rate far inferior to that achieved by pile B.[30]

Granted, gold provides some industrial and decorative benefits as Mr. Buffett mentions, but the demand for those purposes is paltry compared to the vast stockpiles of gold already mined throughout the world. The value of gold rises and falls primarily based on what other people are willing to pay for it in the moment, not because of anything it produces.

When we buy gold, we can only make money on it if someone else is willing to pay more for it at a future date, also known as the "greater fool theory." That is more like gambling than investing.[31]

How has gold fared compared to stocks in both risk and return for the past several decades? In January 1980, gold prices reached an all-time high of $850 per ounce, then crashed 40 percent in just two months. The value continued melting over time, finally settling at around $272 the day before September 11, 2001.[32] Can you imagine suffering a 68 percent loss as a reward for your loyalty to gold over the course of almost 22 years?

Gold struggled for 28 years total to return to its former high—three years longer than it took the stock market to recover from the crash of 1929 and the Great Depression. More importantly, gold never paid any dividends or interest over that 28-year period. Conversely, according to Yale economics professor Robert Shiller, the dividend yield of the overall stock market during the Great Depression was as high as 14 percent per year.[33]

As you can see in Figure 11, gold prices finally began to recover around 2001 for the first time in a very long time, mainly due to fears surrounding the aftermath of the dot-com bubble burst, 9/11, and the subprime mortgage crisis in 2007-2009. (This chart only displays month-end values, so it doesn't show the exact prices detailed in this chapter.) [34]

Figure 11: Gold Monthly Prices, Jan 1980 to Dec 2022

You may recall an overabundance of articles and advertisements during the Great Recession promoting gold as a safer alternative to stocks and real estate by fear-mongers cashing in on people's emotions. The price of gold skyrocketed, fueled by all this fear-based hype, until it peaked at a new all-time high of $1,900 per ounce in August 2011.[35]

However, as the public began regaining confidence in stocks, bonds, and real estate, gold plummeted again, revealing its true identity as a volatile imposter for a safe haven. It sank to about $1,050 by December 2015, a 45 percent loss over a little more than four years.[36]

It took almost nine years for it to reach $1,900 per ounce again in July 2020. You'll never guess what sparked its growth this time. Yep, you're a genius. The fears surrounding COVID-19 and the stock market's steep but short-lived decline sent gold prices to another record high of over $2,000 per ounce, but not for long. The prices came right back down again as soon as the public realized COVID-19 was not going to wipe out half of the human race as it threatened to.[37]

Yes, over the past several decades there have been periods where you could have made a lot of money in gold. However, there have also been many periods of severe losses, which hardly makes it a stable alternative to stocks and bonds.

Most investors who buy large amounts of gold tend to do so during times of economic turmoil. They wait until after they have lost a lot of money in stocks and the price of gold has already skyrocketed. Then they buy it just in time for another steep decline and extraordinarily long road to recovery.

With all the ups and downs for gold over the period we have been discussing, what was its actual rate of return in the end? If you had bought gold in January 1980 when it was $850 per ounce and patiently held it for 43 years until the end of December 2022, your average annual rate of return would have been 1.8 percent.

In other words, $1 million invested in gold in 1980 would have been worth about $2.2 million at the end of 2022. Of course, this does not include the high cost of acquisition, storage, insurance, and other issues we haven't discussed yet.

In comparison, the average annual return for U.S. large stocks over that same period was a staggering 11.3 percent.[38] The same $1 million invested in the S&P 500 from January 1980 to

December 2022, assuming the reinvestment of all dividends, would have grown to almost $100 million!

Yes, you read that correctly: $100 million. That's almost $98 million more than you would have if you had invested $1 million in gold. I know, I was just as surprised as you.

How can so many people believe that gold is a safer alternative to stocks? The S&P 500 has certainly endured its share of choppy waters, but gold has suffered much larger declines and has typically taken much longer to recover.

The worst performance for the S&P 500 during this period was October 2007 to March 2009 when it lost about 46 percent. As painful as that was, it only took about five-and-a-half years to recover—much less than the 28 years it took gold to recover from its long, painful 68 percent loss.[39]

One reason some people invest in gold is that they expect it to be a good hedge against inflation, but history has not proven it to be so. How could anyone assert with a straight face that gold's less than 2 percent average annual return over the past 43 years was a better hedge against inflation than U.S. large stocks' more than 11 percent average annual return?

You may contend that 43 years is a long time period to measure and doesn't relate to investors today. Okay, let's look at more recent history. Did gold come to the rescue in 2022 when we needed it most to combat the highest inflation we had seen in decades? Just the opposite—its value steadily declined throughout most of 2022. Bye-bye inflation hedge.

Besides the historically dismal returns and extreme volatility, gold can be very expensive to buy and store. Typically, the hidden markup when you buy gold is 5 to 10 percent, but could be as high as 200 percent, even when they say the "commission" is only 1 percent. On top of that, annual storage fees can be as high as 2 percent per year.[40] Remember that gold doesn't pay any dividends or interest to offset any of these costs over time. Furthermore, gold gains are taxed as collectibles, which are normally taxed at higher rates than stocks.

The gold sales industry is also fraught with fraud. False gradings on coin quality, the use of undisclosed cheaper alloys, overinflated historical or numismatic values, and never being able to take physical possession of the gold you buy are all-too-common scams that fool many unsuspecting investors.[41]

In 2020, the Commodity Futures Trading Commission published a warning that "precious metals dealers often times are not licensed or registered to provide investment or trading advice to retail customers. They are typically salespeople who are paid commissions based on the products they sell. Unlike financial professionals who have a fiduciary responsibility to you, these dealers are not obliged to have your best interests in mind. As a result, commissions and profits often drive their recommendations…with expensive monthly fees for administration, handling, storage, or insurance…some dealers will boost their profits by charging hidden one-time or monthly fees. In some cases, customers have reported losing half of their investment to fees."[42]

As an extreme example of fraudulent gold dealers, one of my CPA friends told me that one of his clients sold $3,500,000 of high-quality stocks to buy gold because someone convinced him stocks were going to crash and gold was much better. His client paid a huge capital gains tax for selling his stocks because they had grown a lot in value over the years. Then he was defrauded of the full $3,500,000 he thought he was buying gold with. He never received any gold or his money back.

I have spent a lot of time talking about gold because it is one of the most popular and liquid tangible assets people invest in, but obviously it is not the only one. What about silver, the second most popular precious metal? As you can see in Figure 12, it is no less volatile than gold and has produced even worse average annual returns since 1980.

Once again, please don't misunderstand me. You certainly can make a lot of money in precious metals, but predicting their price movements is just as hard as predicting the stock market, and most people jump in after a big spike just in time to ride the next big wave crashing down.

For example, silver was up 435 percent in 1979. Anyone who bought it at the beginning of 1980 expecting that type of return would have suffered a 52 percent loss, then *another* 47 percent loss the next year. It would have taken them 31 years to get back to break-even. Moreover, if they didn't cash out at the perfect time after that long road to recovery, they would likely still be waiting to break even. At the end of 2022, silver prices were about a third lower than they were at the beginning of 1980.[43]

Figure 12: Silver Monthly Prices, Jan 1980 to Dec 2022

Other popular tangible assets, also called commodities, include crude oil, natural gas, grain, and yes, even cattle. I won't bore you will the details of all these, but similar principles apply. It's all about supply and demand, and the price swings can be very volatile and unpredictable.

For example, take the price of crude oil, which is used to produce gasoline, diesel fuel, jet fuel, lubricants, solvents, asphalt, plastics, and a host of other important products. Yes, you could have made a lot of money during certain unpredictable price spikes, but it was very volatile and took a long time to recover from several large drops in recent decades. The average annual return for crude oil from 1980 to 2022 was 1.9 percent, surprisingly similar to gold.

Warren Buffett hit the nail on the head: the main problem with investing in gold and other commodities is that they don't produce anything once they have been extracted or harvested. Gold, silver, gas, grain—they all just sit there and look at you.

They will never earn any money for you unless someone else happens to be willing to pay more for them than you did. If that's your investment strategy, you might have a lot more fun and make a lot more money investing in baseball cards, Barbies, and Beanie Babies.

On the other hand, organizations that produce these commodities, such as mining, energy, food, and agriculture companies, consistently pay very strong dividends. They have been largely responsible for the remarkable stock returns I've been quoting, so I encourage my clients to own them as part of their overall investment holdings.

Ponder the perspective of Napoleon Hill, who was persuaded by Andrew Carnegie to write the first "philosophy of success," *Think and Grow Rich*: "More gold has been mined from the thoughts of men than has been taken from the earth."[44] The human ingenuity that converts gold and other commodities into useful products and services is much more valuable and of greater benefit to society than raw commodities by themselves. When we invest in the stocks of companies that provide these products and services, we participate in this exciting creation of value.

Sadly, there is no silver bullet, gold bullet, or even beef bullet that can magically solve all your investing woes. If you like the look and feel of gold better than Beanie Babies, then buy some and stick it on your finger or in your safe, but don't rely too heavily on it for your financial future or happiness. Most of all, promise me you won't sit and caress your gold or other *precious* metals for too long; one Gollum is more than enough.

THEY'RE NOT MAKING ANY MORE LAND

Another popular tangible asset many investors flock to after losing money in other assets is real estate. If you consider Mark Twain to be an investment expert, you might be wise to follow his advice from the late 1800s: "Buy land, they're not making it anymore." Although not exactly an expert in 21st century investing, Mark Twain was a smart man, and his reasoning sounds logical, but it does not always play out quite so simply in the real world.

Real estate is an amazing investment with many benefits, and I feel strongly that everyone should own some. However, I know a lot of people who lost everything by counting on the notion that real estate is a safe investment that will always be in demand. The fact that it cannot disappear and that no more land can be created does not mean it's always a good investment.

They're not making any more gold or silver either, and look at what has happened to those prices. Like commodities, real estate values can fluctuate wildly based on what other people are willing to pay, due to changes in supply and demand.

Consider the impact of the Great Recession on real estate values. If you owned real estate in 2006, you remember how painful that was.

I have lived in Las Vegas since 2001, where we enjoyed one of the hottest real estate booms in the country during the early 2000s. Alas, this frenzy also made Vegas one of the hardest-hit cities when the house of cards finally came crashing down.

We bought a home at the end of 2002, which just about doubled in value within three years. That was an exciting time of "irrational exuberance." Everyone was in a rush to buy bigger and better homes they couldn't really afford before prices rose again.

Few planned to stay in their homes for more than a few years so they could leverage the equity to buy something even better. If you could double the value of a $500,000 home in three years, why not buy a $1 million home and turn it into $2 million?

Banks were happy to extend interest-only loans that didn't even require full interest payments, with nothing down and no verification of income. Everyone fancied themselves a real

'Your pocket money is for sweets – you weren't meant to buy a house'

estate expert because everything seemed to be going up, no matter what, where, or when they bought.

A young guy I knew at the time signed the paperwork to buy 10 homes under construction within a few months with very little or no money down. He never intended to close on any of them, and certainly couldn't afford to.

Prices were rising so fast that he figured by the time

the homes were finished being built, he could quickly sell them to someone else for at least 20 percent more than what he was under contract to pay for them. Unfortunately, housing prices started sliding in 2006, so when it came time for these homes to close, no one would buy them from him, and he was forced to declare bankruptcy.

Despite my efforts to exercise prudence during this very rough period, my family and I were not immune to its effects. Over the course of the next several years, the house we bought in 2002 continually dropped in value until it was worth about half of what we paid for it.

We patiently held onto it for many years in hopes that it would eventually recover its value. We were fortunate to be able to collect rent on it for more than the mortgage payment and other expenses. We eventually sold it for a profit, but I believe it took about 15 years for the value to return to what it was before the crash—much longer than we anticipated having to wait to recover.

As you know, many people were not able to hold onto their homes long enough to recoup their losses, or they simply chose to walk away because they gave up all hope of recovery. Since home prices had risen so rapidly in the Southwest compared to most of the country, when things turned south, our area was hit especially hard. Hundreds of thousands of homes went into fore-closure each year in Nevada during that time—more than three times the national average.[45]

Others lost vast portions of their net worth by being lured into real estate deals where they had no control. A popular way to make money during the real estate boom without having to buy houses was loaning money to developers through hard money lending, also known as trust deeds. When banks refused to loan more money to developers because they were already too lever-aged, developers turned to the public for additional funds.

As we discussed in the introduction, trust deeds paid as high as 14 percent guaranteed interest. If you allowed the developer to hold the interest until the project was complete rather than send-ing you monthly payments, you could earn up to 16 percent. Those who sold trust deeds were required to disclose the risks, but many ignored or downplayed them. Most investors thought of them as risk-free investments because the guarantees were backed by the value of the land. If the developer ever failed to pay the interest or your deposit back on time, you could take owner-ship of part of the land securing the deed.

When the real estate market fell apart, developers couldn't (or wouldn't) complete their outstanding projects, so most people never got their money back. True, they technically could have taken ownership of the land, but speculative raw land and un-sightly incomplete projects became practically worthless as demand for new construction fell and funding dried up.

Besides, ownership of each project was typically spread among hundreds of investors, making it cost prohibitive to equitably split up and transfer ownership to all respective parties. Much of the remaining cash for each project, if any was left, was spent on at-torney fees.

Some of my clients eventually succeeded in taking ownership of the land securing the trust deeds they bought in 2006, but it is still a complicated mess for several of them because so many in-vestors are involved. As of the time of this writing they have yet to receive their money back, with no apparent resolution in sight.

Other popular investments during this time included limited partnerships (LPs), tenant-in-common deals (TICs), and nontraded real estate investment trusts (REITs). Through these structures, you could pool your money together with hundreds, if not thousands of other investors.

A management company would raise money and collect a fee to purchase, develop, and manage one or more properties held by the entity—typically commercial real estate. You would be promised a certain "guaranteed" monthly return, maybe 7 to 8 percent per year, with the expectation of a larger payout later if the deal ever went public or if they sold property for a profit.

Needless to say, most of these deals lost quite a bit of money, too. One of my clients invested several hundred thousand dollars and only got $18,000 back after countless hours in meetings with attorneys and other investors over the course of several years.

Another challenge with some of these deals is that the management company could require investors to pay in additional capital proportionate to their ownership percentages if they needed more money to cover expenses. Some people I know who had already invested at least $1 million were required to invest hundreds of thousands more over the next several years to satisfy these "capital calls." Of course, these calls often came at times when their other investments and income were down, so it was quite a sacrifice to continue paying into a project that had lost so much money.

If they didn't meet these capital calls, they could be forced to sell their portion to the other investors in the fund at steep discounts, pay penalties, or be subject to legal proceedings for damages to the fund. A few people I know were able to hang in there for the long term, but it took them 10 to 15 years just to break even, after investing a lot more than they originally wanted to. Most investors were not able to keep up and had to simply walk away.

A friend of mine who had lost a lot of money in the stock market in the early 2000s decided he was done with stocks and put it all in a brand new strip mall. It made him feel a lot better that he could always see it and feel it, that it would never disappear like some of his stocks did.

Due to the extreme oversupply of commercial real estate during that time, his strip mall sat vacant for years. At least he could go look at it whenever he wanted to, though. Commercial real estate in Vegas took more than 10 years to return to normal occupancy levels.

VACANT MULTI-MILLION-DOLLAR STRIP MALL
YOU CAN LOOK AT AND TOUCH

Las Vegas was lucky compared to the poor residents of Detroit, Michigan. Real estate there was hit even harder during the financial crisis due to its economy's dependence on the three largest auto manufacturers in America: General Motors, Ford, and Chrysler, who were on the verge of bankruptcy in 2008.

From 2005 to 2015, more than a third of Detroit properties were foreclosed on due to unpaid mortgages or taxes. Many of these homes were never reoccupied, leading to an unbelievable increase in squatters, theft, demolition, and arson, causing huge declines in real estate values.

In the fall of 2014, the national average home sale price was $193,000. In Detroit, it had fallen to a meager $22,000. One lady bought a home there in 2002, when all houses on her block were occupied. In 2015 it only appraised for $5,000 because so many homes in her neighborhood had been abandoned and vandalized.

She was stuck with a $82,000 mortgage with a $900 monthly payment.[46]

According to *BridgeDetroit*, in 2021, "The median sales price plunged by 82 percent between 2006 and 2008 and housing values are still only a little more than half what they were before the collapse."[47] Did anyone warn Detroit homebuyers in 2006 that they could possibly lose 82 percent over the course of three years, and that 15 years later it would still only be worth half of what they paid for it? I dare you to remind them that real estate is always a good investment because they're not making any more land.

Another painful lesson came from the blazing boom and bust of Williston, North Dakota. In the late 2000s, while so much of the country was reeling from the effects of the financial crisis, tens of thousands of people were migrating to Williston to find their fortune in fracking during the oil boom, reminiscent of the California Gold Rush of 1849.

Real estate prices in Williston soared because there was not enough housing for such a sudden influx of people. Developers scrambled to meet the demand. The town had grown by 67 percent from 2010 to 2014, and North Dakota had become the fastest-growing economy in the country.

Sadly, demand for real estate can fall as quickly as it rises. By the end of 2015, oil prices had fallen 70 percent and people began abandoning Williston almost as fast as they flocked to it.

I personally know people in Vegas who lost a lot of money in real estate there, as they were trying to cash in on the "amazing" growth opportunity. Another friend of mine lost his shirt trying to start a construction business there just as the boom turned into a bust. He is still trying to recover financially from those losses.

These are not the only cities whose real estate values have struggled to keep up. Although not as dramatic, other major cities have suffered similar fates over longer periods of time. Pittsburgh, Scranton, Cleveland, Dayton, Buffalo, Newark, and many other cities that once enjoyed explosive growth have experienced a gradual dwindling of their populations as their main industries dried up or moved elsewhere. Believe it or not, the values of land and buildings tend to fall when populations decline, even though you can still look at and touch them.[48]

Let me pause here to acknowledge that most real estate ventures are not so destined to fail. I love real estate and feel strongly that everyone should own some, as I mentioned earlier. I have been focusing on extreme examples because I want to help you avoid the tempting traps where people get burned the most—chasing outrageous returns in a short amount of time without understanding the risks.

Contrary to other investing strategies I have been criticizing throughout this book, real estate can be a very smart investment when done the right way. Real estate is the best tangible asset to complement an investment portfolio because it can produce significant income. It doesn't just sit there and stare at you like precious metals and other commodities, with one exception: raw land, which tends to be more speculative like commodities because it doesn't produce any income and drains your potential returns with taxes, insurance, and other expenses.

This isn't a book about real estate investing and I wouldn't consider myself a real estate expert, so I won't dig very deep on how to do it properly. But I know a lot of people who have been extremely profitable in real estate, and I have enjoyed some success myself, so I will share a few basic pointers from what I have learned.

Most of the people I know who have consistently succeeded in real estate take a more prudent approach. They understand that it's more about when you buy than when you sell. It's less about the visual and emotional appeal of a property, and more about the numbers.

They know it's a long game, so they tend not to buy into the urgency and hype of real estate booms. They patiently wait for the right opportunities to come along. The best deals are not usually the type that average buyers would be interested in. They don't look very pretty, and they seldom get caught in bidding wars.

More money can be made in bad times than in good times, but the real estate market is just about as unpredictable as the stock market. Those who try to time it perfectly are prone to getting burned. You improve your chances of success if you plan to hold for the long term, much like investing in the stock market.

A friend of mine sold her house in 2019 and moved into a rental because she thought real estate prices were about to tumble. She was trying to take advantage of what she expected to be a great buying opportunity in the near future.

Unfortunately for her, home prices continued to climb by at least an additional 50 percent over the next three years, so she was priced out of the hope for an upgrade even more than before. Now it would cost her 50 percent more just to get back into where she was living before, not to mention the lost opportunity cost of realtor commissions, transfer taxes, closing costs, and all the rent she has been paying to someone else rather than reducing her own mortgage balance.

Keep in mind that it is practically impossible to invest in real estate without incurring additional ongoing costs, such as taxes, insurance, HOA dues, utilities, maintenance, repairs, landscaping, potential lawsuits, and so on. When you measure your potential return on a real estate purchase, you should estimate net income after all expenses, as well as the value of your time spent.

You would be wise to overestimate expenses and underestimate rents. If your success depends on rosy assumptions, you will surely be disappointed because it almost always costs more than you think it will.

One way you can keep yourself out of trouble is to not over-leverage. In other words, don't borrow too much money to buy real estate. Just because banks are willing to offer you a mortgage with a payment representing half of your monthly income doesn't mean you should take it, unless you don't care about extras like furniture, fridges, and food.

Most banks don't really care about your overall financial well-being or happiness—they just want to earn as much interest as possible and ensure they get their money back. Why do you think your mortgage broker's commission is based on the size of your loan? If you keep your mortgage payment to no more than 15 percent of your monthly income, you will have sufficient breathing room to enjoy life and hang onto your home if your income drops.

A big reason so many people lost their homes during the Great Recession is that they put little or no money down, they took the biggest mortgage the bank would give them, and the affordability of their monthly payment was dependent on an artificially low, temporary payment. As soon as payments reset to what they were really supposed to be, most people could no longer afford them, and they were forced to let their homes go. I will more specifically outline a sad example of how this worked in Chapter 6.

The risk of foreclosure due to overleveraging compounds when you buy more than one property. Make sure you can afford to cover the mortgage payments, taxes, insurance, HOA dues, utilities, maintenance, and repairs for all properties you own even if rents drop or if some of your properties are vacant for a while.

You can't assume rents will always stay the same or increase and that your properties will always be fully rented out. Rents and vacancy rates fluctuate based on supply and demand, just like everything else.

Keep a generous slush fund to cover other unexpected costs. What if it takes you a year to find a tenant? What if the air conditioning, flooring, or roof needs to be replaced? What if an irate tenant vandalizes your home and steals the appliances when they move out? What if someone is injured on your property and they sue you? All of these costs will fall on your shoulders.

Successful real estate investing in real life is more like playing Monopoly than Minecraft. Your resources are not unlimited. If you rush out and buy everything you land on and spend all your cash on houses and hotels, you could be forced to sell it all for half of what you paid for it when you land on Boardwalk.

And believe me, if you play the game long enough, eventually you will figuratively land on Boardwalk in the form of very large unexpected expenses. Hoping you don't is not a sound investment strategy. If you really want to win the game of real estate investing and build real, sustainable wealth, you have to maintain positive cash flow and be prepared for the unexpected.

Another issue with real estate is that the income derived from it is not quite as passive as beginners expect it to be. It takes time, energy, and money to manage properties, or you have to hire someone else to do it, which eats into your returns.

In fact, the people I know who have made the most money in real estate have made it their full-time job. They put a lot of time, energy, and money into improving property to create value for others.

For example, a friend of mine has been very successful buying dilapidated houses for really low prices, fixing them up, and renting them out or selling them for much more than what he paid for them. Not everyone can do what he does. He was an appraiser for over a decade so he can more easily determine what is wrong with every house he evaluates and how much it would cost to repair it.

This allows him to calculate up front how much he can afford to buy a house for and still turn a healthy profit after the cost of fixing it up. On top of that, he can make repairs for much less than you or I could because he employs a whole team of home repair experts that work only for him.

He can easily recognize a steal that amateurs would walk away from due to something as simple as a bad smell, and he walks away from many properties others might think are a steal. He also has the capital to pay cash for every deal he does, which allows him to offer much better terms and a quicker closing than most people could. It would be very difficult for most investors to generate the returns he can, due to his resources and expertise.

Another way some people I know have profited in real estate by creating value for others is through developing new property. Anytime I drive through a new master-planned community that is being developed, it blows my mind. I can't wrap my head around how anyone could conjure up and fulfill the vision of such a massive, beautiful, functional place out of nothing—especially in Vegas, where it was literally just dirt and rocks. These are true visionaries who deserve to be paid well for the incredible value they create for so many people.

Even for full-time real estate experts, the grind can get old for the size of the actual returns over time. A client of mine who is a true real estate expert told me he recently met a seasoned investor who is in his mid-70s and owns about 3,500 rental properties throughout the country, mostly single-family residences. This investor observed that after all the hard work and risk he has endured to build such a massive real estate portfolio, at the end of the day his average annual return has been just 7 percent per year. On some properties he made over 50 percent, but on others he lost over 50 percent. Often the ones he thought would earn the most ended up being the biggest pains or costing a lot more in the long run. Overall it worked out to be an average of 7 percent per year, net of all expenses.

Due to the unpredictable expenses, vacancies, time, and stress of real estate investing, many of my clients grow tired of managing it by the time they retire, especially when they realize they might not be making quite as much as they thought they were after factoring in the true costs and losses over the years. At that point, they often choose to convert some of their real estate holdings to truly passive assets like stocks and bonds that don't require any additional work or capital to succeed.

In summary, you can make a lot of money in real estate, and it can be a great complement to other assets like stocks, bonds, mutual funds, ETFs, and your business. Just remember, the fact that they're not making any more land doesn't mean it's sure to make you money. It usually involves a lot more risk and work than most people realize. If you are going to invest in real estate, do it prudently and patiently with a long time horizon.

CRYPTOCURRENCY: THE FINAL FRONTIER?

When you hear that the first 10,000 bitcoin spent on two pizzas in 2010 would have been worth almost $688 million in November 2021, you start to understand why Bitcoin has turned so many investors' heads.[49] However, like other hot investments we discussed, the largest potential returns may have already passed.

Bitcoin launched in January 2009 while distrust of traditional banking was exceptionally high during the financial crisis that led to the Great Recession.[50] It is the "world's first widely adopted cryptocurrency... [where] people can securely and directly send each other digital money on the internet," according to Coinbase, the largest, most popular U.S.-based cryptocurrency exchange.

The technology supporting Bitcoin is very complex, but Coinbase boils it down for us: "Every transaction involving Bitcoin is tracked on the blockchain, which is similar to a bank's ledger, or log of customers' funds going in and out of the bank. In simple terms, it's a record of every transaction ever made using bitcoin. Unlike a bank's ledger, the Bitcoin blockchain is distributed across the entire network. No company, country, or third party is in control of it; and anyone can become part of that network."[51]

Since Bitcoin's birth, tens of thousands of additional cryptocurrencies serving many different purposes have been created. They are all fighting to stake their claim in what promises to be the biggest revolution in our economy since the proliferation of the internet in the late 1990s.

This is truly the Wild West all over again—perhaps even the "final frontier" as my Trekkie friends would call it. It feels a lot like the early days of the internet in both good and bad ways. No person, company, or even government entity can control or predict where it's going.

Everyone is trying to get in on the ground level of the next big new idea, and FOMO is kicking in big time. The problem is, how can you know which ones are the best to buy out of the tens of thousands available, when to get in and out, and how much to invest in each?

Let's take a closer look at Bitcoin, since it is the largest, most popular cryptocurrency, representing about 40 percent of the $800 billion crypto market at the end of 2022. As a side note, the crypto market was worth almost $3 trillion in November 2021, to give you an idea of how quickly it can lose massive value.

In the beginning, you couldn't really buy Bitcoin—the only people who owned it were the people who mined it (computer programmers who created new Bitcoin by adding to the blockchain). It first became available to buy and sell in 2010, and in April 2011, the price of one bitcoin exceeded $1 for the first time.

The next 10 years were a wild ride with many extreme ups and downs, landing in April 2021 at more than a 200 percent average annual rate of return for the decade. In comparison, the S&P 500 average annual return was about 14 percent over the same period.[52]

Anyone with a brain would clearly prefer a 200 percent average annual 10-year return over 14 percent, so why not dump all your U.S. stocks and invest it all in Bitcoin? This is where things get tricky. If you had done so in April 2021, you would have lost about 50 percent over the next three months.

If you were patient and brave enough to hold onto it until reaching its all-time high in November 2021, you would have earned a whole 10 percent return for all that risk. However, if you didn't sell at the peak, you would have lost all your gains within a few days. Then you would have suffered a long, painful slide all the way down to a 74 percent loss by the end of 2022. And you thought stocks were risky![53]

The funny thing is that in spite of this extreme volatility, Bitcoin is considered the most stable, least-risky cryptocurrency on the market. What does that tell you about the risk of investing in other cryptocurrencies? It is exceptionally speculative.

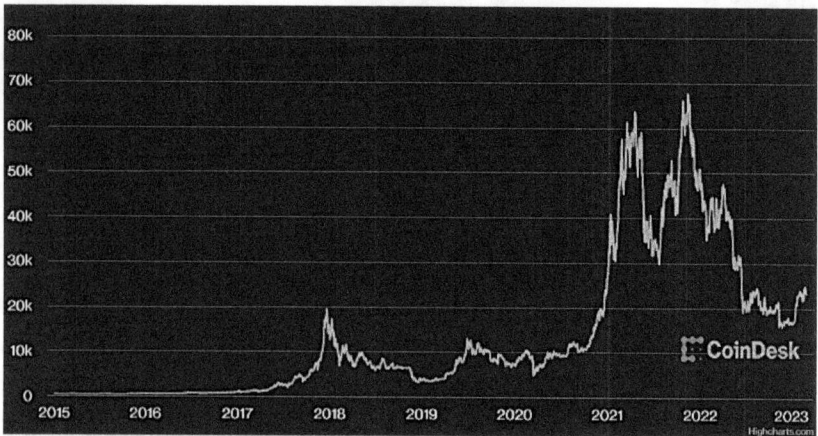

Figure 13: Bitcoin Prices, Jan 2015 to Feb 2023[54]

I personally believe cryptocurrency is here to stay. It is a fascinating technology that has the potential to dramatically improve the efficiency and security of financial transactions, as well as the exchange of many other forms of value and information.

In many ways, our society is already largely run on digital currency, so this is a natural next step. When was the last time you paid cash for something? When you split the costs of a trip or night out with friends, did you write each other checks or exchange funds over Venmo or Zelle? The last time you attended a concert or sporting event, did you hand them a paper ticket or enter with your phone? These are all forms of digital currency.

However, this does not necessarily mean you should rush out and invest in crypto—it is still very young and extremely speculative. Although it is likely to change the way we do business, much like the internet did, good luck predicting who the important players will be and how it will affect our lives. Most cryptocurrencies currently in existence are not likely to survive. If you invest too much in them you may suffer a fate similar to those who lost almost all their money in dot-com stocks in the early 2000s.

Several crypto giants have already tumbled, sending shockwaves throughout the cryptocurrency universe. The popular Luna crypto network, founded in 2018, boasted astronomical returns in 2021 and early 2022, with a final 135 percent burst in March and April 2022. The very next month it collapsed, wiping out an estimated $60 billion in digital currency. Although what caused its sudden unexpected demise is still under investigation at the time of this writing, experts suspect that insiders exploited vulnerabilities in the system through price manipulation and short selling, causing a chain reaction of widespread panic and collapse of the whole system.[55]

In similar fashion, FTX was a $32 billion crypto exchange that started in May 2019 and suddenly went bankrupt in November 2022. Not long before its failure, it boasted high-profile Super Bowl ads and celebrity endorsements, advertising itself as "the safest and easiest way to buy and sell crypto." The founder and CEO, Sam Bankman-Fried, was arrested and indicted "on eight criminal counts, ranging from wire fraud to conspiracy to commit money laundering and violating campaign finance laws," according to NPR. The SEC also accused him of misappropriating customers' funds "to make undisclosed venture investments, lavish real estate purchases, and large political donations."[56]

Besides the typical risks associated with investing in a pioneering company in an industry that is still trying to find its way, the crypto world is also a fraudster's paradise. One of its greatest appeals to investors is that many cryptocurrencies cannot be monitored or controlled by any central government or institution. However, this is also one of its largest risks, with steep potential costs.

Billions have been lost due to exchanges being hacked. Countless scammers have also posed as employees of crypto exchanges, tricking investors into divulging their passwords, then locking them out of their digital assets forever with no enforceable recourse.

Many investors have attempted to reduce these risks by storing their crypto holdings on their own digital hardware wallets. Unfortunately, this approach introduces a new form of risk because if you lose your wallet or forget your password, you may never be able to recover your crypto holdings. Several people have lost hundreds of millions of dollars this way. Experts estimate that up to 20 percent of all Bitcoin has been lost forever.[57]

Some people believe they are better off owning their cryptocurrency on nonregulated exchanges. They want to minimize the chance that the government might be able to track or regulate it in the future, and they are hoping to avoid taxation on any gains.

Using a non-U.S. based exchange can be risky. If the exchange goes under, you will lose all your cryptocurrency value. You are technically required to report crypto gains on your U.S. tax return anyway, whether the exchange reports your earnings or not. If the exchange does not report gains and losses to the IRS and you lose money, you may also lose the opportunity to write off your losses.

Many crypto enthusiasts are passionate about its potential role as a hedge against inflation and possible devaluation of the U.S. dollar. Obviously we are all concerned about the national debt, inflation, and whether or not the dollar can maintain its relative strength. However, crypto has not yet proven to be a viable alternative. It is much more volatile than the value of the dollar and has suffered much steeper losses overall so far. As I mentioned earlier, most crypto is likely to be totally worthless at some point.

Like commodities, most cryptos don't pay dividends or interest so you can only make money if other people are willing to pay you more for them later. Unlike commodities, they could vanish overnight because they have no intrinsic value.

Due to the excessive risks at the time of this writing, only invest in cryptocurrency if you're comfortable with more volatility than the stock market, you're willing to continually do a lot of your own research, and you limit your crypto holdings to a small percentage of your total investments. Yes, you could make a killing with crypto, but it could also kill your portfolio in a heartbeat.

IF IT SOUNDS TOO GOOD TO BE TRUE...

We have all heard this warning a thousand times. Yet some promises are very difficult to ignore because we really want them to be true. Sometimes when we least suspect danger, we allow ourselves to be seduced by the siren song of high returns with no risk, not realizing our mistake until it's too late.

This section is perhaps the most difficult for me to discuss because it hits very close to home. I personally know a lot of people who were victims of a $450 million Ponzi scheme in the Las Vegas area that was exposed in 2022, affecting over 600 investors. A Ponzi scheme is a fraudulent plan in which early investors are paid fake returns from the funds of subsequent investors, rather than from actual investment returns.

I will try to tread lightly out of respect for my friends who lost a lot of money, some of them as much as $1 million, due to this dreadful debacle. As painful as it is to talk about, I feel this issue must be addressed in some detail to help you recognize future threats. This wasn't the first Ponzi scheme to decimate investors, and I'm sure it won't be the last.

From 2017 to March 2022, a small group of people sold interests in slip-and-fall insurance settlements promising unusually high returns with no risk. Investors could deposit funds with this "investment group" in increments of either $80,000 or $100,000. These funds were intended for advance payments to people who had already reached a settlement agreement with the insurance company for a personal injury claim. They supposedly already knew how much they would be paid by the insurance company and when, hence the purported lack of risk.

Allegedly, the claimants were willing to pay a 25 percent fee to the investment group in exchange for a $80,000 to $100,000 90-day loan. When the insurance claim was paid 90 days later, the investment group would be paid back the amount they loaned to the claimant plus the 25 percent fee.

Half of this 25 percent fee would be paid to the investor, and the investment group facilitating the deals would pocket the rest. Investors were promised a 12.5 percent return every 90 days if they kept their money in the fund and continually reinvested in a new deal each time a claim matured, resulting in a 50 percent annualized return. I understand why so many people invested in this—who wouldn't want a 50 percent annual return with no risk!

The attorney who orchestrated the whole thing claimed to have relationships with personal injury attorneys from 66 different firms around the country who referred him a large number of these cases for a fee. Unfortunately, it was all too good to be true.

In the end he admitted that he never even spoke to any of the attorneys he had listed on the deals. In fact, he used the same case names and details over and over to fabricate multiple offerings to different investors.

None of the money collected from investors was ever invested in a single personal injury settlement. Instead, according to the Nevada District Court, they "used a portion of investors' money to make periodic payments of fictitious 'returns' on the purchase agreements to investors in a Ponzi-like fashion, but used the bulk of investor money to fund lavish lifestyles, including purchasing luxury homes and properties, a private jet, ATVs, boats, and numerous luxury cars for themselves and their relatives." It was also used to pay off huge gambling debts.[58]

Most of the people I personally know who were drawn into this deal are very smart and successful, which begs the question, how did the Ponzi scheme perpetrators convince so many people that it was legitimate for so long? I wouldn't profess to fully understand all the reasons, but here are some possible explanations:

At first glance, a 12.5 percent 90-day return may not have sounded too outrageous to investors, especially if they thought of it as more of a short-term unique opportunity, even though a 50 percent annualized return is really high. Some of them started with smaller amounts in the beginning to test whether it was legitimate. When they got their first payments back, it seemed like it was working and they were encouraged by the awesome returns, so they put a lot more in and told their friends.

Many people who wouldn't normally invest in something like this felt comfortable with it because they knew and trusted the people who sold it to them. They also knew several other investors who seemed to be having success with it.

After the fraud was exposed, one of my clients who invested in it observed that looking back now he recognizes all the warning signs were there, but he disregarded them because he really wanted it to be true. He quipped that he learned something about himself—he is motivated by greed.

The natural instinct of greed may influence our investment decisions more than we realize. Most of my friends and clients are generous, service-minded people who I would not call greedy, including my client who claims he is motivated by greed. Still, we all want to maximize the growth of our money as quickly and easily as possible because that's human nature. Whether we call this desire greed or not, its ability to blind and skew the judgment of smart, good people can be frightening.

Besides the fact that the promised returns were so high, were any other warning signs present that could have helped these 600 unsuspecting investors recognize the fraudulence of this deal? Fortunately, yes. We're not doomed to rely only on chance when it comes to vetting investment offerings.

All legitimate investments would have been able to answer "yes" to the following four questions. Use these questions to help you identify future potential frauds:

1. Does it appear to be a legitimate business with the proper experience, licensing, and staff to produce what they are promoting?
2. Are the investment offerings marketed openly through legitimate channels with detailed documentation, including full disclosure of all risks?
3. Do expected returns, volume of deals, and terms seem reasonable for the amount of risk described?

4. Can the flow of money, returns, and other aspects of the deal be verified by other sources?

Now let's break down how this Ponzi scheme specifically failed each of these four tests. I acquired these details from three main sources: friends of mine who invested in it, the SEC's court case against the perpetrators, and an article written by a research firm that investigated the scam in depth and reported it to the regulators:[59]

1. Does it appear to be a legitimate business with the proper experience, licensing, and staff to produce what they are promoting?
   a. None of the people involved in this Ponzi scheme held any investment licenses or had any experience in litigation finance.
   b. Neither the company nor any of its investment offerings were registered with the SEC and/or FINRA (investment regulatory agencies) as they were legally required to be.
   c. No physical address, website, or active social media pages could be found for the operation.
   d. Besides the marketing people, they only had one employee: the managing partner's son. Managing this type of business typically involves a lot of due diligence, paperwork, and follow-up on every case, requiring at least a few dozen people to handle the number of cases they claimed to manage.
   e. Each marketer handled all administrative duties, paperwork, and money flows for their respective investors. These are tedious and technical tasks that would normally not be assigned to marketers.

2. Are the investment offerings marketed openly through legitimate channels with detailed documentation, including full disclosure of all risks?
   a. They had no website or marketing materials. You could only learn about the details through undocumented calls and meetings with the scheme's marketers directly.

b. They veiled this "amazing opportunity" in a shroud of secrecy, forcing investors to sign non-disclosure agreements so it wouldn't "leak out to the broader investment world."

c. They relied heavily on relationships of trust through church and gym memberships to attract potential investors, apparently steering clear of institutional investors and financial professionals who might do more due diligence. This exemplifies the SEC's description of affinity fraud.[60]

3. Do expected returns, volume of deals, and terms seem reasonable for the amount of risk described?

a. They promised investors a 50 percent annualized return with no risk. Litigation finance is a highly competitive industry with most companies targeting a 20 percent annualized return with substantial risk. How could they produce more than double the return with no risk?

b. They claimed to have closed over 20,000 cases with zero defaults. The industry average default rate is 1 percent, so at least 200 of their cases would have defaulted under normal circumstances.

c. The median case size for these types of settlements is typically $50,000, but their median case size was supposedly $225,000 to $350,000. How could they find 20,000 cases that much larger than the norm?

d. The national average amount advanced to personal injury claimants is $5,000, with a wide variety of case sizes. This scheme only financed contracts for $80,000 and $100,000 (16-20 times the national average size), with no logical reason for such homogenous amounts.

e. Would 20,000 people really be willing to give up 25 percent of such a large advance because they couldn't wait 90 days? Would you pay $20,000 to $25,000 to receive $80,000 to $100,000 just 90 days sooner? That's 100 percent annualized interest!

f. If the return was really that certain, why wouldn't the marketers of the scheme just invest their own money and make a lot more? When questioned, they claimed altruistic motives for sharing half the returns with investors.

g. Due to legal ethics rules, it is highly unlikely that so many attorneys from 66 different firms would be willing to risk losing their licenses by collecting referral fees for something like this.

4. Can the flow of money, returns, and other aspects of the deal be verified by other sources?

a. They never used any sort of third-party custodian, administrator, or auditor to provide independent accounting, monitoring, or reporting for investors. Every credible investment manager provides this sort of transparency and protection for investors.

b. Some marketers manually created their own basic reports to give investors, but others never produced any reports confirming amounts deposited or withdrawn, status of cases, or interest earned. They instructed investors to track their own deals on a spreadsheet.

c. Although they claimed to place liens on each settlement case to ensure repayment, not a single lien could be found on public Uniform Commercial Code (UCC) databases.

d. Legal documents stated that no marketers would be paid any commissions, but marketers' verbal statements and motives indicated otherwise.

e. Several suspicious investors called the attorneys listed on their cases to confirm details, but they all denied any knowledge of or involvement with the company or the cases mentioned in their purchase agreements. When confronted, the principals of the scheme argued that the attorneys probably denied involvement to protect client confidentiality.

Of course I wouldn't expect any of the investors in this Ponzi scheme to have known to check all of these issues before investing in it. I'm just sharing them now in hopes that they can help you and others avoid future scams.

Some of the warning signs of this Ponzi scheme were admittedly fairly technical matters that many investors might have had difficulty verifying on their own. However, most of these examples should be able to help the average investor detect fraud. Just to be safe, anytime you are seriously considering a deal that sounds almost too good to be true, it might be a good idea to run it by a trusted attorney, CPA, or wealth advisor to help you verify its legitimacy and understand the potential risks, regardless of any nondisclosure agreements the salesperson asks you to sign.

As I mentioned, unfortunately this wasn't the first Ponzi scheme to harm investors. The largest Ponzi scheme in history was exposed during the financial crisis of 2008, run by the infamous Bernie Madoff. In several ways it was similar to the Vegas Ponzi scheme, so let's briefly compare characteristics and lessons learned for additional insight on how to detect fraud.

Madoff was well-respected on Wall Street, helped pioneer electronic trading, and even chaired the NASDAQ stock exchange from 1990 to 1993, so few people dared to question his unusually high and consistent returns. Over the course of several decades, he grew his "hedge fund" to about $65 billion, which claimed to invest in blue-chip stocks with a hedging strategy. However, the funds were not invested. They just sat in a bank account, and he paid out fake returns to investors from the deposits of new investors in classic Ponzi manner.

When the market crashed in 2008 and panic ensued, his fund was flooded with more redemption requests than he could fulfill, so he could no longer keep the sham going. In December 2008, he confessed the truth to his two sons, who were senior managers of the firm. They reported him to the authorities the next day, and Madoff eventually pled guilty to 11 federal felony counts. He received the maximum sentence of 150 years in prison with restitution of $170 billion.

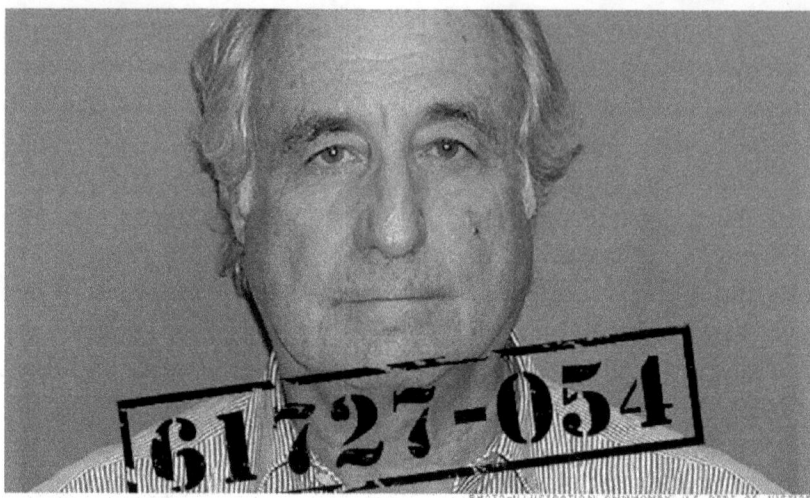

BERNIE MADOFF, U.S. DEPT. OF JUSTICE PHOTO, 2009

Similar to the Vegas Ponzi scheme, Madoff's firm fabricated their own trading records and monthly investor statements with no verification from any third-party custodians. He consistently paid 10 to 20 percent annual returns in both up and down markets. Note that although these returns were not realistic, they were not as outrageous as the 50 percent annual returns the Vegas scheme promised. This might be one of the reasons Madoff was able to fool both investors and regulators for so long.

Bernie Madoff also portrayed an air of exclusivity. Not everyone was "lucky" enough to participate, so it was considered a prestigious honor to be invited to invest in his fund. Thus he attracted many wealthy and famous people to invest.[61] As with the Vegas Ponzi scheme, although these characteristics and others were warning signs that it might be too good to be true, many people were blinded by their respect for Madoff and by their strong desire for high returns with no apparent risk.

As if the crippling financial losses caused by Ponzi schemes were not already painful enough, they also often result in even more tragic consequences. The shock of learning that people you trusted with your life savings were lying to take advantage of you, or not adequately evaluating investments they recommended, can be devastating. Your relationships with close friends or family members who got you involved may never be the same again.

Some fraud victims lose all hope for the future and feel they will never be able to trust again. They vow never to invest in anything else because they can't stomach the pain of losing another penny. Others become paralyzed in their future decision-making, no longer able to trust their own judgment, afraid of making another huge mistake.

What about those who innocently recommend these types of "investment opportunities" to friends and family members, genuinely intending to do them a great service? How would they feel knowing they played even a partial role in causing them to lose all their money?

In contrast to legitimate investments, one of the great tragedies of Ponzi schemes is that everyone involved loses in the end, including those who set it up and profited most from it. The attorney who started the Vegas Ponzi scheme almost shot himself in the head when the FBI showed up at his house, then he allegedly pointed a gun at the FBI agents, so they shot him. He survived, but now awaits trial in prison. So far the managing partner and salespeople involved have lost homes, cars, personal assets, friendships, and the trust of many in their community, but they may lose more as the investigation continues.

Look at what happened to Bernie Madoff. In addition to losing everything and living out the rest of his days in prison, at least two people committed suicide because of his Ponzi scheme—his own son and an investment manager who placed $1.4 billion of his clients' money in the fraudulent fund. Madoff died in prison at age 82 in 2021, and his widow lives a modest life in Connecticut.

How do you think he felt knowing that he was responsible for those suicides, as well as for ruining the lives of tens of thousands of investors who are likely still trying to recover from those losses, and may never recover? While in prison, Madoff admitted he wished they had caught him many years earlier because he had lived in constant fear for decades. What good did all that money do for him in the end?

Both of these Ponzi schemes are stark reminders of the troubling reality that we are all susceptible to fear and greed, which can lead us to make irrational decisions that can be extremely harmful to ourselves and others. We must be vigilant of potential fraud by checking investment opportunities against the four questions I mentioned earlier.

Don't ignore that gnawing feeling in your gut when something appears too good to be true. The warning signs will always be there, so don't overlook them, no matter how badly you really, *really* want the promises to be true.

If you choose to participate despite the warning signs, you may not realize the truth until it is too late. The costs to you and others you care about can be astronomical.

Even investors who succeed in withdrawing their funds from these types of shams before the fraud is discovered could be required to pay back a large portion of it, since they were not legitimate investment earnings. This is called a "clawback," which seeks to balance out the restitution paid to all innocent participants in a Ponzi scheme.

If you have been a victim of a Ponzi scheme or any other type of fraud, please don't lose hope, and please don't take the wrong lesson from it. This does not mean you should never trust anyone again, that you should never invest again, or that you will never be able to recover.

There is always hope for the future. You can rebuild. Most people are genuinely good people who can be trusted. You must continue to invest to reach your financial goals.

Now you have more tools to recognize fraud so you can better protect yourself and others you care about from future potential threats. With that knowledge, you will be able to improve your chances of success without letting your fear or greed get in the way.

KEY POINTS OF CHAPTER 3

1. No one can consistently predict which fund or area of the market will perform best in the future.
2. Trying to chase last year's top performing fund, asset class, sector, and so on often results in severe losses.

3. Wait to invest in IPOs until at least a year after they first go public.
4. Meme stocks like GameStop are especially risky and should be avoided.
5. Don't borrow money to buy more stocks.
6. If you are going to invest in bonds, stick with high-quality, investment grade bonds and avoid junk bonds.
7. Don't buy too much gold or other commodities. They are more risky than they seem and have low historical returns.
8. Real estate is a great asset if you invest in it prudently, but you can lose a lot if you expect big returns too quickly.
9. Cryptocurrency is likely here to stay, but is still very speculative and impossible to predict which ones will survive.
10. Watch for the warning signs of potential fraud, especially when someone promises high returns with very little risk.

CHAPTER 4

GOING BROKE SAFELY

GETTING OUT OF BED IS RISKY

This book has been quite a downer so far, hasn't it? I warned you that it would be. At this point I'm sure you're more excited than ever to jump up and invest more of your hard-earned dollars.

As I mentioned in the introduction, you *can* make a lot of money by timing the market, picking stocks, and chasing what's hot. However, even those who get lucky usually end up losing a lot with these strategies over time, so I don't recommend any of them. The good news is that you can be a successful investor without them.

In Chapter 7 we'll discuss more reliable methods. First I wanted you to see the potentially devastating results of common approaches that involve more risk than necessary. Brokerage firms and the media have done an excellent job guiding us to invest in ways that benefit them.

Unfortunately, after being badly burned by one or more of the risky tactics I have shared up to this point, some people give up on investing altogether. They can't stand the thought of losing another penny, so they shove it all in the bank, under the mattress, or in guaranteed insurance products. Who could blame them, especially if they lost everything in one rosy bet after decades of hard work and sacrifice?

The problem is that no one can totally avoid all risk. You're always just trading one risk for another.

For example, if you never invested again, you would avoid the risk of investment losses, but you would increase at least two other risks at the same time: the risk of not being able to retire with the lifestyle you want, and the risk of losing the value of your savings to inflation over time.

The principle of competing risks doesn't just apply to investing—it applies to almost every aspect of life. Have you ever noticed how risky it is just to get out of bed in the morning?

You could slip and hit your head on the bathroom counter, then die of a brain bleed. You could fall down the stairs and break your hip, then never wake up from surgery. You could electrocute yourself by sticking your fork too far in the toaster to pry out a stubborn blueberry bagel.

It's even worse when you leave the house. Walking in the sun could give you skin cancer. Running in the sun could give you a heart attack. Swimming in the sun could give you a shark attack. I should have written a book about all the ways you could die after getting out of bed—kids these days would love it.

But would staying in bed eliminate all risk? Hardly. You could die of starvation if no one ever brought you breakfast, lunch, or dinner in bed. You could die of abdominal poisoning for never visiting the toilet. On a more serious note, back pain, bedsores, obesity, heart disease, diabetes, depression, muscle and bone deterioration—these are all proven consequences of staying in bed for excessive periods of time.[1] It turns out that staying in bed is much less likely to lead to a happy, healthy life than confronting all the risks of that cold, cruel world outside the comfort and safety of your favorite blanket.

Life is not about avoiding all risks at all costs. Success in any endeavor requires taking at least some risk. There are no guarantees in life, but we can reduce the overall risk of negative outcomes by engaging in activities that will improve our chances of success.

If someone were to sit on the couch and watch Netflix 16 hours a day and eat nothing but Ruffles Cheddar & Sour Cream potato chips, they still might live to age 100, but it's not likely. If they were to run five miles a day and eat nothing but salads, they still might die of heart disease at age 40, but that's not likely either. Chances are they will live a longer, healthier life by exercising regularly and eating healthy food.

Investing works a lot like that. If I take my chances with risky bets on every dollar I earn, I might strike it rich, but it's not likely.

Even if I were lucky enough to make a lot of money, I probably would not be able to keep it for long.

Conversely, if I patiently stick to prudent, disciplined investment strategies and ignore all the hype and market noise, I might still lose money. However, I would be much more likely to reach my financial goals and my life would be a lot less stressful.

The chance that things won't turn out the way you want will always be looming in the background whether you invest or not. If you do invest, some things will turn out far better than you expected, and others will disappoint you. But I can almost guarantee that if you don't invest at all, you're much less likely to reach your financial goals.

TAMING THE BEAST

Horses are naturally wild, skittish beasts with an instinctive fight-or-flight response. Handling and riding horses can be very dangerous, causing serious injury or death when not done properly. In fact, approximately 700 people are killed in the U.S. each year due to horseback riding accidents.

However, these risks can be dramatically reduced by understanding the nature of horses, learning how to properly handle and ride them from trained professionals, and ensuring proper gear setup before each ride. Studies show that the majority of horseback riding injuries are preventable. The three most common causes are broken tack, slipped saddle, and no safety check.[2]

For centuries, horses played a critical role in the success of farming, and still do in some parts of the world. Horses were used to plow fields, plant, fertilize, and harvest crops, and haul them to market much more efficiently than a farmer could on his own before the invention of modern machinery. Can you imagine a farmer doing all that by himself? Or a rancher trying to herd cattle running around on his own two feet?

If a farmer chose not to use horses so he could avoid the risk of horse-related injuries, he likely would not have been able to produce the crops necessary to earn a sufficient living. In other words, he could not have eliminated all risks simply by avoiding the use of horses. A wiser approach would have been to minimize risk by learning how to properly handle horses.

Successful investing is very similar. The key is not to eliminate all risk, but rather to understand the nature of investing and how to prudently manage risk so you can improve your chances of success. With this knowledge, risk becomes much less threatening and you can channel it to your advantage.

These are the most important aspects of investing risk and basic ideas for how to effectively bridle each one:

1. **Business Risk** refers to the viability of a company's on-going operations. Can they stay profitable and continue to grow in a constantly evolving marketplace? Investing in many different companies rather than relying on a single enterprise or handful of stocks is the best way to minimize this risk.

2. **Concentration Risk** can hurt you if you are too focused on any one company, industry, or type of investment. For example, if all your money is in tech stocks, you will suffer larger losses when technology struggles than if you were better diversified. Be sure to invest in many different companies, industries, and types of investments to soften the impact of this risk.

3. **Interest Rate Risk** can affect the value of stocks but it more directly affects the value of bonds. When interest rates rise, bond prices fall, and vice versa. Holding individual bonds with a variety of maturity dates helps to reduce the effects of this risk.

4. **Reinvestment Risk** is the chance that you might have to reinvest a bond, CD, or other fixed income security at a lower interest rate when it matures. This risk can be reduced by purchasing longer-term fixed income (when it makes sense to do so) and avoiding callable bonds, which tend to be paid off early when interest rates fall.

5. **Credit or Default Risk** is the risk that a bond issuer, typically a government entity or corporation, will not be able to make its interest or principal payments to you on time. Highly rated, investment-grade bonds have lower default risk. Low-rated, junk bonds have higher default risk.

6. **Horizon or Duration Risk** also mainly applies to bonds and other fixed income. The longer you lock up your money, the more its value will be affected by interest rate fluctuations. If you cash out early to cover an unexpected cost, you could be forced to sell it at a discount. As with interest rate risk, this is best mitigated by buying bonds with a variety of maturity dates. Avoid locking up all your money for too long so you can cover short-term needs.

7. **Liquidity Risk** measures how easily you can access your money when you need it. With low liquidity, an unexpected cash need may force you to sell at a loss. In some cases you may not be able to access your money at all. For example, private placements, limited partnerships, and certain real estate deals often have strict rules about when investors can withdraw funds, with no way for you to sell your portion to others if you want out early. Avoid investing all your money in assets with little or no liquidity.

8. **Country Risk** relates to the inability of a country to meet its financial obligations, most likely in emerging markets or countries with severe deficits. This risk is mitigated by investing throughout the world and avoiding countries with excessive risk, like Russia at the time of this writing.

9. **Foreign Exchange or Currency Risk** involves the fluctuation in value of investments in a foreign country simply due to changes in the exchange rate between its currency and the U.S. dollar. This risk can be reduced with currency hedging, but if not properly executed, hedging can increase costs and reduce the benefits of global diversification. Foreign exchange rates are just as unpredictable as the market.

10. **Regulatory or Political Risk** measures the potential impact of changes in government regulation on certain companies or industries. Outside the U.S., major changes in government policy or political control can have even greater impact on investments in foreign countries. Investing in a variety of industries and countries, and avoiding those with extreme political instability, are smart ways to reduce these risks.

11. **Market Risk** is the risk of investments losing value due to unwelcome news or economic conditions that affect the whole market. The collapse of stock, bond, and real estate values due to the financial crisis in 2008 is an example of market risk. Stock values fell even for companies that were in a strong position to continue succeeding, simply because of the public's response to the crisis. This risk cannot be completely mitigated through diversification. The best protection from market risk is not taking on more risk than you can stomach and avoiding the temptation to time the market. Stick to your strategy through the ups and downs.

THE RISKS OF NOT INVESTING

Of all these risks, perhaps the most insidious is the risk of not investing at all. It truly is like farming without a horse.

As I mentioned in the introduction, most of the best things in life require some effort and risk. If we stop exercising, we lose energy and strength. If we stop learning and thinking, we lose our ability to reason. If we stop nurturing old friendships and forging new ones, we suffer socially and emotionally.

Investing is no different. There is no such thing as remaining static with your wealth. It is always either growing or shrinking. If you don't invest, it's likely to dwindle away and vanish over time through your spending and the impact of inflation.

Keeping up with inflation was a major concern for investors in 2022 and 2023 because inflation levels were the highest we had seen in 40 years. Even with "normal" inflation of just 3 percent per year, your money would be worth half what it is today in about 24 years if you don't give it a chance to grow. At 6 percent inflation, the value of your assets would be cut in half in only 12 years.

Inflation is the silent wealth-killer. You may not feel it each day, but over time you will literally go broke safely if you don't invest.

Another major risk of not investing is "longevity risk." This is the risk that you will run out of money before you die.

According to the Social Security Administration, the average life expectancy for those who reach age 65 is about 20 years. In other words, if you live to age 65, you are likely to live to at least age 85.

But don't plan on spending all your money by age 85 because about a third of those who make it to 65 will live to age 90. One in seven will live longer than 95 years.[3] These figures may expand with future advances in medicine, so be financially prepared to enjoy life for a long time!

Furthermore, the goal is not just to avoid running out of money. Don't you want to enjoy at least as good of a lifestyle in retirement as you do now? Would you like to leave a legacy to your children, grandchildren, or favorite charities when you pass away? Investing wisely increases your chances of attaining all of these goals. Hoarding cash decreases your chances.

At the end of Chapter 1, I mentioned a retired client who invested almost $2 million with my firm in 2003 and has gradually spent about $1.3 million of it since then. Amazingly, his account is worth $3.4 million at the time of this writing, even after the big losses of 2008 and many others along the way.

That might sound really good now, but the journey was not always smooth. For five of the past 20 years, his annual return was negative, even with a well-diversified mix of stocks and bonds.

In 2008 he lost 36 percent and ended the year with even less money than he invested with us in 2003. Since he was patient and stuck to the plan, the very next year he gained 28 percent, then another 17 percent in 2010.

Eventually he fully recovered his losses and ended up with a lot more money than he would have if he hadn't invested. If he had kept it in cash for the past 20 years, he would currently only have about $700,000, nearly a fifth of its current value. Was it worth the risk he took?

Another retired client of ours invested $4 million with us in 2015 and has spent $1.5 million of it over time. At the time of this writing his account is worth $4.1 million, even after losing 8 percent in 2018 and 10 percent in 2022. If he had kept it in cash the whole time to avoid the pain of potential losses, his account would likely only be worth $2.5 million today instead of $4.1 million.

This doesn't just work for investors who are retired, though. Another client who invested about $500,000 with us at the end of 2017 has gradually invested another $1.7 million with us since then. Their account is currently worth over $2.6 million. In other words, they have earned $400,000 more than they deposited over time, even after losing 9 percent in 2018 and 13 percent in 2022 (their investments are a little more aggressive than the previous example). If they had kept it all in cash, they would have avoided these losses. However, they would only have the $2.2 million they saved, rather than their current $2.6 million balance.

I won't bore you with too many examples, but many of our clients have enjoyed similar results. Although no one can guarantee that you will make money investing, these are typical examples of the benefits of investing in a diversified, disciplined manner over long periods of time. People who don't have enough faith in the market to ride through the ups and downs may never realize what they are missing.

Keeping your money literally in cash can be risky for other reasons besides its inability to grow. Some people I know stashed tens of thousands of dollars in cans buried in their backyard, then decades later couldn't find them or the cans had deteriorated, and the cash had been destroyed by soil, water, and insects. Storing cash in your house may subject it to theft or fire damage. Although these risks are minor compared to the lack of growth potential, their consequences could still be devastating.

Keeping all your money in checking or savings accounts at the bank does not avoid all risks, either. At the time of this writing, the U.S. government's Federal Deposit Insurance Corporation (FDIC) only insures bank accounts up to $250,000 per person. If you store millions of dollars at one bank and the bank goes out of business, you could lose most of it. What are the chances of your bank going out of business? According to the FDIC, 561 banks failed from 2001 to 2022. Most banks are very safe, but this demonstrates that it could happen.

YOUR BANK IS LAUGHING ALL THE WAY TO THE BANK

Speaking of banks, do you have any idea how much money your bank is making on your deposits? They would never deposit all their funds in other "risk-free" assets. In other words, if you're not willing to invest your money, the bank is happy to invest it for you, but they will keep most of the profits.

Don't get me wrong, I love the banks I work with and I'm grateful for the extremely valuable products and services they provide. Can you imagine life without the safety and convenience of checking accounts, savings accounts, debit cards, credit cards, online banking, online bill pay, direct deposits, automatic withdrawals, and the ability to pay people electronically?

Even more importantly, think of how few people would be able to purchase a home, buy a decent car, further their education, or acquire a business without banks. They are critical to the growth of our economy because they allow people and businesses to borrow money with relatively low interest rates and reasonable monthly payments.

I'm legitimately pleased that banks make a profit for providing these vital services to our modern society. They deserve to be fairly compensated for that. However, I believe strongly in win-win relationships, not win-lose. If you let banks make all the profits off your money, they are winning and you are losing.

As you know, banks typically charge much higher interest for loans than they pay you for your deposits. They profit from the "spread" between the low interest rate they pay you and the higher interest rate they charge borrowers.

Bank savings accounts pay a low rate that rises and falls as interest rates fluctuate. If you're willing to lock up your money for a certain period in a certificate of deposit (CD), you can earn a little higher interest rate than a normal savings account.

CD terms usually range from three months to ten years. The longer you lock up your money, the higher the interest rate you can earn. But if you take a withdrawal before the maturity date, you will lose anywhere from three months to two years' worth of your interest earned, depending on the bank and the CD term.

As of the time of this writing, one of the largest, most popular banks in the country pays 0.01 percent interest on their savings accounts. That's right, only 1/100th of 1 percent annually. They currently charge about 6 percent for a 5-year auto loan or 30-year mortgage. That's 600 times the amount they would pay you for depositing your money with them! Oh, and how much interest can you earn if you lock up your money in a 10-year CD with them? A whole 0.03 percent. No wonder they are so huge and profitable.

Thankfully, other banks are currently willing to pay you 3 to 4 percent for depositing your money with them, but that's still a lot lower than 6 percent interest on a loan. If you didn't have impeccable credit, the loan interest rate would be much higher, resulting in an even wider spread in the bank's favor.

Banks also make more than they pay you by investing in stocks, bonds, and real estate, and by charging you fees for a variety of products and services they provide for *your* money. What do you get in return? A very safe, very low rate of return.

That's how it works. Those who are willing to take even just a little risk tend to make a lot more than those who won't. Most people who leave gigantic sums of money at the bank for years will probably never realize what it's costing them.

THE PROMISE OF HIGH RETURNS WITH "NO RISK"

For investors who are fed up with low rates on bank deposits but still want safety, banks and insurance companies offer a variety of products promising high returns with little to no risk. These are some of the most complex products the financial industry has ever invented, and most people have no idea how they really work. This makes it easy for those who sell them to exaggerate potential benefits and minimize potential risks. Remember, if it sounds too good to be true, it probably is, even if it's issued by your favorite bank or insurance company.

One example is market-linked CDs, which claim to provide market-based returns with principal protection. They are FDIC-insured, but they don't have a guaranteed fixed interest rate like normal CDs. Instead, the interest rate varies based on the performance of an underlying asset like the S&P 500 index. Who wouldn't want S&P 500 returns with no risk? If only it were that simple.

Unfortunately, most market-linked CDs don't turn out nearly as well as investors expected. One study of 147 market-linked CDs from 2010 to 2016 discovered that 62 percent of them paid less than a conventional five-year CD over the same period, and 25 percent of them paid no interest at all. This was during a period when the stock market performed very well.[4]

How could this be? There are several reasons. First of all, they tend to be laden with high fees that reduce returns. Some say they have no fees, but they're often hidden in the spreads on options or other derivatives linked to the underlying assets. Banks and the people who sell market-linked CDs tend to make a lot more on these than they do on traditional CDs.[5]

Second, you don't usually get to participate in the full performance of the investments linked to the CD. Many of them limit your return to a percentage of the underlying asset's return, called a "participation rate." If the S&P 500 earns 10 percent in a year, you might only earn 7 percent.[6]

Third, you don't benefit from any dividends paid. When you own a stock directly and the company makes a profit, you are entitled to receive your share of the profit, called a dividend. Likewise, if you own a fund that invests in the S&P 500 index, you are entitled to receive the dividends paid by all 500 stocks in the index. Dividends are important because historically about a third of the S&P 500 total returns have come from dividends.[7]

In a market-linked CD, you don't own any of the stocks, so you are not eligible to receive any dividends. You only participate in price changes of the underlying stocks, which makes it almost impossible to keep up with actual S&P 500 returns over time.

Some people may argue that the principal protection is more valuable than being able to participate in dividends. True, market-linked CDs limit how much you can lose each year, but the trade-off is that they also limit how much you can make during the good times. These upper limits (caps) often hurt you more than the lower limits (floors) help you, severely reducing overall performance.

For example, one market-linked CD issued in 2010 tied to the performance of 20 stocks only paid a $40 total return per $100,000 invested over five years because of the timing of its caps and floors. Those same 20 stocks collectively more than doubled in value over the same period. Investors would have made a lot more by investing in a regular CD or in those 20 stocks directly.

To be fair, I'm citing extreme examples to make a point. Obviously, not all market-linked CDs perform so poorly. Sometimes they do make more than you would have made in a regular CD or in the market directly, but not often enough to be considered as a reliable long-term investment strategy.

If you want the chance to earn more than a regular CD while maintaining FDIC principal protection, and you recognize that you might earn substantially less than a regular CD, maybe a market-linked CD would be okay for a portion of your investments. Just don't expect them to produce market returns with no risk as they are frequently sold.

How would you feel if after locking up $1 million for 10 years you only got your initial deposit back? What if you found out you could have earned hundreds of thousands of dollars in a normal CD or grown it to more than $2 million by investing directly in the market over that time? If you're not okay with the possibility of missing out on that much growth, don't invest in market-linked CDs, because that outcome is more likely than you may realize.

Most of these are not liquid, either, meaning that if you're not happy with the performance, you can't get your money back without steep penalties until the end of the term. They also tend to be taxed at higher rates than stocks. Keith Amburgey, who used to design these for a large investment bank, explained, "I've worked in the kitchen and seen how it's made, so I'm not interested in consuming them."[8]

Structured notes are another popular banking product similar to market-linked CDs, but they are riskier because they are not FDIC-insured and tend not to have the same principal guarantees.

They may promise even higher returns than market-linked CDs with some downside protection. However, if the underlying investment performs below a certain level or if the issuer declares bankruptcy, you could lose your *full* deposit amount. This is not likely to occur, but most investors probably don't realize that it's possible.

Although I don't recommend structured notes to my clients, they can work for some investors looking for higher potential returns than traditional CDs with a measure of principal protection. They just need to understand that they could end up earning a lot less than CDs, and that they might even lose some or all of their principal if the underlying assets perform badly enough.

Unfortunately, many salespeople downplay the risks and overstate the expected performance, giving investors an unrealistic expectation of market-based returns with little to no risk. In response, the SEC and FINRA (regulators for the financial industry) have issued several warnings to investors about them, including the following: "structured notes with principal protection can have complicated pay-out structures that can make it hard to accurately assess their risk and potential for growth...while [they] have reassuring names, they are not risk-free...chasing a higher yield by investing in these products could mean winding up with an expensive, risky, complex and illiquid investment."[9]

Indexed annuities are a classic example of an insurance product touting undeliverable promises of high returns with no risk. Like market-linked CDs and structured notes, they are among the most complex and confusing financial instruments ever invented, making investors susceptible to unreasonable expectations.

Since their performance is typically tied to the S&P 500 or other indexes, people who sell them often make it sound like you're investing in the index with downside protection, but it's not true. You're not actually investing in the index. As we discussed with market-linked CDs and structured notes, you are not likely to earn returns comparable to the index after the drag of hidden fees, rate caps, limited participation rates, and the lack of dividends.

Proponents of indexed annuities may say you can expect to earn at least an 8 percent average annual return with no risk, since that was similar to the average annual return in the S&P 500 for the past 20 years. The truth is you're more likely to earn as little as 3 percent to 5 percent. Annuity salespeople are eager to exaggerate hypothetical returns and minimize the costs and risks because they can earn up to a 10 percent commission for selling them.

Due to the high commissions and other expenses involved, if you try to withdraw your money early, you could be subject to steep surrender penalties for as long as 10 years. If you withdraw funds before age 59.5, you will also be required to pay a 10 percent penalty tax on top of ordinary income taxes. Although they may claim your principal is protected from market loss, you can still lose significant value over time due to excessive internal costs.[10]

As with market-linked CDs and structured notes, indexed annuities can work for investors who are okay with much lower potential returns than the market in exchange for some principal protection and perhaps even some guaranteed lifetime income. However, most of my clients prefer to invest in the market directly and control their risk in other ways so they have a lot more flexibility and higher potential returns than these complex, stringent products normally provide.

Indexed universal life insurance can be even more problematic than indexed annuities. Let me be clear: I am a huge fan of life insurance for the right purposes. It is a critical tool that provides tremendous financial stability to families, businesses, and society in general. However, if you don't need a death benefit for estate planning purposes or to cover a potential financial loss to your family or business resulting from your premature death, it's probably not worth considering.

Most people I talk to who are contemplating the purchase of an indexed universal life insurance policy are not doing it for the death benefit. They are mainly interested in the promise of high returns with no risk and the potential tax benefits. My observation is that people who purchase any type of life insurance solely for these purposes generally end up disappointed with the outcome.

Why? Because indexed universal life insurance policies combine all the drawbacks of indexed annuities with substantial additional life insurance costs. And those costs increase each year as you get older.

When you are young, the internal costs of insurance are relatively low and increase gradually. As you near retirement age, they really start to ramp up. Around the age of average life expectancy, the costs skyrocket exponentially each year, causing most policies to lapse before the death benefit is paid. That's right—these policies are purposely designed to accomplish the insurance company's goal of collecting your premiums for decades without ever having to pay a claim. Are you shocked?

Let me explain more specifically how this works. The "savings account" component of a universal life policy is called cash value. Your cash value grows based on the amount of premiums you deposit and the performance of the index it's linked to, limited by all the same factors we discussed with market-linked CDs and structured notes. Your cash value shrinks by the amount the insurance company automatically takes out each month for the cost of insurance and other expenses.

In the beginning, the premiums you pay and any interest the cash value earns are likely to be higher than the insurance costs and other expenses. However, as you age, the insurance costs typically exceed the amount of the premiums you're able to pay and the cash value's ability to grow. This is where lower than expected returns due to rate caps, limited participation rates and lack of dividend earnings can really hurt you, especially if you were projecting an 8 percent annual return for the rest of your life.

Many people have purchased these types of policies with the hope of withdrawing large amounts of tax-free income throughout retirement with much less risk than the stock market. Unfortunately, far too many of these policies get to the point where the owner not only loses the ability to take income from the policy, but also is required to pay significant additional premiums to keep the death benefit going. If they don't, they could be subject to a very large tax bill on most of the "tax-free" income they had taken from the policy up to that point, called a phantom tax.

This happened to the father of a friend of mine. He had paid premiums for many years on a large universal life insurance policy.

When he was in his 80s, he became incapacitated, so his children had to handle his financial affairs.

The insurance company sent him a notice stating that his cash value was no longer sufficient to cover the insurance costs. If he didn't send them a check for about 40 percent of the death benefit amount, his policy would lapse. His doctors predicted he would only live another six months, so his children figured it was worth paying such a high premium because they would get even more money back in six months.

A year later he was still alive! The insurance company sent another notice requiring an even higher premium to keep the death benefit going since he was a year older. What would you do if you were his children? Would you pay another 45 percent of the death benefit amount hoping he would die within the next year, or lose every penny of the hundreds of thousands that had already been paid into the policy? What if he lived for another year?

Some universal life insurance policies guarantee that the death benefit will not lapse for a certain period if you pay a specified premium amount much higher than the minimum. The guaranteed period could be anywhere from 20 years to age 110. The longer the guarantee, the higher the premium—a guarantee to age 110 is very expensive. If you ever touch the cash value or miss a single premium payment, the guarantee goes away. Most people don't have these guarantees on their policies for very long because the premiums are too high, they miss premium payments, or they need to access the cash value.

There are hundreds of ways to structure indexed annuities and indexed universal life policies, so comparing options and measuring potential performance can be very difficult. If you are considering a purchase of any of these products, be sure to read the fine print and understand the worst-case scenarios. I can almost guarantee that whoever is selling it to you has never read it, so they are not likely to fully understand the risks.

I have attended many training meetings over the years to learn as much as I can about these. I usually walk away frustrated because they tend to focus on how to sell the potential benefits and gloss over the risks. In talking to hundreds of other advisors and insurance agents throughout my career, I have found that most who sell these types of products have never read any of the contracts and don't really understand how they work. However, they seem to be very familiar with the most important part—how large of a commission they will receive for selling them.

On illustrations showing projected performance, take the "non-guaranteed" optimistic columns with a grain of salt and focus more on the "guaranteed" columns to understand what you're really getting yourself into. Your actual performance will probably land somewhere between the non-guaranteed and guaranteed projections, but at least you'll better understand the worst-case scenarios.

If you already own an indexed universal life policy, ask the insurance company or the agent who sold it to you for an in-force illustration every year or so. This will give you updated estimates on how your policy is expected to perform based on your actual earnings, cash value, death benefit, outstanding loans (if applicable), expenses, and planned premium payments.

Be sure to get a version showing how long the cash value and death benefit would last if the policy only earned 3 to 5 percent per year. If it looks like it might run out too quickly or doesn't otherwise meet your expectations, here are three potential solutions:

1. Significantly overfund the policy (pay much higher premiums than required for as long as you can). This will maximize your chances of outpacing the increasing cost of insurance throughout your lifetime so you don't lose the death benefit before you pass away.
2. Reduce the death benefit to lower the cost of insurance and prolong the life of the policy.
3. Cancel the policy while you're still ahead, but not until after you get a new policy with better terms if you still need a death benefit.

Some who read this section may assert that these types of banking and insurance products have worked out great for them. If so, that makes me happy. As I mentioned, they can work, just like timing the market, picking stocks, and investing in cryptocurrencies *can* work. They especially can look like heroes when the market takes a dive, giving very risk-averse people some chance of a better return than a bank savings account.

My point is that they are not likely to earn the same or higher returns than you could earn by investing in the market on your own over time, regardless of what unscrupulous or ignorant salespeople may tell you. Neither banks nor insurance companies have exclusive access to any magic investments that can guarantee high returns with no risk. They generally invest in the same stuff you could invest in without them, and they charge hefty fees for the guarantees, substantially reducing your potential return.

There is no such thing as high returns with no risk. Too many people are going broke safely by putting too much of their hard-earned money in banking and insurance products without realizing the costs.

KEY POINTS OF CHAPTER 4

1. No one can totally avoid all risk. When you avoid one risk, you often trade it for another.
2. Prudent investors reduce overall risk by engaging in activities that improve their chances of success.
3. Understanding the nature of different investments and types of risk can help you manage risk more effectively.
4. One of the greatest risks is not investing at all. If you don't invest, you are not likely to reach your financial goals, enjoy a decent lifestyle throughout your entire life, leave a financial legacy, or keep up with inflation.
5. Banks and insurance companies provide valuable products and services, but if you leave too much money with them, you can miss out on big opportunities for wealth creation.
6. Beware of the promise of high returns with no risk. Due to high internal expenses and complex limitations, many banking and insurance products have lower long-term expected returns than the investments they are tied to.
7. Don't buy life insurance unless you need a death benefit. Universal life insurance can be especially risky because of the ever-increasing cost of insurance and other variables.

CHAPTER 5

IGNORING COSTS

THE HOUSE ALWAYS WINS

Another way many smart people lose money unknowingly is by ignoring the costs associated with their investments. The financial industry is notorious for downplaying and burying them.

Thankfully, many of these costs have become more transparent in recent years, but most people don't understand their implications, and some are still hidden. Whether you see them or not, they are there. Chances are you have no idea how much they impact your investment performance. After reading this chapter, you will.

I am not a gambler, but after moving to Las Vegas in 2001 I have learned some interesting things about how gaming works from friends and clients in the casino industry. As I'm sure you've already figured out, those colossal casinos were not built by chance.

Several years ago, some friends and I were invited to tour an exclusive section of a large casino in Vegas reserved for "high rollers" who bet tens of thousands if not hundreds of thousands of dollars per hand. It was a beautiful place! We even got to visit their high-roller baccarat room, which I believe normally requires at least a $1 million credit line just to enter.

Baccarat is a popular card game played at casinos. As one of the dealers explained how the game works, we asked how much money high rollers tend to win or lose there. He shared that one bettor was up $17 million but kept playing until he was down $25 million, then the casino made him quit. I guess they only let you dig so deep of a hole to ensure you can repay the loan. Can you imagine owing $25 million to a casino?

It blows my mind to think that even if he had quit when he was up $17 million, the casino would have been fine and would surely have invited him back. In fact, several casinos fly private jets as far as China to pick up these high rollers, house them in the finest luxury suites, and feed them gourmet food, all at no cost to the players. Why? They know that over time they will make a lot more than these perks cost.

If guests spend too much time enjoying their luxury suites or the fabulous restaurants, shows, and shopping in Vegas, they send them home right away, and may never invite them back. Bettors earn their perks by spending time at the gaming tables.

Casinos also closely monitor every inch of the gaming floor through security cameras and security guards to ensure no one is stealing, cheating, or consistently winning more than statistically plausible. They don't hesitate to throw out and blacklist anyone who appears to be a threat to their profits. They go to great lengths to ensure that the house always wins in the end.

How do casinos make money so regularly if gambling is a game of chance? Everyone knows they can lose money gambling, but they may not realize how much of every dollar bet is kept forever by the casino, never paid out to any bettor.

Every game has a built-in "house edge," which is the percentage of total bets that the casino retains. This percentage can vary widely from game to game. The house edge is about 1 percent for baccarat, 5 percent for American roulette, 2 to 25 percent for slot machines, and 25 to 29 percent for keno.

Most gamblers know the casino has an edge, but they don't fully grasp how it plays out. The house edge applies to every bet, not to the total amount you wager. In other words, if you were to play baccarat starting with $100, expecting over time to walk away with $99 on average because of the 1 percent house edge, you would be mistaken. If you place 80 bets per hour at $100 per bet, your total expected loss would be around $80 ($1 per bet), not just $1.[1]

This is part of why you could easily walk away empty handed even with just a 1 percent house edge. The more you play, the greater your chances of losing, and the more likely your overall losses will approximate the house edge.

Based on a study of thousands of gamblers over a two-year period, the chances of winning on any given day weren't too bad. About 30 percent of the days they gambled they won something. But the more they gambled, the more they lost.

Over the two years analyzed, 83 percent of those who bet the least frequently (bottom 10 percent) lost money overall. During the same period, 95 percent of those who bet the most frequently (top 10 percent) lost money. This study confirms that the more you play, the greater your chances of losing.[2]

Why don't casinos retain an even higher house edge to increase profits? They must remain competitive with other casinos and they want their edge to be as imperceptible as possible. If they retained half of everything players bet, no one would place any more bets because they wouldn't have a sufficient expectation of winning. Just enough has to be paid out to give gamblers the insatiable hope that next time they will win big, continually luring them back for more.

Brokerage firms are similar to casinos in the sense that they stack the deck in their favor and encourage investor behavior that serves their interests. Believe it or not, brokerage firms also have their own version of a "house edge" that ensures they make money regardless of your outcome. The more you trade stocks, bonds, and other securities, the more they make, and the greater chance you have of losing money. They don't really care whether you win or lose, as long as you keep trading.

I don't mean to vilify all brokerage firms. Like banks and insurance companies, they provide an extremely valuable service. Investors wouldn't be able to buy or sell securities so easily without them. Wealth advisors like me wouldn't be able to operate our investment advisory businesses without them, either. They deserve to be paid well for the benefits they provide.

However, I'm not okay with them receiving all the value at your expense. Some are blatantly predatory. Learning how they make money will increase your awareness of the motives behind their constant barrage of market updates, marketing messages, and website and mobile app designs. It's up to you (and your advisor) to ensure your relationship with them is a win-win. If you're not on your game, it could deteriorate into a win-lose scenario, and they won't be on the losing side.

How can you tell if it's a win-win? Generally speaking, investment strategies with high fees, frequent trading, and excessive cash positions are in brokerage firms' best interests, not yours. Whose interests are you more interested in serving?

THE TRUE COST OF FREE TRADING

Brokerage firms used to charge high commission percentages on every stock trade, up to hundreds or even thousands of dollars per trade depending on the size of the order.[3] This was a huge revenue source for them and the brokers who worked for them.

At the time, brokers could only make money when they convinced their clients to place a new trade, so they would regularly call their clients with new investment ideas. Often these "hot new stock tips" were simply stocks the firm was trying to sell, so they would pressure their brokers to unload them onto their clients.

As electronic trading technology improved in the 1990s and competition intensified, many firms migrated to a flat commission dollar amount per trade. Discount brokerage firms like E-Trade and Scottrade were touting commissions as low as $7 per trade, which was unheard of at the time.

That sort of pricing became the norm for a long time. Then in October 2019, industry giant Charles Schwab rocked the brokerage world by announcing they would no longer be charging any commissions on most stock or ETF trades. They decided they were tired of making so much money and wanted to be more like Mother Teresa by serving investors for free.

Ha! Obviously nothing is truly free, at least in the investing world. They had a strategic business motive behind this move and still make plenty of money without charging those commissions. In fact, less than 4 percent of Schwab's net revenue was from stock and ETF commissions before this change.

Surely they expected to easily make up the difference by attracting additional assets with lower trading costs. Popular trading app Robinhood showed the power of free trading as a marketing

strategy when it started in 2013. They opened four million brokerage accounts in their first five years, even surpassing E-Trade,
and grew to 23 million accounts by 2022.[4] When Schwab made
the switch to free trading in 2019, several other brokerage firms
were forced to immediately follow suit in order to compete.

Schwab still charges fees on trades for bonds, options, foreign
stocks, penny stocks and certain mutual funds, but these fees are
a drop in the bucket compared to their main revenue sources. Like
banks, a huge portion of their revenue comes from the interest
they earn on cash in client accounts, margin loans, and securities
lending. Additional profits come from revenue sharing on mutual
fund expenses and "payment for order flow," a cut of the bid-ask
spread from market makers who fulfill their trades.[5]

What is the bid-ask spread? It's the difference between the
highest price a buyer is willing to pay and the lowest price a seller
is willing to accept for trading a stock or other security. The spread
can range from a few cents per share to more than a dollar per
share, which could represent as much as 2 percent of the price of
the stock.

The largest, most frequently traded stocks like Apple and Amazon tend to have the smallest spreads because they are high in
supply and demand. Smaller stocks and foreign stocks that are
traded less frequently tend to be more volatile and have larger
spreads. Bonds tend to have larger spreads, too.

Who gets to keep the difference between the buy price and
the sell price? The market maker, which is typically a large firm
that facilitates the trade. Market makers are often even able to set
the amount of the spread, determining their own profits.[6]

Every time you trade a security, you lose value to the spread.
The more you trade, the more money you lose to spreads. This is
a huge revenue source for investment firms, explaining why they
want you to trade as often as possible even if they don't charge a
commission on the trade.

Brokerage firms exploit our hard-wired belief that we always
have to be active to be productive. If we don't exercise, we lose
muscle. If we don't work, we don't make money. It's natural to
think we must constantly tinker with our investments to ensure

that they grow, but investing in the market doesn't work like that. Activity does not equal productivity.

Investing is more like growing grass. It needs you to leave it alone for a while even though it might not look like it's doing anything. How well would your lawn grow if you were to constantly walk on it, trim it, hand-water it, and fertilize it? You would severely stunt its growth or kill it.

Prudent investing can be pretty boring, just like watching grass grow. It doesn't need much from you. Give it time and be patient with it. Don't place very many trades. Brokerage firms don't want you to know this, because if you leave it alone for too long, they don't make much money.

Speaking of "lazy" investing—ironically, keeping too much cash at a brokerage firm can be almost as harmful as trading stocks and bonds too often. I recently received an ad from a bank offering an automated robo-advisor investment platform with no advisory fee. The only catch is that you have to keep a full 30 percent in cash at all times. That's a lot of cash!

They describe it as a 30 percent buffer against market volatility "to balance out potential risk should market conditions change." This is smooth marketing language to make it sound like a smart strategy, but we know the real reason they require such a large "buffer" is that they make a lot of money on that cash.

According to their website, you cannot access the cash like a normal money market account, and it's not FDIC insured. If you pull funds out of your account, they immediately sell some of your investments and replenish the buffer to ensure you always retain a 30 percent cash balance because that's how they make their money. It's not really free.[7] This is great for them, but not so great for you if you're trying to grow your money.

POISONOUS FREE LUNCHES

Economists have taught for decades that "there is no such thing as a free lunch," meaning that giveaways often come with costly strings attached. This saying refers to the once-common practice of saloons giving away free lunches with high salt content to entice customers to buy more drinks, but it has many applications today.[8]

We are easily suckered into accepting freebies because the costs are usually hidden very well. Don't be fooled—there is always a cost to you or to society as a whole. The chefs who concoct today's "free lunches" in a wide variety of industries have become masters at making them more irresistible than ever, but they can be laced with poison and lead to devastating consequences.

My twin boys have always loved video games as most kids do, but when they discovered Fortnite Battle Royale at age 10 in 2018, they thought they had died and gone to heaven. In fact, you can even do one of those two things in the game.

Fortnite is an online cooperative survival game, and their 10-year-old brains couldn't get enough of it. For a school assignment, they even wrote "getting better at Fortnite" as one of their most important life goals.

Many video games require a one-time purchase somewhere between $10 to $100 to download and play the game, but Fortnite allows all players to download it for free. At first I thought this was a great deal, but now I wish it would have cost them $500 to download. That would have been a lot cheaper in the long run.

At the time of this writing, Fortnite has about 400 million registered users and rakes in over $5 billion in revenue each year. How could a "free" game make so much money?

In Fortnite you can exchange real dollars for in-game currency to buy cosmetic customizations of players' characters, such as the way their outfits, pickaxes, and gliders look. You can even buy dance moves! That's it. You can't buy anything that improves your abilities, weaponry, or any other strategic advantage in the game.

Active users spend an average of 6 to 10 hours per week playing, which highlights its addictive nature.[9] Now my sons regret how much time and money they spent on Fortnite because they don't care about it anymore, and they have nothing to show for it. One of them estimates that he probably spent about $2,000 on customizing his characters over the course of a few years. My other son may have spent a similar amount.

While sleeping over at my mother-in-law's house one time, she loaded her credit card onto their account so they could play it there. In her absence, they figured out how to buy more in-game currency on her credit card without her permission. They absolutely had to buy more upgrades right at that moment before they disappeared from the online shop in the game.

Later they felt horrible, fessed up, and worked for a while to pay her back. Still, we were terrified to realize how addictive this game could be, driving players to irrational, impulsive, and even immoral behavior.

I am alarmed at the ability of Fortnite's designers to manipulate the thoughts and actions of its users. My sons are generally honest, respectful boys who have been taught how serious stealing is. How could they be so desperate for something as pointless as customizing the look of their video-game characters that they would even be willing to steal from their beloved grandma for it?

I wish I could say the investment industry was immune to devious developers like the creators of Fortnite, but the gamification of investing has become even more poisonous. Some of the greatest threats to personal wealth, health, and happiness are free stock trading apps like Robinhood, which we discussed earlier.

At first glance Robinhood looks like a knight in shining armor, making investing more accessible to all people through unlimited free trades, no minimum deposits, and an easy-to-use interface. The company's mission is to "provide everyone with access to financial markets, not just the wealthy," hence the name Robinhood.

But how much good are they really doing and what is their true motive? Addiction experts accuse Robinhood and other similar trading platforms of purposely employing systems of cues and rewards that induce gambling and addictive behavior in its users.

According to Addiction Center:

> When a new member joins the platform, an image of a digital scratch-off lottery ticket pops up on their screen. The picture is a welcome stub, a gift for joining Robinhood's community. The app's stub promises a free share of stock worth anywhere from $2.50 to $200.00. If the new trader wants the prize, they have to play by 'scratching off' the image like a lotto ticket.

> At first, the interaction seems harmless, even fun. Yet, Keith Whyte, the National Council on Problem Gambling

executive director, warns that Robinhood's styling has features like common betting apps. He claims it encourages immediacy and frequent engagement. Through its design, Robinhood induces dopamine rushes (pleasure neurotransmitter).

By promising a free yet unknown gift, the company immediately triggers dopamine responses among their new users. The trigger is what keeps them coming back.

Some of Robinhood's many alleged dopamine inducing features include:

- Green confetti to celebrate transactions.
- A constant update of stock related articles.
- A colorful, eye-catching interface.
- Emoji phone notifications.
- One-click trading for instant gratification.
- Free stocks in the shape of lottery tickets.
- Waitlists where users can improve their position by tapping up to 1,000 times per day.

Research indicates that a flow of uncertainty and rewards hooks users. Much like drugs or alcohol, incertitude stimulates the brain's reward system. Over time this repeated exposure can lead to addiction....

Inexperienced investors are not actively warned about financial dangers. Instead, the app's design is drawing them to the riskiest forms of trading like options. The app also highlights more risky investments with dazzling neons like cryptocurrencies.[10]

If Robinhood really wanted to help people make sound investment decisions and build real long-term wealth, wouldn't they recommend safer options like well-diversified ETFs, especially for the novice investors they are targeting? Robinhood makes a lot more money when investors trade options and cryptocurrencies, though, so it's no wonder they heavily promote those. In fact, as of May 2022, almost 90 percent of their revenue came from the trading of options and cryptocurrencies. They collect hundreds of millions of dollars from the hidden fees on these "free" trades.[11]

The zero-commission trading on Robinhood, which sounds like a good thing, is also a major driver of addictive behavior in its users. Investors mistakenly believe there is no cost for each trade, so many of them buy and sell stocks as often as they like throughout the day in response to every little market movement. They have no idea how much they are reducing their potential returns and racking up tons of profits for Robinhood.

Addiction Center continues, "According to filings, Robinhood received $18,955 from trading firms for every dollar in the average customer account. Schwab only received $195 for the same deal." This shows how much more actively their users trade than Schwab users, and how much money they can make through the spreads of high-volume trading.

In 2020, Robinhood was forced to pay $65 million to settle charges by the Securities and Exchange Commission (SEC) that it was misleading investors about its revenue sources and failing to satisfy their duty of best execution on trades (rules of fair pricing and timing of trades). This means investors would have received better trade prices at other brokerage firms.

Even after taking into consideration the savings for not paying commissions, their customers were robbed of $34 million in value due to bad trade execution.[12] How would the "real" Robin Hood feel about a firm named after him robbing from the poor to give to the rich?

The Financial Industry Regulatory Authority (FINRA) also ordered Robinhood to pay about $70 million in fines and restitution to investors harmed by their "false or misleading information." This was FINRA's largest penalty ever levied.[13]

Too many people have lost more money than they could afford to lose on Robinhood by taking way more risk than they realized. Since most of Robinhood's users are new to investing, 2022 was the first big market drop they experienced, and it blindsided them big time. No one was there to hold their hand and help them make wise investing decisions through the most challenging market environment since the 2008 financial crisis.

Robinhood lost about a third of its active users in 2022. Its stock price plunged 90 percent, erasing tens of billions in shareholder value. Hundreds of thousands of these shareholders were Robinhood users.[14]

Tragically, money isn't the only thing people have lost by investing with Robinhood. Many have lost their emotional wellbeing and hope for the future.

A 20-year-old college student even took his own life due to a $730,000 loss he mistakenly thought he had incurred trading stock options. The lawsuit his family filed against Robinhood stated, "This case centers on Robinhood's aggressive tactics and strategy to lure inexperienced and unsophisticated investors…to take big risks with the lure of tantalizing profits. Robinhood built out its trading platform to look much like a videogame to attract young users and minimize the appearance of real-world risk." [15]

Obviously, I don't blame Robinhood for this heartbreaking suicide, nor do I blame Fortnite for my sons' stealing from their grandma. Everyone is accountable for their own actions.

However, I do believe Robinhood and other free trading apps like them should be held accountable for fooling investors into believing there is no cost for trading on their platform. They should also take responsibility for seducing investors to engage in highly addictive, speculative behavior that is profitable for the company but harmful to investors' long-term success.

Investing is not a game, and there is no such thing as a truly free lunch. I can neither confirm nor deny whether free lunches at school contain radioactive material as many students suspect. But when it comes to the financial world, "free lunches" are often quite literally laced with poison and may cost you dearly in the end.

THE TERMITES IN YOUR PORTFOLIO

Investors who understand the perils of excessive trading tend to hold their investments for longer periods to reduce these costs. However, some mutual funds or ETFs they own might buy and sell stocks frequently behind the scenes, subjecting them to expenses they thought they were escaping.

These hidden costs are not reported anywhere and are practically impossible to measure. The best indication of a fund's trading frequency is its "turnover ratio." This measures the percentage of holdings in the fund that have changed over a one-year period. A fund's turnover ratio can usually be found in the fund's fact sheet, prospectus, or on a fund analysis website like Morningstar.

A mutual fund or ETF with 100 percent turnover is the equivalent of replacing every stock or bond in the fund over the course of a year. In other words, each security in the fund is held for an average of one year. That's a lot of unnecessary buying and selling!

A 200 percent turnover signals that each security is held for an average of six months, which would be even worse. The funds I recommend to my clients typically have a turnover of only about 5 percent to 14 percent. This means that each security in the fund is held for an average of seven to 20 years.

Whenever I meet with a new potential client, my team does an in-depth analysis of their current portfolio to help them understand what they're doing well and how they might improve. I have yet to meet an investor who was fully aware of the hidden costs of their portfolio, including turnover ratios.

The average turnover is usually much higher than I recommend, but the highest I have seen is over 300 percent. Can you imagine the bid-ask spread costs associated with buying and/or selling every security in your account three times over the course of one year? But that's nothing compared to the Vesper U.S. Large Cap Short-Term Reversal Strategy ETF, which boasts an insane 4,280 percent turnover, holding its stocks only eight days on average!

How could any fund manager justify that much turnover? Some boast they can make up for these high trading costs by outperforming the market through their superior skills. They can promise whatever they want, but the proof is in the pudding.

In the first three chapters we discussed the problems with trying to time the market, pick stocks, and chase what's hot. Active fund managers with high turnover utilize these strategies in an attempt to outperform the market. Sometimes they might get lucky, but as a whole they tend to significantly underperform the market.

No doubt most of them are really smart, but they face two major challenges that would be almost impossible for anyone to master: they must outperform the market *and* make up for the higher costs of their strategies. As a result, high-turnover funds, in general, have lower returns, worse tax consequences, and go out of business more often than low-turnover funds.[16]

I recommend low-turnover funds because they increase your chances of success. Anything below 30 percent is reasonable, but the lower the better. Some prudently managed funds require higher turnover than others due to the nature of their holdings, such as small-cap stocks, foreign stocks, and short-term bonds.

Excessive taxation is another silent-but-deadly cost associated with high-turnover mutual funds. Normally you don't have to pay tax on any increase in the value of mutual funds you own until you sell them. However, whenever the fund manager sells a security (such as a stock or bond) inside the fund, any gains or losses in the value of that security are passed on to you and the other fund shareholders. If sold for a gain, you must claim it on your tax return.

If the manager held the security for less than a year before selling it, your tax bill would be much higher than if he held it for more than a year. Imagine the tax bite on a fund that is changing every position more than once a year, potentially subjecting every security to short-term capital gains. Add that to the excessive trading costs, and it's no wonder these types of funds tend to underperform. This is another reason why I prefer low turnover funds—they are much more tax efficient.

As a side note, one way to defer annual tax costs associated with turnover is to hold your funds in a retirement account such as a 401(k) or IRA. Retirement accounts are not subject to any taxes until you withdraw funds. However, withdrawals are subject to ordinary income taxes, which are usually taxed at a higher rate than the long-term capital gains you would pay for holding your investments more than a year outside of a retirement account.

Many ETFs can also provide greater tax efficiency than the average mutual fund. Their structure allows them more flexibility to minimize capital gain distributions sent to shareholders each year, even if the sale of securities within the fund generates capital gains. ETFs still must distribute some capital gains, as well as any dividend or interest income paid throughout the year by the underlying stocks, bonds, or other securities held.

Despite these tax benefits, mutual funds have some advantages over ETFs, so I don't necessarily always recommend ETFs. For example, mutual funds are not subject to bid-ask spreads when you trade them, but ETFs are. Mutual funds are also slightly more liquid and less volatile than ETFs and can be nearly as tax-efficient when turnover is low.

Unfortunately, the excessive trading costs and taxes associated with high turnover funds are not the only termites that silently eat away your returns. Two other deadly parasites are exorbitant fund expense ratios and unreasonable advisory fees.

I've met many people throughout my career who felt like they never made much money with other advisors they had worked with. This is often the result of advisors' attempts to time the market, pick stocks, or chase what's hot. However, excessive trading costs, unnecessary taxes, and over-priced fees also dramatically reduce returns, and most investors have no idea of their impact. These truly can be like termites silently nibbling away at your financial house until it crumbles to the ground.

You may not realize it, but every mutual fund and ETF carries an expense ratio that reduces your returns—even "no load" funds. You will never see it listed on your account statement, but it is listed on the fund prospectus. It covers the costs of running the fund, including payment to fund managers and administrative, research, marketing, and other expenses.

No one can invest without any fees, including Warren Buffett. Even low-cost fund companies like Vanguard and Dimensional Fund Advisors carry expense ratios on all their funds. Every fund company is a for-profit enterprise, and I'm not opposed to them making money. Like brokerage firms and banks, they deserve to be compensated for the valuable services they provide. However, I'm not okay with them making all the money at your expense.

Fund expense ratios can range from less than a tenth of 1 percent to more than 10 percent per year. The average is probably somewhere between half a percent and 1 percent. Hedge funds usually have even higher expenses than regular funds because they often charge an additional 20 percent of the returns in the fund on top of the normal expense ratio.

Why would anyone invest in a fund with such high fees? As with high-turnover funds, fund managers with high expense ratios claim they can deliver higher returns than the market even after expenses. However, it typically doesn't work out very well for investors.

Brokerage firms love funds with high expense ratios because they get to collect a significant portion of this fee. This "revenue sharing" is required of most funds simply for the privilege of being listed as an investment option on their platform. These costs are passed on to investors through higher fund expenses that enrich brokerage firms. Some firms even produce their own funds, allowing them to keep the whole expense ratio for themselves.

Obviously, the lower the expense ratio, the higher the potential returns, so I recommend funds with low expense ratios like Vanguard and Dimensional Fund Advisors. They normally do not share revenue with brokerage firms because they are committed to keeping costs as low as possible for investors. They are well-known enough that most brokerages have to list them to satisfy investor demand even though they cannot share in their revenue.

Another cost you need to be aware of is the advisory fee. This fee is charged by your advisor in addition to the fund expenses. It typically starts at about 1 percent per year but can drop well below 1 percent for very large accounts. I have seen advisory fees as high as 2 percent per year, which I believe are unacceptably excessive, especially for large accounts.

Maybe I'm biased because this is how my team and I are paid, but I believe advisory fees are less devious than some other costs because they are fully transparent and cover a wide variety of client services. We always list our advisory fee clearly on the quarterly reports we send to clients. We also strive to deliver greater value than the fee amount by providing many other services in addition to investment management for no additional cost. However, advisory fees still impact returns, so you need to be aware of what they are, confirm that they are reasonable, and ensure you are receiving adequate value for the fees you pay.

What is the potential impact of excessive fund expenses and advisory fees over time? Let's compare 3 percent in total annual fees (fund expenses plus advisory fees) to a more reasonable 1 percent total annual fee. If you had invested $1 million in the S&P 500 for 20 years (2003 to 2022), reinvested all dividends, and paid 3 percent in expenses (not including taxes), your average annual rate of return would have been 6.6 percent. This means your $1 million would have grown to about $3.6 million. Not bad, huh? But if your expenses were only 1 percent over the same period, your average annual rate of return would have been 8.6 percent and your $1 million would have grown to about $5.2 million![17]

The last type of expense I want to briefly touch on might be the most egregious of all—commissions. Thankfully, commissions are playing a smaller and smaller role now that investors are more aware of their impact on returns and the conflicts of interest they present to advisors.

We have discussed some of these already, so I won't spend a lot of time on commission-rich financial products here. Structured notes, annuities, A-share mutual funds, private placements, and precious metals all typically pay commissions to the salespeople who sell them to you.

The amount of the commission varies by product, but can be as high as 12 percent or more. That means if you invested $1 million, the person who sold it to you would immediately be paid $120,000 without any further obligation to you. It might look like it's free because you don't see an itemized fee on your statement, but I promise you either the amount you gave them to invest is reduced by the amount of the commission, or the commission is baked into the ongoing expenses of the investment.

That is part of why structured notes, annuities, and other similar products charge huge penalties if you withdraw funds too soon after investing with them. They want to ensure they can cover the costs of the large commissions they paid to the salespeople who set them up for you.

Some annuities claim they don't charge any expenses, but they are built into the contract. Some annuity expenses can be as high as 4 percent or 5 percent per year, especially if loaded with riders like guaranteed lifetime income.

EVERYONE CAN WIN

As I mentioned earlier, you can't invest without incurring any expenses, so don't obsess over trying to eliminate all of them. Just focus on learning what your costs are and make sure they are reasonable for the value you receive.

This might sound like a daunting task, but it doesn't necessarily require any work on your part. If you have an advisor, ask them what all your costs are. Now you know what questions to ask.

Banks, insurance companies, brokerage firms, fund companies, and even registered investment advisors are all for-profit organizations that deserve to be compensated for the valuable services they provide. You can make a lot of money by utilizing their services. Just make sure you know what they're really charging and ask the tough questions about hidden costs so they don't take advantage of you. It has to be a win-win.

My company, an independent registered investment advisor, is also a for-profit entity. My firm's revenue comes from advisory fees, which are paid directly by our clients and are clearly listed on their account statements. We do not receive a single cent from any of the brokerage firms or investments we recommend to our clients.

We feel this is important because it helps us be more objective in our advice. We have a fiduciary duty to recommend only what is in the best interests of our clients, so we have established a compensation structure that allows us to answer only to them.

While no one can be totally free of biases and conflicts of interest, we feel that charging a low quarterly investment management fee most closely aligns our interests with our clients' interests. We don't make more money for recommending any specific investment over another. When our clients' account values increase, we make more money. When they lose money, our income drops.

We also must continually earn our clients' fees because we don't receive any up-front commissions for the investments we recommend. If we fail to deliver the value they expect, they can fire us at any time with no penalties or any further obligation.

That's one of the biggest issues I have with the commission model—it doesn't give advisors the incentive to continue providing excellent service to you. If an advisor sold you an investment or insurance product and you never heard from them again, they probably received an upfront commission and are not receiving sufficient ongoing compensation to make it worth their time to continue serving you. They're too busy hunting for their next commission opportunity. Would you rather pay 12 percent upfront and never hear from your advisor again, or 1 percent per year for 12 years to ensure that you continue receiving excellent service, financial planning, and other services, with the option to fire them whenever they stop meeting your expectations?

I like feeding my family and purchasing Fortnite character customizations for my boys, but not at the expense of my clients' success. My team and I always charge reasonable fees and strive to deliver much greater value than our clients pay. We also constantly evaluate how we can improve.

Our advisory fee covers much more than just investment management. At no additional cost, we also provide ongoing concierge-level service, financial planning, collaboration with our clients' CPAs and other professionals, behavioral coaching, market updates, financial education for our clients' children and grandchildren, estate planning, philanthropic planning, business succession and transition planning, insurance review, tax planning, and a variety of other services. Sometimes we also feel like marriage counselors and psychotherapists, but we're not licensed for that so please don't tell your friends we can fix their investments *and* their marriage!

At the end of 2017, we began serving a new client in his early 70s who had previously been working with an advisor at a very large, well-respected firm you would recognize. He gave his old advisor $6.5 million to invest 10 years earlier. He was appalled when he realized that over time it had dwindled to $5 million even though the market had grown exponentially over that period.

He had been clear from the beginning that he didn't want to erode his principal. He wanted to ensure a healthy income for the rest of his life and leave a generous inheritance to his children and grandchildren. He felt like his advisor was "asleep at the wheel" and hadn't heard from him for at least two years.

Upon analysis of his portfolio, we found that several factors contributed to this unwelcome erosion of principal over time. Most of his investments were held in underperforming, risky junk-bond funds that did not allow him to participate in stock market growth. He was also spending more from the portfolio than it was making.

When we pointed this out, he grew very frustrated that his former advisor never told him he was spending his principal. The advisor just kept sending him more money than he needed without informing him of the consequences.

Another major factor was the outrageous internal costs of his portfolio. His advisory fee was 1.5 percent per year, which we felt was astonishingly high for a $5 million account value, and his weighted average fund expense ratio was 1.8 percent. This means that his total combined expenses eating away at his returns were about 3.3 percent per year. No wonder he was losing money!

We switched his account to significantly lower-cost investments with better expected returns and a much more reasonable advisory fee. His total costs are now about a fourth of what he was paying before.

What kind of difference has this shift made? Over the past five years, he has spent about $1.2 million from his account. At the time of this writing (beginning of 2023), it is worth the $5 million he gave us, even after all expenses and after losing almost 12 percent in 2022 due to the worst market since 2008.

I don't want to give the impression that his experience with us has been all sunshine and rainbows, though. The ride has been very bumpy at times, with his account dropping as low as $4.2 million in 2020 due to COVID-19 and rising as high as $5.7 million at the beginning of 2022.

This highlights the potential benefits of a disciplined long-term investment strategy with low costs. He is very happy with the outcome so far despite two very rough market periods over a short five years.

Perhaps even more importantly, he is no longer stressed about his investments and can focus on enjoying his retirement and sleeping well at night. Of course we couldn't guarantee the same outcome for everyone, but it's gratifying to see how we were able to simplify his life and enhance his peace of mind by substantially reducing his costs, helping him determine a reasonable spending rate, and shifting to an investment strategy that would improve his chances of success. We are grateful for the opportunity to serve him because he is an absolute pleasure to work with—a win-win as it always should be.

STACKING THE DECK IN YOUR FAVOR

To wrap up this chapter, I would like to end where we started, with a final thought about gambling. Although investing can sometimes feel like a gamble, one important distinction between gambling and investing is that gambling is a zero-sum game. In order for one party to win, another has to lose.

In contrast, everyone can win with investing. When it works properly, businesses receive the funds they need to execute their vision and meet consumer demand, society benefits from enhanced products and services, and investors earn a healthy profit. This is part of why the stock market generally continues growing over time.

Another key difference is that the longer you gamble, the greater your chances of losing money, but the longer you invest, the greater your chances of making money. Based on historical returns of the stock market from 1971 to 2022, if you had chosen to invest for only one day, you would have had a 52 percent chance of a gain and a 48 percent chance of a loss—hardly better than the flip of a coin. These odds are a lot better than the 30 percent chance of winning in the gambling study cited earlier, but still not high enough for me to feel comfortable moving in and out of the stock market each day.

If you stayed in the market for three months, you would have increased your odds of success to 66 percent. Staying invested for a full year would have given you a 73 percent chance of a positive return.[18]

Investing for five years straight would have increased your chance of earning a profit to 87 percent, and 10 full years of investing without pulling it out would have given you a 94 percent chance of coming out ahead.[19] Over 20 years, your chances would have grown to almost a 100 percent probability of success.

By the way, these stats also indicate the likelihood that you will be frustrated with your returns, depending on how often you look at your account. If you look at it every day, then on average you will be disappointed every other day, subjecting yourself to a lot of unnecessary pain. Usually it works itself out, so you can decrease your stress and increase your chances of success by avoiding the temptation to continually check on your account.

Another interesting phenomenon is that the longer you invest, the lower the variability of returns for each period. According to one study going back to 1872, investing in the U.S. stock market for only a one-year period would have given you a maximum possible loss of -37 percent and a maximum possible gain of 53 percent. Investing for 10 years would have limited your range of average annual returns to a -4 percent maximum potential loss and an 18 percent maximum potential gain.[20]

Note that even though there is still a chance of loss over longer time periods, the potential loss decreases significantly as you stay invested longer. Also note that in this study the maximum possible gain (18 percent average annual return) is much larger than the maximum possible loss (-4 percent average annual return).

Compare the gambling odds at the beginning of this chapter to the odds of success in the stock market over 10 years. If the stock market were a game at a casino, how often would you play and how much money would you bet with these odds?

- You only have a 6 percent chance of losing money.
- The most you could lose is -4 percent on average per year.

- You have a 94 percent chance of earning a profit.
- You could earn as much as five times your original investment (18 percent annual compounded 10-year return).

If casinos gave these odds, I'm sure they would be attracting tens of millions more players than they already do, and they would probably not stay in business long. I find it fascinating that the investing odds of success are almost exactly the opposite of the gambling odds of success. Remember in the study I cited earlier, 95 percent of the most active bettors *lost* money over a two-year period. If you extended the study to a 10-year period, I'm sure almost 100 percent of all gamblers would have ended up with a loss. Conversely, almost 100 percent of investors would have earned a profit over the 10 years cited.

If you choose to "play the game" of investing, you can benefit from these amazing odds, but they come with two important rules:

1. They only play out for the stock market as a whole, not necessarily for individual stocks. You must adopt a very broadly diversified strategy and stay invested through the ups and downs to reap the benefits of these odds.
2. You might have to stay invested for 10 years or longer to earn a profit in the stock market. Investing more when the market goes down typically shortens the time frame for coming out ahead.

Is investing just a gamble? Hardly—in many ways it is the opposite of gambling. You can stack the deck in your favor by adopting a diversified and disciplined approach, staying invested for longer periods, and ensuring your costs are reasonable and justified by the value you receive. Most importantly, with investing, everyone can win.

KEY POINTS OF CHAPTER 5

1. Most people have no idea how much they are losing in their investments due to excessive and hidden costs.
2. The more frequently you buy and sell investments, the more brokerage firms make, so they encourage people to trade stocks, bonds, and other securities frequently.
3. There is no such thing as truly free trading. When you trade securities too frequently, bid-ask spreads can reduce your returns significantly even if no commissions are charged.
4. Some do-it-yourself platforms have gamified investing and created an illusion of unlimited free trading to foster addictive, impulsive behavior that makes the company a lot of money but costs investors dearly over time.
5. Know your investing costs, including fund expense ratios, turnover ratios, advisory fees, and commissions.
6. Financial institutions deserve to be compensated for the valuable services they provide, but you need to make sure you're receiving fair value for the fees you pay.
7. Investing is very different from gambling because everyone can win and the longer you invest, the greater your chances of success.

CHAPTER 6

DISREGARDING DISCLOSURES

WHO READS ALL THAT GIBBERISH?

Don't you love it when you're in a rush at the Verizon store with five people in line behind you and they ask you to sign a document acknowledging that you read, understand, and agree to the terms of their 47-page contract before they'll set up your new iPhone? Yeah, yeah, I agree not to use it for espionage, identity theft, or ordering pizza with canned tuna fish and anchovies. Click, click, click—just give me my new phone.

Have you ever tried to actually read a contract before signing it? It's a great way to make new enemies. Believe me, I've tried.

You should have seen the look on the escrow officer's face when I started reading all the documents my wife and I had to sign for our last home purchase. The escrow officer insisted, "Oh, you don't have to read them right now—just sign and we'll give you copies that you can read later. You can cancel within three days if you change your mind." How many people do you think actually read it later?

Most of the time it probably doesn't really matter that much. Let's be honest, we're all busy and the last thing we want to do is drudge through a heap of legalese we may not understand anyway. Besides, contract laws protect consumers to some extent by limiting what can be included based on the contract's purpose. Thank goodness I can't accidentally agree to give away my first-born child in a cell phone contract, but I might get stuck with a three-year plan when the sales rep said it was only a two-year plan.

Still, sometimes it's a really good idea to at least ensure you understand the most important elements of a contract *before* signing. The first time I financed a new car at a dealership, I told the salesman I didn't want to add any extra bells and whistles. When we were finalizing the deal and he handed me the contract to sign, the five-year loan payment was about $150 more per month than I calculated, so I asked him to show me the breakdown of the costs.

He had thrown in an extended warranty, gap insurance, paint and fabric protection, tire and wheel protection, and other add-ons I didn't want. When I reminded him that I specifically asked not to include any of that stuff, he was flustered and said he must have "forgotten" to take them off. Reading the main aspects of the contract enabled me to catch his error, whether it was intentional or not, and saved me about $9,000. I wonder how many of his customers sign without realizing how much more they're paying than they should be.

Sometimes not double-checking or understanding the terms of your contract can cost you a lot more than $9,000. You might be surprised at the amount of leeway financial firms have when it comes to contract design for financial products. You might *not* be surprised to learn that most of the language tends to protect their interests, not yours.

Many intelligent people have lost a lot of money by not fully understanding the implications of the agreements they have signed. It's not just a bunch of meaningless gibberish. I promise every word is in there for a reason even if it's a ridiculous 47 pages long and doesn't make much sense to you. It was carefully crafted by the party giving you the contract and their well-paid attorneys.

The smallest print often screams the loudest in court. Why do you think they make it so small, lengthy, and complicated? They want you to gloss over it, while the sales pitch is highlighted in bold letters and neon lights.

This reminds me of the long string of possible side effects rapidly rattled off at the end of a prescription drug commercial. Of course, most of the commercial boasts how easily this wonder drug is going to solve all your problems. Then in the last few seconds you can barely understand the disclosures read at double speed and half volume while everyone in the background is having a great time, happily accepting their increased chance of…what did they say? Hallucinations, amnesia, and premature death?

Tell your doctor immediately if you develop puffiness in your face, changes in urine, swelling of your stomach area and feeling of fullness, or dizziness or feeling faint.

I know these agreements can be tedious, confusing, and ex-cruciatingly boring. But if someone were to pay you $10,000 to read your contract and explain it to them, would you do it? How about for $100,000? Okay, fine—if you really hate reading con-tracts it's still probably not worth $100,000. Would you read it for $1 million?

I'm not exaggerating, you really might save $1 million or more by understanding the terms of an agreement dealing with your life savings before jumping into something that sounds better than it really is. Even if it just means understanding the fees you pay, the long-term impact could be worth more than $1 million to you. Toward the end of Chapter 5, I showed how a 1 percent fee could have made you $1.6 million more than paying a 3 percent fee over 20 years.

If you don't have the time, patience, or ability to read and un-derstand these types of agreements, the good news is that you don't have to do it by yourself. Just promise me that you'll find someone who can help you understand it sufficiently before in-vesting.

Any financial advisor worth hiring should be able to fully explain the terms to you. Don't let them gloss over the fees, withdrawal limitations, worst-case scenarios, and other fine print. Also keep in mind that if they are the one selling it to you, they may have a conflict of interest, so anything they say must be verifiable in writing. In other words, don't just take their word for it. Have them walk you through the agreement as they explain it.

Unfortunately, in my experience many financial advisors have never read the fine print and don't fully understand or care about how the product really works. They were just taught how to sell it by emphasizing the best-case scenarios. If they can't explain the potential cons and answer all your questions to your satisfaction, don't invest in it, or find another advisor who can explain it well.

You could also hire a reputable attorney or CPA who is familiar with investment deals and financial products to review important contracts involving a lot of money. They can verify whether or not it looks like a good deal and explain the terms to you in plain English. You may have to pay them a few hundred to a few thousand dollars to thoroughly review a complex deal, but it's totally worth it. Would you pay a few thousand dollars if you knew it could save you $1 million?

TRUST, BUT VERIFY

Beware of advisors who say you don't need to know how an investment deal works or that you won't understand it. Especially avoid those who claim to have a proprietary secret sauce they can't share with you.

Also be wary of advisors who talk way over your head and use complex jargon to impress or intimidate you. This could be an indication that they don't really understand how it works or don't want you to know. Sometimes this is a "smoke and mirrors" technique to distract you from what's really happening.

In the words of Albert Einstein, "If you can't explain it simply, you don't understand it well enough." That's the advisor's job—to do the research for you and explain their recommendations in clear and simple terms that make sense to you.

Some advisors prefer to keep clients in the dark and are offended when they ask questions. They may complain, "Don't you trust me?" This is a major red flag.

Starting a new relationship from a place of trust is healthy, but full trust must be earned over time through repeated verification that the person or organization is indeed trustworthy. We prove our trustworthiness by openly answering any question the other party wants to ask. As Ronald Reagan often quoted the famous Russian proverb during nuclear disarmament discussions with the Soviet Union in the 1980s, "Trust, but verify."

If a married man were to repeatedly come home from work a couple hours later than expected every night for weeks and fiercely guard his cell phone, his wife might grow suspicious and start asking questions. Wouldn't it be reasonable for her to expect a valid explanation for his perpetual tardiness and secrecy?

How likely would she be to continue trusting him if he simply responded with, "Come on, baby—don't you trust me?" It would not be her fault if she began losing trust in him under these circumstances. If he wanted to strengthen her trust in him, he would need to earn it by being as transparent and reliable as possible so she would never have a reason to wonder.

Likewise, your advisors need to earn your trust by happily providing anything you ask them to verify in writing or from other sources. They should not get defensive or dodgy when you ask them questions.

I'm not saying you always have to get every word in writing. I'm just saying they must be able to back up key components of their claims when you ask them to. Over time, as you realize they can be trusted, you shouldn't have to do as much due diligence all the time. After all, you hired them to save you time and hassle, right?

My team and I strive to educate our clients so they understand the most

Trust, but verify.
– Ronald Reagan

important aspects of their investments and our process. Not everyone is as interested in the details as we are, so we don't force it down their throats. But as we meet with them over time, we reinforce and expand on their knowledge of our strategies and how markets work. We feel this is an essential aspect of earning their trust over time and enhancing their peace of mind.

We made our client agreement as short, transparent, and easy to understand as possible. It's only four pages long with our fee listed clearly on the first page. No one should have to hire an attorney to understand it, and it doesn't have any fine print, long-term obligations, or penalties for termination. We hope this simplifies our clients' lives and shows we're not trying to trick anyone or hold them hostage.

Sometimes investors mistakenly assume that if someone is an honest person they can trust them with anything. In Chapter 1 we discussed Steven M. R. Covey's book *The Speed of Trust*, in which he teaches that trustworthiness is not just a matter of good character. Remember that an equally important element of trust is competence, which requires knowledge, skills, and experience.

If your best friend or brother-in-law becomes a financial advisor, don't invest with them until you verify that they really know what they're doing or that someone you trust is training and supervising them. Their honesty and good intentions will not come to the rescue after you have lost hundreds of thousands of dollars in an investment they didn't fully understand.

An extreme example of this principle is the Ponzi scheme in Las Vegas we discussed at the end of Chapter 3. Obviously, those at the top who structured the deal knew they were ripping people off, but I believe that at least some of the marketers had good intentions.

I personally have known a couple of them for years, and I don't believe they knew it was a Ponzi scheme when they got involved. They never gave me any reason to believe they were not trustworthy from a character standpoint. They invested large amounts of their own money and that of close family members and friends in the deal, so I strongly doubt they knew it was fraudulent at the time. They really are great guys, so I understand why so many people trusted that it was a legitimate investment.

However, if these marketers truly didn't know what was really happening behind the scenes, they must have lacked either the ability or the willingness to verify whether what they were selling was really as good as it was purported to be. As the SEC (securities industry regulator) put it, they "knew or were reckless in not knowing that the purchase agreements were fake and that the investment scheme was a fraud."[1]

This is the part that is most puzzling to me. How could such smart, successful, honest people have been so blinded to the truth about what they were selling? They were very close to the action with at least 20 red flags in plain sight, as we discussed in that section of this book.

Maybe they avoided digging too deep when questions came up because they really wanted it to be true, much like those who invested in it. Maybe they were really just that trusting of the people on top.

With some basic verification, they should have been able to discover the truth, protect their clients from suffering devastating losses, and protect themselves from painful lawsuits, embarrassment, and the erosion of trust from those they were trying to help. It is good to be a trusting person, but when millions of dollars are on the line, why not do at least a little homework?

I believe that for at least some of the marketers, this was a competence issue, not a character problem. Regardless, the end result was the same, showing that competence is just as important as character when evaluating whether someone can be trusted.

This is why I said in Chapter 3 that a lack of investment licenses and relevant experience can be good indications of potential trouble. If the marketers were honestly trying to help people and were able to demonstrate their competence through proper licensing and experience, they would have more easily detected the fraudulent nature of the deals they were selling.

I'm not suggesting that you should assume everyone you meet is guilty until proven innocent. That would be a horrible way to live your life. Most advisors are probably trying to do what they think is best for their clients, even though various advisors may differ in their recommendations at times. Everyone is entitled to their own opinion because there is no one right way to invest. My point is that you can be badly burned if you trust too blindly without any verification of character *and* competence.

WHAT YOU DON'T KNOW CAN HURT YOU

Recently one of my 14-year-old twin boys came home from a friend's house 45 minutes late. When I asked him why he was so late, he said he and his friends were in the hot tub so he didn't know what time it was. When I asked him why he didn't keep his phone by him so he could keep track of time, he said his battery had died. When I asked him why he didn't keep his phone charged so it wouldn't die, he said his friend wouldn't let him use his charger because he had to charge his own phone.

How do you think I responded? "Got it, no problem, that makes sense. Totally not your fault, those are all perfectly valid excuses. You never need to be home on time when you have no idea what time it is."

Of course not! Whose job was it to know what time it was? His alone. I hope it's as obvious to you as it is to me that he was fully responsible to remove any lame "roadblocks" to being home on time. You can tell I'm not emotional about this at all, and I know what you're thinking: "Adam, your son is totally playing you."

Whether or not he made all that up, the point is that if you need to know something to fulfill your duty or protect yourself from harm, it's your responsibility to learn it. If you get pulled over for speeding, the officer is not likely to let you off the hook simply because you had no idea what the speed limit was. If you don't pay taxes for 10 years, the IRS is not likely to let it slide because you didn't know you had to pay taxes.

If you lose all your money in an investment that clearly spells out the risks in the contract and prospectus that you never read, who is to blame? You can blame the salespeople and the company they work for all you want, but it's not going to bring your money back and it's not going to hold up in court.

In 2016, a very sweet widow in her late 70s asked me to review her $6 million portfolio that another advisor was managing for her at a large, well-respected investment firm. She thought most of it was in FDIC-insured CDs with guaranteed interest and principal protection, so she wondered why her account values fluctuated so much.

Upon reviewing her statements, I was astonished to discover that most of her money was held in structured notes. These are the banking products I discussed at the end of Chapter 4, which often carry more risk than most people realize.

You may recall that many structured notes provide some principal protection, but they are not FDIC-insured. The returns are tied to the performance of specific underlying assets. If those assets drop too much in value, some structured notes allow you to lose your full deposit amount—a far cry from the safety of CDs.

As if that wasn't bad enough, the structured notes this widow owned were all linked to very volatile indexes and an individual stock or two. Each was tied to two different investments and the payout at maturity was determined by which of the two performed the *worst*. To me this seemed like the worst of both worlds.

We asked if she remembered the terms of any of her structured notes, and she responded that she had never even seen any of them. She just trusted the advisor would put her in FDIC-insured CDs like she asked, and he said these were like CDs with higher interest.

Let me share with you a word-for-word sampling of some of the disclosures we found on the summary sheet for one of her structured notes issued by a very large bank (purposely kept anonymous). You tell me if they sound like CDs. These aren't even all the risks and limitations outlined. Would you feel comfortable investing in something like this if you were in your late 70s?

- You may lose some or all of your principal at maturity.
- Any payment on the notes is subject to the credit risk of [the issuing bank].
- If the notes have not been automatically called and the final value of either index is less than its initial value by more than the contingent buffer amount, you will lose more than 50 percent of your principal amount at maturity and could lose all of your principal amount at maturity.

- The hypothetical returns on the notes shown apply only if you hold the notes for their entire term or until automatically called. These hypotheticals do not reflect fees or expenses that would be associated with any sale in the secondary market. If these fees and expenses were included, the hypothetical returns would likely be lower.

- The value of the notes prior to maturity will be subject to changes in the market's view of the creditworthiness of [the issuing bank].

- If the notes are automatically called, the appreciation potential of the notes is limited to any call premium paid on the notes and you will not benefit from the upside leverage factor.

- You are exposed to the risk of decline in the level of each index.

- Your payment at maturity will be determined by the lesser performing index.

- The benefit provided by the contingent buffer amount may terminate on the final review date.

- The automatic call may force a potential early exit.

- No interest payments, dividend payments or voting rights.

- The notes are subject to the risks associated with non-U.S. securities.

- The notes are subject to the risks associated with small capitalization companies.

- As a finance subsidiary, [the issuing bank] has no independent operations and has limited assets.

- The estimated value of the notes will be lower than the original issue price of the notes.

- Lack of liquidity: [The issuing bank] intends to offer to purchase the notes in the secondary market but is not required to do so. The price, if any, at which [the issuing bank] will be willing to purchase notes from you in the secondary market, if at all, may result in a significant loss of your principal.

- Potential conflicts: We and our affiliates play a variety of roles in connection with the issuance of notes, including acting as calculation agent and hedging our obligations under the notes…It is possible that such hedging or other trading activities of [the issuing bank] or its affiliates could result in substantial returns for [the issuing bank] and its affiliates while the value of the notes decline.

- The tax consequences of the notes may be uncertain.

After all that, this is my favorite line:

- The risks identified above are not exhaustive. Please see "Risk Factors" in the applicable product supplement and underlying supplement and "Selected Risk Considerations" in the applicable preliminary pricing supplement for additional information.

Be honest—did you really read every bullet point listed, or did you catch yourself skimming over it and jumping ahead to the end? Can you believe that doesn't even include all the risks?

Sorry, I know that list was way too overwhelming and tedious for a book I'm trying to make really easy to understand. I included it to make a point. This is one of the major reasons so many people lose more than they thought possible in their investments.

Most people never read the disclosures because the wording is so small, lengthy, and confusing. Besides, many advisors who sell structured notes tell investors they are safe, so why would they bother reading about seemingly irrelevant risks?

If you didn't read all the disclosures I listed or fully understand them, let me summarize and translate them for you:

1. You could lose every penny you invest in structured notes for a wide variety of reasons.
2. Once you make your deposit, you may not be able to get your money out till the end of the term without losing a lot.
3. The bank could make a lot of money on your structured note even if you lose all your money.

How would you feel if you found out these were your real risks after being told you were in safe, principal-protected CDs? Now you know why I get so frustrated with advisors who sell these as risk-free investments with awesome upside potential.

This poor widow just about had a heart attack when we explained a few of these disclosures that she had never read. We didn't dare read all of them to her because we didn't want to put her in a coma.

As I mentioned in Chapter 4, certain structured notes can work in some situations, but these were clearly not appropriate for her. The type she owned were some of the riskiest I've seen. She had no idea she was exposed to so much risk with the majority of her investments.

Sadly, the combined value of her structured notes had already lost about 11 percent by the time we saw her statements, and two of them had lost more than 50 percent. Most of them were scheduled to mature in three or four years, but none of them were maturing anytime soon. About $1.5 million of them were not scheduled to mature for another nine years.

That's a long time to be locked into something with that much risk when you're almost 80 years old and you think you own CDs. Any of these could have vanished if both of the underlying indexes or stocks didn't behave for the full nine years.

How do you think the FDIC or courts would have responded if any of these notes went belly up and she complained that she thought they were FDIC-insured CDs? They likely could not have done much to help her.

Luckily, we were able to unwind most of them for her without too much additional loss and put her in new investments that were more consistent with her objectives and risk tolerance. She has made another $1.6 million with us since then, even after the losses of 2022, mostly in very conservative investments. Sure, maybe some of the structured notes could have worked out in the long run, but they were not meeting her expectations and did not align with her goals at all.

She was really lucky she got out as well as she did. She could have been hurt much worse by what she didn't know. She had no idea how much risk she was taking because she never verified anything her advisor was doing.

Obviously, this is not just an issue for structured notes. Be sure to learn the true risks of any investment you are considering. As I mentioned earlier, if you don't have the time, patience, or ability to read and understand them, hire a qualified attorney, accountant, or fiduciary wealth advisor you can trust to help you. If your advisor is the one recommending the investment, make sure they are willing and able to explain the written disclosures and worst-case scenarios to you, especially if you haven't been working with them for very long.

SO SORRY I FORGOT TO TELL YOU THAT PART

I never got the chance to speak with that widow's former advisor. I would be curious to know whether he skipped over the risks of her structured notes or if he was as clueless about them as she was. Something tells me that's not likely. Structured notes typically pay much higher commissions than the regular CDs she asked him to invest in, so he may have had ulterior motives.

If he did know how they worked, he obviously "forgot" to fully disclose the true risks. Where was he when she discovered that some of them had lost more than 50 percent of their value while she thought they were FDIC-insured?

The following is an even sadder tale of the consequences of a salesperson downplaying potential downsides. In 2005, some friends of mine really wanted to buy a new house in a great neighborhood they had their eyes on for years. They were a little nervous and unsure whether they could afford it. The skyrocketing housing prices made it even more difficult to imagine how they could pull it off.

Then a mortgage broker they met through some friends at church came to the rescue, insisting that he could make their dream come true through a fancy new type of mortgage called an "option ARM." Oh yeah, remember those babies? Just writing the words "option ARM" makes my stomach churn.

It sounded complicated and they didn't really understand it, but he seemed like a nice guy and he had recently helped their friends. Besides, this was the key to getting them that house they *really* wanted, so they decided to give it a shot.

During the real estate boom of the early 2000s, option ARM mortgages were very popular because they allowed people to buy bigger and better houses than they could really afford. "Option" means that in the early days of the loan you can choose how much you want to pay each month. "ARM" stands for Adjustable-Rate Mortgage, meaning that your interest rate can change throughout the loan term.

Many of these started with a discounted teaser interest rate as low as 1 percent or 2 percent for the first few months of the loan. Then the regular interest rate would kick in, which was typically much higher and dramatically increased the actual monthly payment. The interest rate and monthly payment could continue rising substantially over time, unlike a traditional 30-year fixed mortgage where the rate and payment stay the same for 30 years.

These were usually the four payment options from which you could choose, depending on how much you felt like paying each month:

1. Fifteen-year amortized payment of principal and interest. This was the highest monthly payment option by far and would pay off your mortgage in 15 years.

2. Thirty-year amortized payment of principal and interest. This was the second-highest payment option and would pay off your mortgage in 30 years.

3. Interest-only payment. This was the second-lowest payment option, covering only the amount of interest charged each month. Since you wouldn't be paying any principal, your mortgage balance would not decrease.

4. Minimum payment. This was the lowest payment option by far, typically based on the initial teaser rate. After the regular interest rate kicked in, you could continue making the minimum payment amount, but your loan balance would increase over time because you wouldn't even be paying the full amount of monthly interest charged.

Which payment option do you think most people chose? That's right—the vast majority, including my friends, only paid the minimum amount due each month.

Which payment option do you think the loan qualification was typically based on? Right again—many buyers were able to "qualify" for a much more expensive home than normal because of the artificially low introductory payment. They figured if the payments increased by too much, they could simply refinance or buy a different home because real estate values were rising so rapidly.

But the party couldn't last forever. Mortgage companies would only allow the loan balance to go so high before they would "recast" the mortgage.

What is a mortgage recast? If your payments didn't cover the full amount of interest charged each month and your loan balance grew to exceed 110 percent of the original loan amount, the mortgage company would recalculate your payment schedule. Your new minimum payment would be fully amortized with principal and interest based on the higher rate for the duration of the loan, typically 25 to 27 years. This was still a variable-rate loan, so your interest rate and payment could continue increasing even more over time.[2]

When this happened to my friends, their minimum payment suddenly jumped from $1,300 per month to more than $5,000 per month, with the possibility of climbing considerably from there. They had only been living there for a few years and had no idea their required payment could increase by that much so quickly.

The mortgage broker who sold them the loan "forgot" to disclose that if they just made the minimum payment for too long it could nearly quadruple overnight. Maybe he was just a great salesman and had no idea how it really worked. Either way, his description of how it was going to play out was far from the truth and held no weight when reality hit.

He also downplayed the potential impact of interest rates increasing. "Sure, your interest rate could increase a little, but no big deal," he explained. "If the payment goes up by too much, you could easily refinance it because your new home will be worth a lot more in a few years."

Except my friends couldn't refinance when they needed to most. Since housing prices had fallen substantially by this point and their mortgage balance was higher than the amount they started with, no one would refinance it. They begged the mortgage company to work with them, but they wouldn't budge. This was during the early stages of the financial crisis so banks had not yet resorted to loan modifications or short sales in an attempt to curtail their losses.

Regrettably, my friends could not afford the new mortgage payment so they lost the home and were forced to declare bankruptcy. They never read the fine print of their contract, nor did they care about it until it was too late. They just wanted the house, so they put their future in the hands of a salesman who walked away with a healthy commission and never spoke to them again. They were totally unprepared for the reality of what could happen, and it took them years to recover from the devastating consequences of that seemingly small decision.

The mortgage broker who sold them the loan was nowhere to be found when the music stopped. He had left the company he was with at the time and bounced around three more times.

Ironically, the mortgage company that refused to negotiate with them, Countrywide Financial, went out of business shortly thereafter. They had been the largest provider of home loans in the U.S. for years, largely due to their aggressive marketing of high-risk subprime, stated-income, and adjustable-rate mortgages like the option ARM loan my friends had.

Due to such high exposure to these types of loans, they faced far more foreclosures during the financial crisis than other banks, and the whole world felt the impact of that. Bank of America bought Countrywide in 2008 at a substantial discount.[3]

So many people and organizations were hurt by option ARM loans that they were effectively eliminated in 2014 by the Consumer Financial Protection Bureau.[4] This illustrates the principle that glossing over the extreme potential outcomes of risky deals can be harmful not only to you personally, but also to the company who writes them and even to society at large. Were the mortgage brokers who didn't fully disclose the risks ever held accountable?

Anyone can say whatever they want to get you to buy what makes them the most money. Unfortunately, not even all financial advisors have a fiduciary duty to recommend what is in your best interests. However, investment advisor representatives at registered investment advisor firms and CERTIFIED FINANCIAL PLANNER™ professionals do have a fiduciary duty to you, so they may be easier to trust. Fiduciary duty is a legal or ethical obligation to put your interests ahead of their own and to always act with prudence.

A good financial advisor will outline all the terms in a way you can understand and be honest about worst-case scenarios. How much money could you lose? What are all the fees? How much money can you take out, and when? What issues could impact the hypothetical projections?

Despite my best efforts to educate clients on potential downsides to my recommendations, I'm sure their expectations are not always fulfilled. Still, I endeavor to set realistic expectations by emphasizing what could go wrong.

My team and I are not interested in making a quick buck and moving on. We strive to nurture deep, long-term relationships of mutual trust and respect, and we work hard to help our clients attain long-term success. That's why it's not in our best interest to "pull a fast one" on them.

Even if you have a good advisor, it's ultimately your responsibility to dig as deep as you can to ensure you understand the risks and conditions of whatever you're signing up for. Don't rely too heavily on verbal explanations from salespeople. They may be holding back or minimizing the most important factors you need to consider to make an informed decision.

If things don't turn out as you expected, their words won't hold any weight in the end. It's all about the written agreement.

The time to discover unwelcome potential surprises and worst-case scenarios is before you sign up. I know it can be tedious and time-consuming, and you may be disappointed to find out it's not the panacea you were hoping for. Just remember that you'll be much better off in the long run if you do a little homework up front or hire someone you trust to do it for you.

LEARNING TO LOVE WORST-CASE SCENARIOS

Call me weird, but I love exploring worst-case scenarios. Do you know why? They give me peace of mind. I can't think of a better way to control risk and sleep well at night than knowing what could go wrong and how likely it is to happen.

Think of investing as a game of chess. I'm not very good at chess, but I know you're more likely to win if you plan many moves ahead and anticipate your opponent's future moves. Supposedly chess grandmasters can see as far as 20 moves ahead or more. That's why they win so consistently. Fully understanding all possible outcomes of an investment opportunity is one way to look several moves ahead and improve your chances of success.

Why are some people reluctant to consider the impact of worst-case scenarios? Maybe they think it's a waste of time or they're afraid to acknowledge something bad could happen. Perhaps it produces too much anxiety and they're worried they won't be able to stop obsessing over it. Maybe they want it to be true so badly that they ignore all potential downsides, like some Ponzi scheme participants.

If you tend to disregard the possibility of unwelcome outcomes, let me introduce you to your new best friend: Mr. Worst-Case Scenario. If you get to know him well, he really can unlock a whole new world of loss aversion, financial success, and peace of mind for you.

Do you want to know a great place to practice evaluating worst-case scenarios? Online reviews—but proceed cautiously because they can be a dangerous time suck.

One time I went down a rabbit hole reading Amazon reviews for 15 to 20 minutes to find the best option for fixing something at my house. I was abruptly awakened from my trance by my inner voice screaming, "Just order the stupid screws, Adam—they're only five bucks!" Okay, fine, not all worst-case scenarios are worth exploring, but I digress.

When you read reviews, do you focus on the positive or negative ones? I like to read some of each, but I prefer to focus on bad reviews because that's where worst-case scenarios hang out. If I'm looking at a promising Airbnb option and the worst thing anyone can say about the place is that not all the flatware matched and they didn't have a copy of *Goodnight Moon*, I'm gonna book that baby!

Not all downsides are created equal with Airbnb rentals or investing. Some people may accept certain risks more easily than others. That's why no particular type of investment is inherently good or bad. They all have pros and cons, but some cons can be quite severe so you need to understand them to make an informed decision.

The problem is that too many people expect some investments to do things they're not capable of doing. That's because most salespeople tend to emphasize best-case scenarios and minimize or totally ignore worst-case scenarios. No wonder investors tend to expect the rosiest projections to come true without a hitch.

What should you be looking for as you evaluate downsides? It would be impossible to list every potential problem with investments you may be considering, but here are several examples of issues you should research before deciding:

1. GUARANTEED MINIMUM RETURNS

Other than individual bonds, I prefer investments without guaranteed minimum returns because they usually come at a steep price. You can see the worst-case scenarios of banking and insurance products by evaluating projected performance when minimum guarantees kick in.

For example, the illustration of a universal life insurance policy has a column labeled "current" and a column labeled "guaranteed." The "current" column projects the outcome if the assumed rate of return and expenses continued unchanged forever. This usually approximates the best-case scenario and is not likely to occur exactly as illustrated.

The "guaranteed" column shows what would happen if the rate of return were to drop to the guaranteed minimum and expenses were to increase to the guaranteed maximum for the duration of the policy. Yes, insurance companies can increase expenses on these policies if necessary. This extreme is also unlikely to occur, but it's helpful because it shows the worst-case scenario, assuming you continue to pay scheduled premiums and the insurance company stays in business.

Your performance will probably be somewhere in between. If you understand the risks and you like how it looks after considering the minimum and maximum possibilities, go for it. If the "current" column is the only acceptable option, you probably shouldn't do it because it's not likely to occur.

If you are considering the purchase of an annuity, you should focus on the implications of the minimum rate of return being paid over long periods of time. You may be surprised to discover how quickly high internal expenses drain your principal with low or zero earnings. Even though minimum guaranteed returns are designed to "protect" you from losses in the market, they cannot protect you from the erosion of principal through fees.

Some structured notes offer principal protection. If they do, the minimum guaranteed return is often zero, meaning that after holding it for 5 or 10 years, they promise to at least give your initial deposit amount back at the end. But is this really a win? What about the impact of inflation and the lost opportunity to make a lot more in another investment over such a long period?

2. MAXIMUM FEES

We already spoke at length in the last chapter about the importance of knowing what your fees are. You should also find out whether the fees can change and how they are calculated.

Annuities charge higher fees than most people realize. Mortality and expense (M&E) fees, administrative fees, investment expense ratios, and fees for popular riders such as guaranteed lifetime withdrawal benefits can add up to 4 or 5 percent per year, as I mentioned in the last chapter about hidden fees.

As if that wasn't high enough, most of these fees can be increased up to double the initial amounts by the insurance company. Evaluating projected performance at the maximum possible fees and minimum guaranteed performance will show you the worst-case scenario.

What about "no cost" indexed annuities? Believe it or not, they're not really free. They are funded through options, and the insurance company takes a cut of the spread on the options rather than charging visible fees. These spreads reduce your returns, and the amount of the spread can increase if the insurance company needs to make more money.

If your interest rate cap or participation rate has been reduced, that could be an indication that your fees were increased indirectly. On annuity illustrations, pay attention to how the maximum potential reduction in these rates can affect long-term performance. If the projected performance of these types of products don't look appealing to you when the fees are increased, you might be better off walking away.

3. WITHDRAWAL LIMITATIONS AND PENALTIES

Lack of liquidity also impacts worst-case scenarios. Know how long your money will be locked up, how much you will be able to access, and what the penalties will be if you must use it sooner than expected. Even common investment vehicles like 401(k)s and IRAs heavily restrict early withdrawals.

Most annuities and universal life insurance policies include surrender periods as long as 15 years and surrender charges as high as 10 percent. Some annuities also employ a "market value adjustment" (MVA) clause—if interest rates rise they can charge you significantly more than the surrender penalty on withdrawals. If you take any money out before retirement age, you may also lose guaranteed benefits the annuity provided.

As we discussed previously, structured notes are not very accessible, either. Once you buy them, banks are not required to repurchase them. If they do, they will likely pay you much less than you gave them. Usually you are stuck until the note matures.

Many real estate investments tend to be highly illiquid as well. If your money is pooled together with other investors to buy real estate or loan money to developers, you may not be able to retrieve your funds for a long time. Some of our clients have had money tied up in real estate deals for at least a decade longer than they originally intended. Things simply didn't work out as well as they hoped, and they didn't have the option to get out as early as they planned.

Limited partnerships, private equity, private debt, hedge funds, and venture capital are additional examples of investments with low liquidity. These can be very expensive if not impossible to exit until after the objective of the investment has been fully realized, which can take years. Avoid tying up too much of your money in illiquid assets because you never know when you might need to access extra cash.

4. ONGOING OBLIGATIONS

As I mentioned in the real estate section in Chapter 3, many deals require ongoing financial commitments called "capital calls." Once invested, you're on the hook for the additional deposits you committed to making whenever they ask for it. Usually you cannot back out without serious ramifications.

Make sure you are able and willing to pay your capital calls no matter what, even if the deal goes south for a while. Otherwise, you could risk losing your initial deposit or be subject to legal action. Learn the consequences of missing capital calls before you invest.

If you own rental real estate directly, be ready to cover additional expenses besides the mortgage, taxes, and insurance. Estimate potential costs of ongoing repairs, remodeling, cleaning, landscaping, utilities, new appliances, new flooring, a new roof, new air conditioning, marketing, property management, and potential lawsuits. Consider how much these costs could increase over time. How would you handle lower rents and longer vacancies than expected? Are you prepared for the worst-case scenario?

As we wrap up this section, I have one last comment about worst-case scenarios. Despite our best efforts, we can't always assess every possible outcome. Life is too unpredictable to be absolutely certain we're aware of how bad or how *good* things can possibly turn out.

In his thought-provoking, yet somewhat cynical book entitled *The Black Swan,* Nassim Nicholas Taleb points out that as a society we don't know as much as we think we do. We tend to look for patterns where none exist to create a false sense of security.

The book description on Amazon reads, "A black swan is a highly improbable event with three principal characteristics: It is unpredictable; it carries a massive impact; and, after the fact, we concoct an explanation that makes it appear less random, and more predictable, than it was. The astonishing success of Google was a black swan; so was 9/11."

We can prepare and predict all we want, but many events cannot be anticipated, much less the impact of those events. Some turn out much better than expected—others, much worse. The author asserts that if we take a more realistic view of the uncertainty surrounding us, we will be better prepared to face the consequences of unexpected events and perhaps even profit from them.

That's why I hope you learn to love discovering worst-case scenarios in every major investment decision you make. You have worked way too hard to throw away years of sacrifice by relying solely on the claims of salespeople who only divulge best-case scenarios so they can make a quick commission and move on. Even if you don't understand every possible outcome, your efforts to learn the cons as well as the pros will dramatically improve your ability to make wise decisions, increase your chances of success, and enhance your peace of mind.

OWNER'S MANUALS ARE UNDERRATED

My wife Andrea often makes fun of me for reading the owner's manual for almost everything we buy, but guess who she always comes to for help when she can't figure something out? She laughed especially hard when she caught me reading the instructions for a new set of expensive cookware we bought. "Come on, Adam—don't you know how to use a pan!"

I sheepishly responded, "Sorry babe, but I was excited about these and wanted to learn how to best take care of them so they could retain their beauty and functionality longer than the last few sets we bought. Is that a crime?"

Did she know it's bad to put water in a pan to clean it while it's still hot because it could warp or crack over time? Did she know it was harmful to leave soapy water soaking in a pan over-night? Did she know that cleaning them with certain abrasive pads and types of cleaners could damage the surface? Did she know that cooking sprays were not necessary and could be harmful for this particular cookware? Did she know certain types of spoons and spatulas could damage the surfaces? Did she know they should never be washed in the dishwasher?

No! She didn't know any of that stuff. Guess where I learned it? That's right: in the owner's manual. I didn't even have to pay extra for all that great info and it only took me five minutes to read. Sorry to waste your time, Andrea. Maybe I should have spent those five minutes cleaning pans the wrong way instead.

Why do so few people read owner's manuals? I know they're not quite as captivating as *People* magazine, but they might im-prove your life a lot more. Maybe you don't have the patience, think you already know enough about what you purchased, or would rather figure it out on your own. Reading the manual doesn't take very long, though. Even just skimming through the important parts can save you a lot of time, hassle, and money in the long run.

My brother-in-law is one of the coolest and smartest guys I know. He is incredibly handy and can fix or build just about any-thing—houses, furniture, cars, boats, teeth, you name it (yes, he is an orthodontist, too).

Several years ago we bought a new trampoline for our kids for Christmas—err, I mean Santa brought it—and I was grateful my brother-in-law offered to help me set it up. Luckily, he loves doing that kind of stuff.

We opened the box and pulled out all the parts. I opened the instruction booklet and started reading, but he got right to work putting poles together and screwing things in place. I was nervous about setting it up the right way because I had never assembled a trampoline before and wanted to ensure it was safe for the kids.

I suggested that maybe we should follow the instructions, but he insisted that we could figure it out on our own. Like I said, he's really handy and smart when it comes to this kind of stuff, so I didn't challenge him. I didn't want to sit around reading while he was doing all the work, so I jumped in to help set it up.

After more time and hassle setting it up than we had antici-pated, we were ready for the final step of attaching the safety net to the tall poles protruding from the base of the trampoline. It wasn't until that moment that we realized we had put the poles on backward, so we had to take almost the whole thing apart and start over.

I didn't know whether to laugh or cry. I was somewhat amused that it didn't work out for us because we didn't follow the instructions like I wanted to, but it was very frustrating to realize how much time and effort we had wasted. True, sitting down and reading the assembly instructions might have felt like an annoying waste of time to my brother-in-law at first, but it would have saved us a lot of time in the long run.

Of course, this was far from a life-and-death situation, and there was no chance it could cause us to lose our life savings. But sometimes when we don't read instructions, warnings, or disclo-sures, the consequences could be that severe.

Most of this chapter has been about bad things that can hap-pen when you don't read agreements or disregard disclosures, but reading contracts can have a positive side, as well. One reason I like owner's manuals is that they help me better understand all the features and benefits of what I purchased so I can maximize its value to me. Usually I discover additional features that benefit my life in meaningful ways, even though I wasn't looking for them.

Investment agreements can do the same for you. Maybe you can take out more money than you thought you could. Perhaps you have more investment options than you realized. Maybe your advisor is willing to do a lot more than simply manage your assets, without any additional fees. You might never know what you're missing out on until you read your agreements.

Well-written and well-understood agreements are a beautiful thing. They clarify and confirm understanding between parties to ensure a win-win for everyone involved. Too many agreements are too one-sided because the only party who reads them is the party who created them.

It's time for you to put the power back in your hands by read-ing and understanding all the important, potentially life-changing documents you sign. Only then will you more fully protect yourself from the devil in the details and live a more prosperous, peaceful life.

KEY POINTS OF CHAPTER 6

1. You can lose a lot of money if you don't understand the implications of the agreements you sign.
2. It's your responsibility to know what you are signing.
3. Don't ignore the fine print—it's in there for a reason and just as important to understand as the large print.
4. If you don't have the time, patience, or ability to read and understand important contracts dealing with a lot of money, hire a reputable attorney, CPA, or fiduciary wealth advisor you can trust to review and interpret them for you.
5. Building relationships from a position of trust is healthy, but be sure advisors' claims can be verified in writing or from other sources.
6. Only trust people who demonstrate good character *and* competence to deliver the results you need in the areas of expertise for which you hire them.
7. One way to measure character and competence is to observe whether an advisor can explain complex concepts in simple terms. This demonstrates they understand the issues and are willing to help you understand.
8. Salespeople tend to exaggerate best-case scenarios and downplay potential downsides, so dig deep and ask tough questions to make sure you fully understand both.
9. Focus on the worst-case scenarios of every deal before signing so you can make an informed decision and sleep better at night. If the magnitude and likelihood of worst-case scenarios are not acceptable risks to you, walk away.
10. Reading owner's manuals and other instructions can save you a lot of time, hassle, and money in the long run. They can also help you reap the full benefits of what you buy.

CHAPTER 7

HARNESSING THE POWER OF THE MARKET

DISCOVER WHAT DRIVES INVESTMENT RETURNS

Finally we arrive at the happy ending of this gloomy book! Have you heard enough about the seemingly endless ways even smart people lose money investing? I hope so, because I certainly am tired of writing about them. Thanks for hanging in there—hopefully I haven't killed all your hope for investing success.

You really can make a lot of money investing without taking so much risk. Now that you know why many popular practices often ruin returns, you're ready to discover a more reliable approach to building long-term wealth.

If you're feeling perplexed as to what you should do next, I have good news for you. You don't have to time the market, pick stocks, or chase the hottest trends to be a successful investor.

If any of those strategies have worked for you, I'm happy for you. However, most people who try them eventually end up losing quite a bit. While no method can guarantee 100 percent success, I'm more interested in helping my clients find solutions with a high likelihood of accomplishing their goals.

There is no single "correct" way to invest, but throughout this chapter we will discuss prudent approaches that have worked well for my clients over time. It's not about predicting the future—no one can do that consistently. It's all about improving your chances of success through more dependable strategies and keeping your costs low.

As you can see, the market is a powerful force that can be highly constructive or destructive depending on how you interact with it, similar to the power of the wind. Like the market, the wind is unpredictable and uncontrollable, but when you understand its nature and utilize effective tools to harness its power, it can propel a large ship across the ocean and power millions of homes.

Although the wind's strength and direction constantly change and are unpredictable from moment to moment, several general patterns are quite predictable over time:

1. For hundreds of years, sailors have relied on the steady, predictable Trade Winds, Westerlies, and Polar Easterlies, which always blow in the same direction due to patterns of how air flows through the atmosphere in response to the Earth's spin.[1]

2. Wind consistently moves from large bodies of water towards the land during the day (sea breezes), and from land towards nearby bodies of water at night (land breezes). This is due to differences in atmospheric pressure as the sun heats land faster than water during the day, and land cools off faster than water at night.

3. In mountainous regions, wind tends to flow up the mountain during the day and down the mountain into the valley at night, also mainly due to temperature differences between slopes and valleys at various times.[2]

While the market is even less predictable than the wind, certain general patterns are observable over long periods of time that can help you harness its power to achieve your goals:

1. **Time** in the market improves your chances of success. As we discussed in Chapter 5, if you were to invest for just one day in the broad market, you would have only a 52 percent chance of a gain. If you held your investments for 10 years, your chances of earning a profit would increase to 94 percent.[3]

2. **Bonds** tend to outperform savings accounts over time because they are not quite as safe or as liquid. A bond is a loan to a government entity or corporation for a specified period in exchange for guaranteed interest payments and return of principal at the end of the period. They must pay higher interest than the bank to make it worth the slightly higher risk and lower liquidity. High-quality bonds are

safer than stocks, but they can still fluctuate in value due to changes in interest rates or credit ratings.

3. **Stocks** tend to outperform bonds over time because most stocks do not carry any guarantees. When you buy a stock, you become an owner of the company. When the company does well, you benefit from any increase in its value (capital appreciation) and any profits it pays to shareholders (dividends). When it struggles, you lose money. Stocks in general must pay higher returns than bonds over time, or investors would not be willing to take the additional risk.

4. **Small stocks** tend to outperform large stocks because they are riskier and have greater growth potential than large stocks. At time of this writing, Apple is the largest company in the world, with a market cap (company size) of $2.3 trillion, but they started as a small stock like everyone else.[4] If you had invested in Apple when it first went public in 1980, you could have grown $10,000 to over $14 million today, but it would have been quite a bumpy ride for the first 20 years.[5] Now that Apple is so massive, do you think it has the same growth potential it had in 1980? Not a chance. Since they are large and successful, they are a safer bet now, so investors do not deserve to be rewarded as much as they would be for taking a chance on a smaller company. Not all of them will make it, but some of today's small stocks will be the large stocks of tomorrow. The investors who bought them when they were small will earn a lot more than those who wait for them to grow into large stocks.

5. **Value stocks** tend to outperform growth stocks because you can buy them "on sale" typically due to some type of distress. They can also be riskier because they don't always recover from whatever caused their stock price to drop, but as a whole, history has shown that value stocks generally outperform growth stocks over long periods.

The difference in returns among these various types of investments can be quite dramatic. For example, if you had invested just one dollar in each of these asset classes in 1926 and reinvested all dividends and interest through the end of 2021, your one dollar would have grown to the following amounts for each asset class (assuming no fees or taxes):

One-month U.S. T-bills (like savings accounts)	$22
Long-term government bonds	$194
US large stocks (S&P 500)	$14,076
US small stocks*	$47,760
US small value stocks*	$134,192

*Small stock returns shown from 1928 to 2021. Source: Dimensional Fund Advisors Matrix Book 2022. Past performance is no guarantee of future results. [6]

Figure 14: Growth of $1 from 1926 to 2021

Some people who see this might be tempted to put everything in U.S. small value stocks because it has outperformed the others by such a wide margin. However, I would not recommend doing this because small value stocks are much more volatile and can underperform the others for long periods.

I advocate a balanced approach among various asset classes to maximize returns while minimizing risk, but wanted you to see why you might want to own some small stocks and value stocks. Due to their much higher expected return I tend to slightly over-weight them for my clients, but the right mix for you depends on your risk tolerance and time horizon.

Of course these general patterns are not very helpful in predicting the performance of any particular stock or bond, rather the market as a whole over time. As I mentioned in Chapter 2, stocks behave somewhat like fish. The movement of each individual fish in a school may appear totally random. You may not be able to predict which fish will end up in the lead, but you can observe the direction of the school as a whole.

Why do stocks generally continue to rise in value? Will they ever hit a ceiling and stop growing for good?

No one can predict the future of stocks. Still, when you think about what the market represents, you start to understand why it has consistently grown so much over time and always found a way to recover from significant challenges. The market represents millions of people going to work every day, trying to make the world a better place. New products and services are constantly being invented and improved to increase our standard of living.

This is the magic of investing. As I mentioned at the end of Chapter 5, investing is not just a gamble. When the process works properly, everyone can win. Businesses receive the funds they need to execute their vision and meet consumer demand, society benefits from enhanced products and services, and investors earn a healthy profit. This is why the market grows over time, and this is why I believe it will keep on growing as long as people strive to continually improve the value they deliver to others.

Think of how your life has improved just over the past 20 years. What vehicle safety and technology features are standard today that didn't even exist for luxury vehicles 20 years ago? Have packages been arriving on your doorstep any faster than they did back then? How much bigger is your TV now, and how much more can you do on it? What can you do with your cell phone that you couldn't have imagined doing 20 years ago?

2002   2022

My cell phone back then didn't even have a camera or a flashlight, let alone provide me the ability to record high-quality video, keep a calendar, send emails, browse the internet, get turn-by-turn directions, read books, listen to and watch unlimited amounts of music and movies, pay people electronically, enter a concert—the list goes on and on. But I still miss my PalmPilot—not!

What new products and services will we not be able to live without 20 years from now that we can scarcely even imagine today? This is what drives market growth and investment returns.

Yes, the market can be a powerful place to grow wealth, but it can also drown you if you don't exercise prudence. Anyone could make it across a large body of water if the sailing was always smooth and the wind was always at your back, but weather conditions can change rapidly. Wise travelers choose a strong sailboat and an experienced captain to ensure they reach their destination safely and in a timely manner, regardless of which direction the wind might blow or how turbulent the storms may become.

Likewise, prudent investment strategies take into account the impact of various market conditions to improve your chances of success regardless of potential circumstances outside your control. Throughout the remainder of this chapter we will discuss effective tools for harnessing the power of the market. Once you determine your strategy, a qualified guide can help you implement the strategy to improve your likelihood of a positive outcome.

EMBRACE UNCERTAINTY

After a particularly large investment loss, have you ever wished you could eliminate all uncertainty from your investments? Wouldn't it be nice if we could all live rich, abundant lives with no challenges or fear of ever losing anything?

Yes, it would be nice, but that's not how investing works. In fact, that's not even how life works, and that's a good thing.

Why do we find predictable movies boring and love movies with an unexpected twist at the end? Why is it so much less exciting to watch a recording of the Super Bowl after you already know who won? Predictable outcomes are boring and rarely happen in real life.

We tend to think of unexpected outcomes as a bad thing, but some things turn out even better than we expected. When I married my sweetheart, Andrea, I really hoped our marriage wouldn't fail because I saw how painful my parents' divorce was for them and for us children. Although the future was uncertain, I took a leap of faith by asking Andrea to marry me.

Since then, I have done everything in my power to increase our chances of having a good marriage. Over 20 years later, I still have a lot to learn about how to be a better husband and father, but so far our marriage has been way more fun and rewarding than I ever expected, and I'm more in love with her now than I imagined I could be. In that sense, I'm glad it hasn't turned out only as good as I thought it would.

Business owners take on a higher degree of uncertainty in exchange for greater potential income and growth opportunities. One of my clients was a CPA for many years, then decided to buy a business in an industry for which he had been doing tax work for a long time. He grew to make 20 times more than he was making as a CPA and increased the value of his assets to more than he ever thought possible.

His life also became a lot more interesting after he started running his own business. When he was in his late 60s I asked him what his thoughts were about retirement. He responded, "Why would I retire? I love waking up every morning not knowing what new challenge I'm going to have to face. What would get me out of bed if I didn't have that?"

Some things in life portray an illusion of certainty when in reality they are not as certain as they may seem. In 2006 I was helping a fairly risk-averse couple with their financial planning and investments. For over a decade he had a steady job working for the county and she was a stay-at-home mom.

Like most government jobs, he received very slight cost-of-living raises every year and never had any opportunities for bonuses or large salary increases. In one of our meetings it suddenly dawned on them that if investors didn't choose to work with me, I wouldn't get paid. The wife exclaimed, "How can you live with that much uncertainty? I wouldn't be able to sleep at night!"

I found her perspective somewhat comical and was tempted to respond, "How can you stand knowing your income will never increase by more than a small fraction each year, and that no matter how good of a job your husband does, he will never receive any bonuses?" But to her point, I wanted to get paid, so I didn't say any of that.

Ironically, when the financial crisis hit just a couple of years later, he was the only employee in his department who survived dozens of layoffs. He was required to take a substantial pay cut and remained fearful of losing his job for several years.

During the financial crisis my income also took a blow. However, I was grateful to be employed by many clients who were extremely unlikely to all fire me at once, rather than a single employer who could cut off all my income. Due to their willingness to embrace uncertainty, business owners often earn higher income and withstand challenges in the job market better than those who enjoy a "safe, steady" income but could be fired at any moment.

Yes, uncertainty can be your friend. Without it, life and movies would be horribly boring and you would never have the opportunity for any big gains. I've never had a client complain about earning a 20 percent return in a year when they were only expecting an 8 percent return. It does happen!

Can you imagine a world where the only investment options were savings accounts and CDs? What if the government outlawed all forms of investment risk to "protect" us from all possible loss?

If that were the case, no one would ever make much money investing, and no businesses would ever receive the funding they needed to build exciting new products and services. Our whole system of wealth building and improved standard of living would crumble.

High investment returns require at least some level of uncertainty. Nothing great ever happens without someone being willing to take a chance. If you are never willing to take any risks, other people will be happy to borrow your money, capture higher returns for themselves, and give you the leftover crumbs.

Of course I don't advocate throwing all caution to the wind. Some risks are not worth taking. Later in this chapter we will discuss how to take prudent risks. The point is that you can't expect high returns with no risk, as we discussed in Chapter 4.

Whether you like it or not, life and investing are uncertain. If you embrace uncertainty and find ways to harness it to your advantage, you will enjoy much greater growth potential both financially and personally. You may also put yourself in a safer position than those who cling to a false illusion of certainty.

IMPROVE YOUR INVESTING EXPERIENCE

No one can guarantee how your investment experience will turn out, but you can significantly improve your chances of success by following these five steps in order:
1. Clarify your goals
2. Develop a plan
3. Determine your risk tolerance
4. Choose your investment strategy
5. Focus on what you can control

Simple, right? Yes, the solutions are simple, but not as easy to implement as they might look.

Prudent investing is a lot like losing weight. Everyone knows they can lose weight if they eat healthier and exercise more, but not very many people do it consistently. Likewise, these prudent investing steps will only help you if you follow them closely. Let's dive into each of these in greater detail.

1. CLARIFY YOUR GOALS

In my first book, *Timeless Principles of Financial Security*, I stated that attaining your goals starts with clearly articulating what you want most. If you don't know what you want, how can you effectively decide what to do?

Lewis Carroll masterfully captured this concept in *Alice's Adventures in Wonderland*, in which Alice asks the Cheshire Cat,

> "Would you tell me, please, which way I ought to go from here?"

"That depends a good deal on where you want to get to," said the Cat.

"I don't much care where—" said Alice.

"Then it doesn't matter which way you go," said the Cat.

No one can do this for you. It's your life. You must decide what you would like to accomplish. Then others can help you get there.

Effective goals contain the following five characteristics, which are commonly referred to as SMART:

- **Specific** – what exactly do you want to accomplish?
- **Measurable** – how will you evaluate your progress?
- **Ambitious** – does it excite you and will it help you grow?
- **Realistic** – is it possible to achieve with reasonable effort?
- **Time-bound** – by when will you accomplish the goal?

When it comes to financial goals, first determine your reasons for investing. Is it for retirement, children's education, a vacation home, or all of the above?

If for retirement, by when would you like to retire, what type of lifestyle would you like in retirement, and how much income will you need to support that lifestyle? Would you like to spend most of your money or leave an inheritance to children, grandchildren, or charity? How much access will you need to your investments for other purposes like a vacation home or expanding your business?

This is just a small sample of potential questions you will need to answer. Ideally, you would ask yourself many more questions to make your financial goals SMART. The clearer you paint the picture, the more likely you will accomplish your goal.

2. DEVELOP A PLAN

If you fail to plan, you plan to fail. Attaining a long-term financial goal like retirement is a marathon, not a sprint.

If you are a bona fide couch potato, you can't just throw down the bag of chips and run out your door like Forrest Gump for

26.2 miles straight without risking injury and burnout. Experts recommend implementing a six-month to one-year regimented training program including gradually increasing run distances, strength training, and specific periods of rest. They also recommend acquiring the proper gear, getting the proper nutrition, and sticking to the training schedule. You may be tempted to skip workouts or run longer than the plan states, but this can be harmful in the long run even if it doesn't seem like that big of a deal in the moment.

Getting to the point where you will have enough money to retire with a prosperous lifestyle may seem like an impossible feat if you haven't done much to prepare for it yet. A well-crafted financial plan breaks down big goals like retirement into bite-sized, realistic chunks. When you have a vision of what's possible with reasonable assumptions, you will know how much you have to save and the rate of return your investments need to attain.

Planning not only tells you what you need to do, but also provides perspective and peace of mind during tough times. Even in down markets, your financial plan may show you that you're still on track to meet your goals in the long run. This can help you maintain discipline and motivation to stick to the plan.

If the plan shows that you're no longer on track, it will outline what adjustments need to be made. Depending on how much time is left to accomplish your goals, these modifications might not be as extreme as you'd expect.

Without a plan, many people are more prone to harmful behaviors in response to market turbulence, such as discontinuing regular investment account contributions or chasing unreasonably high returns. You want to be like Aesop's Tortoise, not the Hare. Slow and steady wins the race.

Financial planning is most useful when it is collaborative and ongoing. Early in my career I often gave clients fancy binders with 50-plus-page printed reports containing their life-long financial plans. These became outdated practically the day after they were printed, so I don't usually hand out those binders anymore. Planning is more meaningful and effective when we use the software in real time during client meetings to evaluate the impact of different scenarios, rather than printing a bunch of static reports.

Financial planning is a process, not an event. All of the assumptions of the plan are merely educated guesses. No one knows exactly how much they will be able to save each year, when they will retire, the amount of Social Security income they will receive, the amount they will spend each year in retirement, what health challenges and other major expenses may come up, or how long they will live. Their actual rate of return, inflation rate, tax rates, and other variables are equally as unpredictable.

According to Stephen R. Covey, author of *The 7 Habits of Highly Effective People,* an airplane is "off course at least 90 percent of the time. Weather conditions, turbulence, and other factors cause it to get off track. However, feedback is given to the pilot constantly, who then makes course corrections and keeps coming back to the exact flight plan, bringing the plane back on course. And often, the plane arrives at the destination on time."[7]

Similarly, the most effective financial plans are updated regularly to determine what course corrections need to be made, if any. This is why I prefer an interactive financial planning process with my clients so we can play around with these variables together over time. I call this "stress testing" the plan so we can evaluate which unexpected outcomes are most likely to throw the plan off and what choices can help them mitigate those risks.

3. DETERMINE YOUR RISK TOLERANCE

Just like an airplane cannot stay 100 percent on course all the time due to weather, turbulence, and other issues, you are not likely to always be perfectly on track for reaching your financial goals because the market doesn't go straight up. You need to determine how much variation in investment values you are willing to stomach to reach your goals. The higher the returns you are trying to achieve, the more fluctuation you must be prepared to endure.

In this sense, skyscrapers are kind of like the market. They cannot stand perfectly straight up all the time because of the force of the wind. The taller the building, the more it must be able to sway to maintain its structural integrity. The tallest building in the world, the Burj Khalifa in Dubai, can sway up to six feet back and forth on its 163rd floor.[8]

According to Kate Ascher from Columbia University's Graduate School of Architecture, "If a building weren't able to move at the top, than various structural elements might be damaged because of the wind pressure. So most skyscrapers will be designed to move at the top. And some, particularly in earthquake zones, will actually be designed to be able to move a little bit on their foundations as well, so they don't take as much pressure as they would do if they were absolutely firm and static."[9]

If you already have a lot of money or if you are able to regularly save a significant amount, you might not need to take as much risk to reach your objectives. This is one of the benefits of having clear goals.

If you feel pressure to earn a high return to accomplish your goals but you cash out every time the market sneezes, you should stick with lower-risk investments and adjust your goals. Saving a little more each month or working a few years longer may be safer and more reliable ways to reach your objectives.

You will never enjoy the higher returns that can accompany higher risk if you don't stay invested during the tough times. It's more important to be true to your gut and only take on the amount of risk you know you'll be able to stick with. You may not earn as much as those who can handle the risk, but you'll sleep better at night and you'll be much better off in the long run.

One way to determine how much risk you can handle is to evaluate how various mixes of assets have performed over time both in good and bad times. Be honest with yourself about how you would have responded to various market conditions.

For example, a historical chart may show a 9 percent average annual return in an all-stock portfolio over the past 20 years, but did you know you could have lost nearly 50 percent in 2008 with that strategy? Would you have had the discipline and patience to stay invested until you earned it all back several years later?

If so, that's probably the right allocation for you. If not, you should probably dial back your risk by investing at least a portion in safer assets like bonds. The 9 percent average annual return included the 50 percent drop, but only those who stuck to the plan would have earned 9 percent in the long run. Those who cashed out after the 50 percent drop would have earned a *lot* less and would have been much better off with a more conservative asset allocation they could stick to.

This is one of the main services my team and I provide for investors. We help them measure the amount of risk they are currently taking and determine how much risk is the proper amount, based on their goals and feelings about risk.

Sometimes people get excited when they see a 9 percent average annual return and ignore the possibility of much lower returns from year to year. They forget that those higher returns come at a price. What is the price of admission? I like to call them stomach exercises because you have to endure a lot of ups and downs to earn a return like that.

A friend of mine told me about a guy she knows who regularly runs ultra-marathons. These can be over 100 miles per race and are usually run on rough trails.

She asked him what he does if he's not feeling well right before a race or if the weather turns bad. He said he loves it when that happens because it gives him an opportunity to grow. He feels like he doesn't learn anything new or increase his stamina when everything goes well. What we do in the face of difficulty reveals our potential to succeed despite obstacles.

When she told me that, I thought, "Wow, that's what separates me from guys like him. I wouldn't have the drive or the discipline to keep going in that situation, so I choose not to enter those types of races."

That's how high investment returns are earned. What we do when things don't go well determines our future returns. Everyone I know who invests more when the market suffers a large decline usually ends up earning much higher returns in the long run than people who bow out when the market drops. Those who can't stick to the plan during the tough times shouldn't enter the race.

A new client of mine was unlucky enough to put a relatively sizeable chunk in the stock market at the end of 2021, just a few months before the market started its significant sell-off in early 2022. Although he was close to retirement age and didn't have much experience investing in the market, he decided to put it all in stocks because he wanted that 9 percent rate of return, despite my warnings that it could drop by 50 percent if we had another year like 2008.

Less than a year later, his account value was down about 18 percent. He asked me what happened to the 9 percent return he thought he was going to get. He didn't have any recollection of our conversation about the possibility of a 50 percent loss in one year.

Of course, I was not happy about this outcome, either. Still, his performance was well within the fluctuation limits he indicated he was willing to tolerate. Thankfully, he was patient and disciplined enough to stay invested, and as of the time of this writing in early 2023 he has recovered almost all his losses. I still believe over time he has a chance of earning a 9 percent average annual rate of return, especially if he is willing to invest more next time a market downturn rolls around.

Unless you're satisfied with the very low, predictable returns of traditional bank CDs, you should never anticipate earning the same rate of return each year that you expect to earn on average in the long run. Your annual results will almost always be much higher or much lower than your average annual return over time. Sometimes this may feel somewhat like you're putting one foot in a bucket of ice water and the other foot in a bucket of boiling water while pretending that on average you're comfortable.

As of January 2023, LeBron James, one of the greatest basketball players of all time, had played more than 1,400 regular-season games over 20 years. He averaged a stunning 27 points, seven rebounds, and seven assists per game. However, can you believe that he never produced this exact number of points, rebounds, and assists in a single regular-season game?[10]

Knowing his average historical stats, you might have thought it a safe bet to predict that he would produce these results in at least one game. But if you had placed that bet for every game, you would have been wrong 1,400 times and lost a lot of money.

That's how the stock market works. Check out the S&P 500 annual returns over the 30-year period from 1993 to 2022 in Figure 15. Can you guess what the average annual return was just by looking at the chart? Not likely. Although the average was about 9.7 percent per year, it never earned that return in a single year.[11]

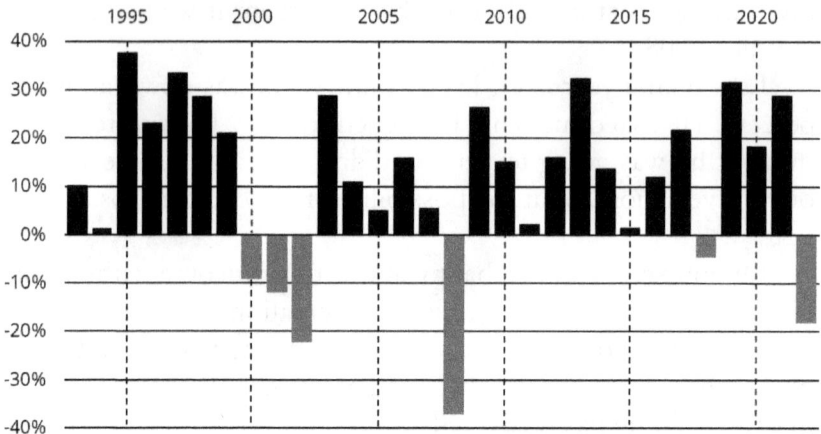

Figure 15: S&P 500 Annual Returns, 1993-2022

As you can see, the returns from year to year varied substantially from a positive 38 percent in 1995 to a negative 37 percent in 2008. You can't count on the market to deliver its average annual expected return to you in *any* year, let alone *every* year, so don't be surprised when it doesn't happen.[12]

This is why it's important to be honest with yourself about how much variability you can tolerate. Your returns will fluctuate quite a bit from day to day, month to month, and year to year. If you're clear about the worst-case scenario for the mix of assets you have chosen, you can rest assured that you are still within reasonable tolerance bands when your losses fall within the maximum expected range of losses.

It's amazing how much your money can grow when you earn interest on top of interest over time. This is called compound interest, which Albert Einstein described as the "eighth wonder of the world." It doesn't work very well unless you stay invested through the ups and downs, though. Figure 16 shows how $1 million invested in the S&P 500 at the start of 1993, with dividends reinvested until the end of 2022, could have grown to almost $16 million despite several large losses along the way.[13]

Year	Annual Return	Year-End Value	Year	Annual Return	Year-End Value
1993	10.1%	$1,101,000	2008	-37.0%	$2,816,870
1994	1.3%	$1,115,313	2009	26.5%	$3,563,341
1995	37.6%	$1,534,671	2010	15.1%	$4,101,406
1996	23.0%	$1,887,645	2011	2.1%	$4,187,535
1997	33.4%	$2,518,118	2012	16.0%	$4,857,541
1998	28.6%	$3,238,300	2013	32.4%	$6,431,384
1999	21.0%	$3,918,343	2014	13.7%	$7,312,484
2000	-9.1%	$3,561,774	2015	1.4%	$7,414,858
2001	-11.9%	$3,137,923	2016	12.0%	$8,304,641
2002	-22.1%	$2,444,442	2017	21.8%	$10,115,053
2003	28.7%	$3,145,997	2018	-4.4%	$9,669,991
2004	10.9%	$3,488,910	2019	31.5%	$12,716,038
2005	4.9%	$3,659,867	2020	18.4%	$15,055,789
2006	15.8%	$4,238,126	2021	28.7%	$19,376,800
2007	5.5%	$4,471,223	2022	-18.1%	$15,869,600

Figure 16: S&P 500 Compounded Annual Returns, 1993-2022, Starting with $1,000,000

4. CHOOSE YOUR INVESTMENT STRATEGY

Successful investing is not about predicting what is going to happen. The key is to maximize your chances of success by taking prudent risks and eliminating excessive and unnecessary risk.

As I mentioned, there is no single right way to invest, yet some strategies yield more consistent results than others. I will share my firm's approach because it has worked well for my clients over time, but be warned, it is not nearly as exciting as investing in Tesla, Bitcoin, or even a Ponzi scheme. You may have guessed this from learning my perspective on the perils of trying to time the market, pick the "right" stocks, and chase the hottest trends.

In fact, my team and I tell new clients all the time that we're the most boring investment advisors they'll ever meet. Can you guess how they almost always respond? "We're ready for boring."

Many investors swing for the fences hoping for a home run but usually end up striking out instead. We strive for singles and doubles because they tend to produce more reliable results. Of course, we might get lucky enough to hit an occasional home run, but our clients don't rely on them to reach their goals.

The Tortoise isn't very flashy or fun to watch, but he sure is rich because all the other animals put their money on The Hare. Slow and steady truly does win the race.

Our investment strategy is largely influenced by Modern Portfolio Theory, a practical method for maximizing expected returns for the amount of risk each investor is willing to take. The economist Harry Markowitz received a Nobel Prize for pioneering this theory in 1952, which revolutionized the investment world.

He taught the importance of diversification—that the performance of an individual stock is not as important as the performance of the whole portfolio. High returns can usually be achieved more safely by investing in a wide variety of assets with "low correlation," meaning that they tend to move up and down at different times to balance each other out.

Mr. Markowitz also suggested that you can only expect so high of a return for the amount of risk you are willing to take. If you only invest in CDs, you should not expect the same returns that stock investors can attain. Conversely, if someone is touting very high returns with no risk, it's not likely to play out as they claim because high returns require a certain amount of risk.

However, taking on more risk does not necessarily always result in a higher expected return, so we advocate taking prudent risks that are worth the potential returns. For example, investing in a start-up company promising you an 8 percent annual return makes no sense when you should be able to earn that much over time in a much less risky diversified portfolio of established companies.

A start-up might be worth considering if the potential return is 80 percent or 800 percent and you're prepared to lose it all, but not for 8 percent. About 20 years ago a friend of mine invested

$100,000 in a local start-up promising only 8 percent annual returns. He never received a single interest payment or any portion of his $100,000 back!

Most people think their investments are broadly diversified if they own a bunch of different funds, but when we analyze their portfolio we usually discover a lot of overlap. You could own a hundred different funds, but if they all hold similar assets, you're not any better diversified than if you just held one fund. Actually, owning various funds with similar assets could hurt you because some fund managers might sell the same stocks others are buying, subjecting you to unnecessary trading costs and taxes.

True diversification requires minimizing this overlap so you can own many different types of assets that tend not to move up and down at the same time. We recommend that our clients own stocks of all sizes in all types of industries, such as large stocks, small stocks, growth stocks, value stocks, U.S. stocks, international stocks, and emerging market stocks.

Our typical stock portfolio holds thousands of companies in dozens of countries. Why not just invest in the United States? We discussed that in depth at the beginning of Chapter 3. As a quick recap, investing outside the U.S. provides additional diversification to balance out periods when U.S. stocks underperform, like they did from 2000 to 2009.

Figure 17: Foreign Stocks You Might Want to Own

Besides, at least 40 percent of the global market cap (total value of shares) of publicly traded companies available for investment are held outside the United States. Many of them are highly profitable, important players.[14] Why wouldn't you want to own a piece of Honda, Toyota, Nestle, Nintendo, Sony, Shell, Bayer, Dannon, Porsche, Yamaha, Adidas, LG, and Samsung, just to name a few?

The amount we invest in each company is determined by a very scientific, systematic approach. We start with each stock's market cap weighting, meaning how large the company is in relation to all other companies. The largest company would represent the largest percentage of our clients' assets, and the smallest company would represent the smallest percentage. This is how the S&P 500 index and many other indexes are constructed. Then we slightly adjust the weightings to take advantage of the higher expected returns that small stocks, value stocks, and highly profitable companies provide.

You may wonder how we do all that for all our clients, because it is quite a complex process. We rely heavily on Dimensional Fund Advisors, which provides extremely sophisticated and diversified investment solutions in a very low-cost, tax-efficient manner through a variety of mutual funds, ETFs, and separately managed accounts (SMAs).

We typically utilize Dimensional Fund Advisors more than index funds because they tend to be more thoughtful about their allocations and have more flexible trading parameters. These and other practices have allowed 79 percent of their funds to outperform their benchmarks over the past 20 years (as of the end of 2022).[15]

For clients who want lower risk and are okay with a lower expected return, we suggest adding high-quality bonds to their portfolio. The ideal percentage of stocks vs. bonds we recommend depends on each client's investment objective, time horizon, and risk tolerance. It's not just a cookie-cutter, age-based approach. Although rare, we do have some clients in their 80s who invest 100 percent in stocks, and other clients in their 40s with only 30 percent invested in stocks, due to their unique circumstances and goals.

If it makes sense for clients to own bonds, we prefer that they own individual bonds in a "bond ladder" with different bonds maturing each year over time, rather than holding bond funds. This helps mitigate interest rate risk while maximizing the total yield of the portfolio.

When interest rates rose at an exceptionally rapid pace in 2022, bond prices fell considerably, but it was only a paper loss for investors who owned individual bonds. As long as they hold them until maturity, they won't lose any value in the end. In the long run, higher interest rates should result in higher returns because as bonds mature they can reinvest them at higher rates.

If all your bonds are held in a mutual fund or ETF, you have no control over when bonds are sold. If too many investors pull money out of the fund when bond prices fall, fund managers may be forced to sell bonds at a loss, so it's harder to withstand interest rate risk. Despite this risk, bond funds can be helpful for providing diversification and liquidity, especially in smaller accounts.

Many of our clients own tax-free municipal bonds. The interest rate is usually a little lower than you could earn in taxable corporate bonds, but if you are in a high tax bracket, the tax-free interest usually gives you a higher after-tax return.

When we build bond ladders, we strongly recommend a high level of diversification, just like we do with stocks. This means you should own bonds from a variety of issuers, serving different purposes, in many different states throughout the country.

Over time, the percentage you originally intended to invest in stocks vs. bonds is likely to drift away from your target allocation. If you start with 50 percent stocks and 50 percent bonds and your stocks outperform your bonds for a few years, your allocation may drift to 60 percent stocks and 40 percent bonds.

When it gets too out of whack, you should trim some of your gains and buy more of what didn't do as well, a disciplined process we call "rebalancing." This is very difficult for most investors to implement on their own because it's counterintuitive.

Most people want to sell what performed poorly and buy more of what recently performed well. However, everyone knows that the key to investing success is to buy low and sell high. Rebalancing assists with that process.

If you never rebalance, your investments could eventually end up with a much higher or lower risk profile than you originally intended. We recommend reviewing your allocation once a quarter to see if anything is getting too overweighted or underweighted. This is what we do for our clients.

You don't need to go crazy on this because you don't want to generate unnecessary trading costs or taxes. Sometimes it corrects itself with natural market movements. As we monitor our clients' portfolios, if their actual allocation hasn't drifted too far from their target allocation (within a certain percentage range), we don't make any changes.

In addition to the ratio of stocks vs. bonds, you should measure your percentage of U.S. vs. foreign stocks, small stocks vs. large stocks, value stocks vs. growth stocks, sectors of the market, and so on. This can get complicated, so you should be able to rely on your advisor to do this for you.

Another thing we love about working with Dimensional Fund Advisors is that they rebalance their portfolios on a daily basis in a very tax-efficient manner as new money comes in, only buying what is under-weighted. This reduces our need to sell clients' assets for rebalancing purposes.

5. FOCUS ON WHAT YOU CAN CONTROL

Worrying is like a rocking chair. It gives you something to do, but it doesn't get you anywhere.
—Erma Bombeck

One of my favorite classes in high school was psychology. My perspective changed forever when the teacher said that great peace comes from learning not to worry about what we cannot control.

He found it comical that some students wouldn't worry about studying for an exam when their efforts could have a huge impact on the outcome, but they would worry for weeks about whether their favorite sports team would win an important game. No matter how long we stress over whether our team will win or how much we scream at the TV when they make a bad play, we can't have any impact on the outcome.

In this sense the stock market is a lot like professional sports. Throughout this book we have talked a lot about how hard it is to predict the market. Perhaps only one thing is even harder: controlling the market. So stop worrying about it.

One of the greatest challenges of an educated, responsible person is to be well-informed without getting sucked into the harmful rhetoric of the media. Remember that fear and greed sell. Prudence doesn't.

The media does not want you to be at peace or stick to your plan. They are paid to give you anxiety so you will keep on watching and regularly make changes to your investments. If you can find ways to tune out the noise, you will be much happier and likely more wealthy in the end.

Roy T. Bennett wrote, "Instead of worrying about what you cannot control, shift your energy to what you can create." This is great advice for investing success. Worrying wastes a lot of time and energy that could be better spent on doing something productive to improve your situation. It also makes you vulnerable to making big mistakes.

If you can't control the market or the outcome of any specific investments, what can you control? You can control the amount you invest on a regular basis regardless of what is happening in the market. The best time to invest is often when market performance is the worst because everything is on sale. Those who continue to invest after a market decline tend to recover more quickly than those who don't.

What else can you control? You can stick to your plan and rebalance as necessary, as I mentioned earlier. When your stocks take a dive and your bonds increase in value, sell some bonds and buy more stocks. This takes a lot of discipline, but can help you make more money in the long run.

You can also focus on your goals rather than your current returns. Update your financial plan to see what if anything needs to be tweaked to make sure you're on track.

You can read books about long-term investing and the history of the market to gain deeper understanding and to keep your current plight in perspective. Remember that high returns are born from uncertainty and volatility, so celebrate it when it happens.

You can hire a good wealth advisor, coach, or mentor to help you manage your emotions and stay disciplined through the unavoidable ups and downs of the market. They often maintain a long-term view more easily because they are not as emotionally involved with your finances as you are.

Lastly, you can control your expectations. Great perspective and peace come from maintaining realistic expectations, learning to let go, and remembering what money is for.

As Mo Gawdat, former Chief Business Officer of Google X, said in his book *Solve for Happy*, our happiness is greater than or equal to our perception of experiences minus our expectations for those experiences. For example, if I expect to earn 20 percent per year in the market year after year without any declines, I am setting myself up for disappointment. If I expect 2 percent average annual returns with a big market downturn every other year, I will probably be very happy with my returns because they are not likely to turn out that bad. These are extreme examples, but you get the point.

Even if the Beatles were wrong and money can buy you love, it surely cannot buy you happiness. Some people I know with tens of millions of dollars have more anxiety about the ups and downs of the market than others with less than a hundred thousand. They can buy anything they want and will never spend everything they have, yet their wealth has become an overwhelming burden to them rather than granting them freedom from worry. If you can't enjoy financial peace of mind with tens of millions of dollars to your name, what's the point of having it?

Shortly after the worst of the market declines in 2022, I met with a retired couple who have invested a little less than a million dollars with my firm since 2011. Since then they have gradually spent almost as much of it as they gave us to invest, but their account balance is still worth close to what they started with.

As I reviewed their recent losses and shared my perspective, they said they weren't worried about it at all. They are fully confident it will come back because they have been through times like this before and it has always recovered.

Then the husband made an unexpected comment that was very humbling to me: "Even if it doesn't come back, God gave it to us, and He can take it away. We'll be fine either way."

This is not exactly a line I would use to calm other clients' fears. However, it was amazing to observe how at peace these clients were because they fully acknowledged they have no control.

I believe their attitude will improve their chances of recovery because they are sticking to their investment strategy. Regardless of whether they fully recover their losses or not, they are very happy and all their needs are being met. After all, isn't that what money is for?

DIY IF YOU DARE

Thanks to modern technology like the internet and easy-to-use phone apps, do-it-yourself investing is more accessible than ever. The internet continues to grow with limitless amounts of information where anyone can learn just about anything they would like to know. If you love learning about investing and following the market, and if you are disciplined enough to not let your emotions get in the way, you might save some money on fees by doing your own investing.

One of my friends who is a successful dentist is a voracious student of the investing world. He spends many hours every week studying the market and simply can't get enough of it.

He even recently sold his dental practice and is thinking he might want to become a financial advisor. He would probably be a good one because he understands the principles of prudent investing better than some financial advisors I have met. He loves doing his own investing, has been successful at it, and has no problem sticking to his strategy through the ups and downs of the market, so I doubt an advisor could provide much value to him.

If that sounds like you, go for it! However, most people I know who have tried doing their own investing have not done very well, for all the reasons we have talked about in this book.

They get excited too easily about "amazing opportunities" without fully understanding the risks. They bail too easily when a barrage of headlines claim things are never going to get better. Ironically, sometimes they pay even more in hidden and unnecessary fees than they would have paid to a wealth advisor, without benefitting from the service and perspective an advisor could have provided.

Fear and greed tend to be the biggest threats to investing success. They can be very difficult to overcome without the aid of a qualified third party who is not emotionally involved in your finances.

Another challenge for do-it-yourself investors is evaluating the quality of investment resources. All information investors need to succeed on their own is out there somewhere in the universe. However, with close to two billion websites providing information and over a trillion megabytes of new data being created every day, determining which information is accurate and useful is more challenging than ever.[16]

How can you be sure you're not being deceived or wasting your time? After discovering reliable information, knowing what to do with that information can be even more difficult.

These are some of the reasons many people who have tried investing on their own eventually end up hiring a wealth advisor. Others never bother trying to do it themselves. The reasons for hiring an advisor can vary widely from person to person, but most of my clients pay my firm to manage their investments for one or more of the following reasons:

1. **Time** – They don't have time to do it on their own. They are busy and successful so their time is valuable and they feel it is better spent elsewhere.

2. **Ability** – They don't know how to do it on their own. They're overwhelmed by it and don't have the confidence to invest without help.

3. **Desire** – They don't want to do it on their own. They don't find it interesting or prefer not to deal with the hassle of it.

4. **Continuity** – They are afraid that if they do it on their own, their family will have no idea what to do after they're

gone. They want someone they can trust to know their financial situation and provide sound advice to their family.

5. **Discipline** – They don't trust themselves to do it on their own. They want a reliable coach with a fiduciary duty to help them make prudent decisions in the face of economic turmoil, call them out on irrational behaviors, and protect them from making big mistakes.

The bottom line is that they hire my firm to help them simplify their lives and enhance their peace of mind. That last point, discipline, reminds me of a client who has several million dollars invested with us, in addition to a small do-it-yourself account at a discount brokerage firm. One day I asked why he didn't invest it all with the other firm so he could avoid paying our fee. He responded, "Because I don't trust myself and it scares me to death."

Nick Murray, one of the foremost thought leaders in the investment industry, thinks the greatest value of the advisory fee is "big mistake insurance" for investors. He points out that although some investors boast they could earn a higher return over time by avoiding an advisory fee, most do not have the ability or discipline to make good decisions in an ever-changing, emotional marketplace. Without a coach helping them avoid big mistakes, many investors earn a lot less on their own than they could have with an advisor, even after paying the fee.

The friend I mentioned in Chapter 3 who sold his rental properties and lost $1 million investing in three individual stocks, much of it with a margin loan, is an extreme example of this principle. He told me if he had to do it all over again he would hire an advisor because he realizes now that he had no idea what he was doing.

He tried to read as much as he could and thought he knew enough, but he underestimated how ruthless the game was. He feels like he was way out of his league, competing in a "big boys" game against millions of investors determined to beat him. The rules he didn't understand wiped him out.

He is convinced he would have a lot more money today if he had hired a qualified advisor to help protect him from the dangers that the brokerage firm downplayed. It's tragic to see investors lose so much money after spending a ton of time, mental exertion, and emotional energy trying to do what they think is best.

As I mentioned earlier, saving money on advisory fees does not necessarily mean you'll have lower costs overall. Some do-it-yourself investors inadvertently pay a lot more in hidden fees than they would be paying an advisor. They have no idea that they're paying exorbitant internal fund expenses or they engage in high-turnover strategies that result in excessive bid-ask spreads, taxes, and other trading costs.

The fees for my firm's investment strategies are extremely low, which helps to offset our advisory fee. Some investors might even experience lower fees overall by investing with us than they would on their own, due to potentially excessive internal expenses they may not be aware of.

Our objective is to provide way more value than the amount our clients pay so we won't be a net cost to them. Sometimes this can be hard to measure because our investments usually drop during the bad times just like everyone else's. However, we do everything in our power to help our clients achieve their financial goals in ways that may be difficult for them to do on their own.

I know how good it feels to receive exceptional value for the fees paid, so I always strive to do that for my clients. I love being able to rely on the expert guidance of my attorneys, bookkeepers, recruiters, compliance advisors, technology specialists, insurance benefits consultants, bankers, and more. It's amazing to pick up the phone and get a quick answer I can rely on without having to do any research on my own, knowing they always have my best interest at heart. They are worth every penny I pay them. Let me share a few more specific examples to see if you can relate.

When I sold my last house, my realtor's fees were not cheap. However, I'm convinced he sold it for a much higher price than I could have bargained for on my own, so he practically paid for himself. He advised me on what to fix and what to leave as-is in preparation for selling. This helped me avoid wasting money on issues that wouldn't improve the sales price. He handled all the photos, marketing, paperwork, offers, and communication with buyers. He also quickly resolved several last-minute obstacles with the buyer that could have delayed or canceled closing. What would

I have done without him ensuring it closed on time? His services were worth way more than the cost.

I'm sure I could learn how to do my own taxes, but when I consider the value of my time, I realize that paying my accountants is way less expensive than the countless hours it would take me to learn the complexities of tax law for business owners. Since they ensure I maximize all available deductions, they probably help me save more in taxes than I pay them anyway. On top of that, they save me the hassle, quickly answer my complex tax questions, and give me the peace of mind that my tax returns are filed correctly and on time so I don't have to fear receiving an unwelcome letter from the IRS. The best part is that they scour hundreds of pages of new tax law every time congress sneezes so I don't have to.

Our business coach is fairly expensive, but for many years he has helped us grow and shape our business in vital ways we could not have done on our own. His advice has led to much higher revenue growth than the fees we pay him, not to mention the positive impact he's had on the development of our amazing team and the quality of our culture.

That's the funny thing about costs. You can't look at them in a vacuum. You have to evaluate whether the value received justifies the cost. You know I'm passionate about cutting excessive and unnecessary costs—I even wrote a whole chapter about it. However, cutting costs at all costs can cost you dearly in the end.

On a recent flight from Las Vegas to Houston to visit family with my wife and four children, I couldn't stop thinking about how much nicer it was flying there than driving. Several years earlier when our kids were younger and still believed in Santa Claus (but not the Santa Claus Rally), we drove from Las Vegas to Houston for Christmas. We had to drive the long, very painful 22 hours over two days so we could transport all our Christmas presents, which were hidden in a bunch of big black garbage sacks. Then we drove another grueling 22 hours over two days all the way back, and I got my first speeding ticket in many years.

A short three-hour flight was a much more pleasant experience to say the least, but was it worth the cost? The plane tickets for six people were much more expensive than the cost of gas would have been for one vehicle. However, when you factor in the cost of meals on the road for four days (two days each way), hotels for two nights, and an extra 3,000 miles of vehicle wear and tear, the gap in cost between flying and driving narrows considerably, especially when you add a couple hundred dollars for that stupid speeding ticket.

Flying was still probably more expensive, but then you would have to factor in the cost of my time for taking four days off of work just for travel time. Not to mention the cost of the other five members of my family sitting in the car for four days instead of doing other more productive things. The cost of our collective wasted time and energy would have been astronomical compared to the cost of the plane tickets. Besides all that, it would have been much less enjoyable and less safe than flying.

As I was thinking about this during our recent flight to Houston, it occurred to me that a commercial pilot's job is similar to a good wealth advisor's job in several ways. If I'm willing to give up some control and place my trust in a well-trained, experienced pilot who has a fiduciary duty to ensure a safe, comfortable, and punctual trip, I am likely to arrive at my destination much more quickly and safely than if I had driven there myself. The trip will also be much less work and much more enjoyable for me because I can focus on other things or even sleep the whole way there instead of having my hands glued to the steering wheel and my eyes glued to the road for 44 hours. And it might even be less expensive than driving.

Likewise, if you are willing to give up some control and place your trust in a well-trained, experienced wealth advisor who has a fiduciary duty to help you attain your goals on time as safely as possible, you are likely to arrive at your financial destination more quickly and easily than if you had tried to do it yourself. The journey should also be a lot less work and much more enjoyable for you because you can focus on other things you would rather do instead of having your hands glued to Robinhood and your eyes glued to CNBC 24/7. And it might even be less expensive than investing on your own. How much is your time and energy worth?

At my firm, Capstone Capital Wealth Advisors, we deliver many additional services besides investment management to ensure that we provide much greater value than our clients pay in advisory fees. Our mission is to simplify our clients' lives and enhance their peace of mind in every way we can.

Recently I met with a couple who owns a successful business. I have loved working with them for over 16 years. We discussed succession planning issues, including partnership options for their son, retirement planning, evaluation of their other assets that we don't manage, pros and cons of other investment options they were considering, an update on what was happening in the market, and a performance review of their investments with us.

At the end of the meeting they said they felt guilty because they always receive way more value from our relationship than they pay for. I told them not to feel guilty because that's the way it should be. It made my day because that is always my goal!

We are committed to creating an excellent client experience by continually increasing our expertise and evaluating how we can improve. Not all clients need or want everything we offer, but for those who do, we provide the following for no additional fee:

THE CAPSTONE CAPITAL COMMITMENT

1. **Competence**
   a. Wealth management
   b. Holistic retirement planning
   c. Risk and tax management
   d. Asset allocation, investment selection/rebalancing
   e. Resource for all investing and financial questions
2. **Coaching**
   a. Honest, objective advice, trusted second opinion
   b. Ongoing education, market and account updates
   c. Measure progress toward goals, stay disciplined
   d. Help you manage stress & complex relationships
   e. Assistance through life and business transitions
3. **Convenience**
   a. Concierge personalized service to save you time
   b. Clear communication
   c. Coordination with your other trusted professionals
   d. Research complex financial issues for you
   e. Secure, easy-to-use technology

4. **Continuity**
   a. Easy transition for loved ones after you're gone
   b. Financial education for children & grandchildren
   c. Multigenerational estate planning considerations
   d. Continuation of your legacy, philanthropic goals
   e. Succession planning for your business

HIRE A COACH, NOT A SALESPERSON

If you decide to hire a wealth advisor, be sure to find a good coach who will always be there to guide you through difficult decisions as you face inevitable changes in your life and in the market. Too many "advisors" are primarily salespeople trying to get you to buy something that will make them a big commission so they can move on to the next sale.

You will probably need to purchase some investment products to meet your goals, and some are higher quality than others, but your behavior will likely impact your outcome far more than the performance of any specific investment. Build a long-term relationship with a qualified advisor you can trust to stand by your side through the ups and downs, who is not afraid to call you out on behaviors that could harm you, and who has a fiduciary duty to always recommend what is in your best interest.

This reminds me of the relationship my kids have with their tennis coach. They respect him a lot because he really knows his stuff (he was one of the top tennis players in the country), he teaches them proven techniques and strategies that help them win games, he truly cares about them and applauds what they are doing well, and he respectfully corrects them when they're not properly implementing what he taught.

We bought our kids high-quality tennis rackets to give them as much of an advantage as possible, but the racket salesperson has had hardly any impact on their performance compared to the influence of their coach. I don't know much about tennis, but I'm pretty sure no matter how much we spent, no racket could guarantee a win every time.

Winning has a lot more to do with how they use their racket throughout each game, especially when they get in a slump. Their coach can't guarantee a win every time either, and he can't play the game for them. However, when they apply what he has taught, they are much more likely to succeed.

I don't mean to throw down rackets too hard. Of course, high-quality rackets and high-quality investments can make a difference. We obsess over ensuring our clients have the best possible tools to maximize their chances of success, but there is no perfect investment product or strategy. Even the best-rated solutions lose money at times, just like the best tennis rackets can lose games.

Investor behavior impacts performance much more than investment selection. Hire a good coach who can help you stay in your seat when everyone else is jumping off the roller coaster.

How can you measure which advisor will be the best coach for you? Just like there is no perfect investment, there is no single perfect advisor for everyone. Finding one you trust can be a daunting task, especially if you have already been burned by other advisors. As we saw with the Ponzi schemes, not all "nice guys" can be trusted.

Unfortunately, no one can guarantee that you will have a good experience with any particular advisor. You will have to be the judge of whether you are receiving sufficient value over time and make adjustments as needed. All you can do is maximize your chances of success by doing a little homework on each advisor you are considering and decide which qualities are most important to you.

This is not an exhaustive list, but here are some of the most important qualities I believe will improve your chances of having a positive experience with a true advisor coach with your best interests at heart:

15 ATTRIBUTES OF EXCELLENT ADVISOR COACHES

1. **Legitimate** – They have a physical business address, up-to-date website, cohesive team, and proper licensing (Series 65 or Series 7 and 66) without serious disclosures (check brokercheck.finra.org and/or adviserinfo.sec.gov).

They also utilize a reputable third-party custodian to hold your assets, like Charles Schwab or Fidelity.

2. **Competent** – They have relevant education, experience, and/or certifications such as CFP® or CFA. Their expertise matches your level of wealth and complexity.

3. **Reputable** – They are well-respected in the community and others can vouch for the quality of their services.

4. **Independent** – They are affiliated with an independent registered investment advisor (RIA) or hybrid firm that gives them freedom to recommend what is in their clients' best interests, rather than being subject to sales quotas or the hidden agendas of "big brother" brokerage firms.

5. **Fiduciary** – They are legally obligated to always put your best interests ahead of their own. Registered investment advisors and CFP® professionals are examples of fiduciaries. You might expect that all advisors would be required to act in your best interests, but many are only subject to a "suitability rule." This means their recommendations must be reasonably suited to a client's needs, even if they're not necessarily the best solutions. Broker-dealers and other commission-driven organizations tend to be held only to a suitability standard and have fought hard against legislation striving to require all advisors to become fiduciaries.

6. **Fee-Based** – Their income primarily or exclusively comes from advisory fees rather than commissions. This helps motivate them to continue serving you over time and reduces conflicts of interest when making recommendations.

7. **Holistic** – They base recommendations on your overall situation, goals, financial plans, and other assets, rather than simply pushing a specific product. They regularly ask about and are willing to advise you on your entire financial picture rather than focusing only on what they manage.

8. **Disciplined** – They don't react impulsively to market movements or media messages and help you stick to the plan when you're tempted to panic. They employ a disciplined investment process that doesn't change on a whim.

They avoid strategies that rely on timing the market, picking stocks, or chasing hot trends, and they keep costs low.

9. **Realistic** – They strive to temper your expectations and ensure your awareness of worst-case scenarios, rather than touting outrageous outcomes with little risk. In other words, their claims are reasonable and they don't say anything that sounds too good to be true.

10. **Honest** – They tell you the truth even when it's hard to deliver, rather than saying what they think you want to hear. This could include bad news about your investment performance, admitting a mistake they made, or respectfully pointing out ways you might be hurting yourself or making irrational decisions. They reveal their true selves and fully disclose all fees, risks, and conflicts of interest.

11. **Clear** – They communicate in simple, direct terms that are easy to understand. They avoid using complex financial jargon to impress or intimidate you.

12. **Proactive** – They reach out to you regularly for review meetings and to keep you informed of meaningful updates. They hold you accountable to follow through on important assignments and help you stay on track to meet your goals.

13. **Collaborative** – They work with you to explore viable solutions rather than taking a top-down, authoritative approach. They continually strive to improve your understanding of the market and their investment process, empowering you to make more informed decisions. They also coordinate their advice with your accountant, attorney, and other trusted advisors.

14. **Respectful** – They pay close attention to your needs, respond promptly and courteously to your requests, and follow through on commitments. They answer your financial questions with respect and take the hassle out of wealth management.

15. **Curious** – They are really good listeners and genuinely want to understand your most important goals and concerns so they can walk in your shoes when making

recommendations. They also continually strive to find better ways to serve clients and improve their abilities.

Does this seem like a very long, unrealistic list of qualities? Believe it or not, I know many advisors with all of these characteristics, so you shouldn't have to settle for anything less. If you can find someone that demonstrates all of these attributes, you will significantly improve your chances of having a good experience. Needless to say, our firm strives to embody these qualities as well.

Under the first point I casually mentioned "cohesive team," but I want to emphasize what I mean by that because it is a particularly important distinguishing characteristic of the best advisors. Most investment firms consist of a bunch of siloed advisors, where every advisor works alone to bring in and service their own clients. At such firms, although many advisors may work under one roof, they are essentially competitors sharing the same conference rooms and copy machine. They have little or no collaboration, and no one takes care of anyone else's clients.

This could be a problem for you. What would you do if your advisor is in the Caribbean or in a coma and no one else can take care of you? Furthermore, not all advisors have the same strengths, so a robust team with complementary skills can provide you better service and perspective than a solo advisor without a team.

In our firm we have gone to great lengths to build cohesive advisory and service teams. Our goal is to ensure our clients feel they have a good relationship with more than one member of our firm and always receive quality advice and service in a timely manner. We empower and encourage every member of our team to share ideas for how we can improve and to hold every other member of the team accountable—including me, the CEO.

On top of all this, be sure to find an advisor that matches your personality, values, communication style, and service needs. You must find someone you trust and enjoy working with because you will likely need to have tough conversations with them at some point.

Remember that a good coach will tell you what you need to hear, not always what you want to hear. If you don't like or trust them enough to be able to take it, you may end up figuratively cancelling your "big mistake insurance" when you need it most.

OPTIMISM IS THE ONLY REALISM

Since I filled most of this book with so many horror stories of people losing money investing, I wanted to end on a positive note. I am an optimistic person. I truly believe that no matter how bad things get, they will always eventually get better for you personally, for the market, and for society as a whole. I have lived long enough to know that although sometimes the night may seem endless, the sun *will* rise and shine again.

Yes, the world is filled with very complex problems, some of which might never be fully resolved. Yes, we have suffered many unwelcome challenges and we will face many more. But we have always bounced back, and I am convinced we will continue bouncing back, better and stronger than ever like a phoenix rising from the ashes.

Nick Murray said it best in his book *Simple Wealth, Inevitable Wealth*: "Pessimism is counterintuitive because no one would look back at history and see a failing worldview….The U.S. economy has seen it all and come back from the brink every time. It has seen wars, crises, recessions, depressions, inflation, deflation, burst bubbles, and the never-ending end-of-the-world whispers and screams….Despite all that, the American capitalist machine was constantly creating, innovating, and driving the economy forward every step of the way….Optimism is the only realism."[17]

Whenever you feel like all hope is lost and the market will never recover, remember what it represents—almost every business you have come to rely on, as well as millions of people working every day to make the world a better place. When you're properly diversified, it's not really possible to lose everything. Although the performance of each individual stock is unpredictable, there is safety in numbers.

As I mentioned earlier, our clients own thousands of companies in dozens of countries, and I doubt they could all go out of business at once. If they did, we would have way more serious problems to worry about than the value of our investments.

On the next page I list a small sampling of only 120 of the thousands of stocks most of our clients own. Do you recognize any of these names? Did you buy anything from any of them in 2008, 2015, 2018, 2020, or 2022, even after the market took a dive in those rough years?

What do you suppose are the chances of every single one of them going out of business at once if we had another market crash like 2008, or even like 1929? It's extremely unlikely.

Keep in mind that this list only represents less than 1 percent of the total number of companies most of our clients own throughout the world. In 20 years I'm sure it will look very different. Some of these companies will decline in value or maybe even go bankrupt. Others will take their place. No matter who the top players are, the market will continue to thrive over time because it represents society's constant drive to grow and improve our world.

What exciting new developments will soon enhance our lives in ways we can scarcely imagine now, while producing awesome returns for investors? Here are some real examples in the works as we speak, at various stages of development and practicality:

- The proliferation of truly autonomous vehicles
- Flying cars
- More accessible space tourism and space sports
- Improved artificial intelligence and machine learning
- New technology and DNA studies to help fight diseases
- 3D-printed bone replacements for surgical use
- Brain-reading robots and brain-controlled prosthetic limbs
- Cleaner, cheaper, and more efficient energy and batteries
- Global high-speed internet for everyone, everywhere
- Radically enhanced virtual reality capabilities for gaming, shopping, training, education, health care, and exercise.

Apple	Target	Dow
Microsoft	Lockheed Martin	Nasdaq
Exxon Mobil	CVS	Netflix
Amazon	Morgan Stanley	Schwab
Johnson & Johnson	UPS	Hartford
JPMorgan Chase	ADP	DR Horton
Berkshire Hathaway	Nike	Oracle
Alphabet (Google)	Tesla	Sysco
UnitedHealth Group	Walt Disney	S&P Global
Procter & Gamble	Adobe	Ulta Beauty
Pepsico	NVIDIA	Reliance Steel
Eli Lilly	Honeywell	Avis Budget
Chevron	Goldman Sachs	Ross Stores
Mastercard	T-Mobile	Kellogg
Visa	Kroger	FedEx
Merck	Abbott Laboratories	Marriott
Pfizer	LPL Financial	Salesforce
Meta (Facebook)	Travelers	PPG Industries
ConocoPhillips	3M	eBay
Verizon	TJX (TJ Maxx)	Deckers Outdoor
Coca-Cola	Dollar Tree	Autozone
Broadcom	Chubb	Aflac
Costco	United Rentals	Ford Motor
Home Depot	Ameriprise	Williams Sonoma
Bank of America	Valero Energy	Intuit
Bristol Myers	McDonald's	Lennar
Union Pacific	Citigroup	Autonation
Texas Instruments	Humana	Phillips 66
Walmart	Sherwin Williams	Moderna
Cisco	Lowe's	Prudential
Comcast	Paychex	Capital One
IBM	General Mills	MetLife
Qualcomm	Progressive	Principal Financial
Caterpillar	Cintas	CBRE
Intel	General Motors	Campbell's Soup
American Express	Discover	General Electric
John Deere	Allstate	Republic Services
AT&T	Best Buy	Tyson Foods
Cigna	U.S. Bank	Estee Lauder
Wells Fargo	Hershey	Starbucks

Our collective global progress and my optimism for the future are not just about financial growth. The research company YouGov conducted a survey in 2016, in which 65 percent of Americans thought the world was getting worse and only 6 percent thought it was getting better. However, in their enlightening book, *Ten Global Trends Every Smart Person Should Know*, authors Ronald Bailey and Marian L. Tupy demonstrate that the world is actually getting much better in a myriad of ways. Here is a small sample of many promising trends they highlight:

- "The global absolute poverty rate has fallen from 42 percent in 1981 to 8.6 percent today."
- "The prevalence of undernourishment in the world fell from 37 percent of the total population in 1969-1971…to 10.8 percent in 2018."
- "Satellite data show that forest area has been expanding since 1982."
- "Natural resources are becoming ever cheaper and more abundant."
- "Since 1900, the average life expectancy has more than doubled, reaching more than 72 years globally."
- "Over the past half century, wars between countries have become rarer, and those that do occur kill fewer people."
- "People today are much more likely to survive natural disasters because of increased wealth and technological progress."
- "Nearly 90 percent of the world's population in 1820 was illiterate. Today almost 90 percent can read."
- In the United States, the percentage of income we must spend on basic necessities has fallen sharply, we have bigger and better housing than ever before, air travel is cheaper than ever, and almost everyone has electricity, plumbing, central heating and air conditioning, a vehicle, refrigerator, microwave, dishwasher, washer and dryer, color TV, computer, smartphone, and internet access.[18]

Considering all these amazing improvements and even more on the way, why are people often so gloomy about the state of the market, our country, and the world at large? The authors cite a few possible reasons:

1. "Johan Galtung and Mari Holmboe Ruge, from the Peace Research Institute Oslo, observed, 'There is a basic asymmetry in life between the positive, which is difficult and takes time, and the negative, which is much easier and takes less time—compare the amount of time needed to build a house and to destroy it in a fire.' News is bad news; steady progress is not news."

2. "Smart people especially seek to be well informed and so tend to be voracious consumers of news. Since journalism focuses on dramatic things and events that go wrong, the nature of news thus tends to mislead readers and viewers into thinking that the world is in worse shape than it really is."

3. "We are the descendants of the worried folks who tended to assume that all rustles in the grass were dangerous predators and not the wind. Because of this instinctive negativity bias, most of us attend far more to bad rather than to good news."

4. Harvard University psychologist Daniel Gilbert explains, "When problems become rare, we count more things as problems. Our studies suggest that when the world gets better, we become harsher critics of it, and this can cause us to mistakenly conclude that it hasn't actually gotten better at all. Progress, it seems, tends to mask itself."

In a humorous interview with Conan O'Brien several years ago, Louis C.K. masterfully described this phenomenon: "Everything is amazing right now and nobody's happy...I was on an airplane and there was high speed internet on the airplane. That's the newest thing that I know exists. I'm sitting on the plane and they go, 'Open up your laptop; you can go on the internet.' It's fast and I'm watching YouTube clips. I mean, I'm in an airplane! Then it breaks down, and they apologize, 'The internet is not working.' And the guy next to me goes, 'This is $%#&.' Like how quickly the world owes him something he knew existed only 10 seconds ago!"[19]

You may argue that just because things have been getting better for a while doesn't mean they will keep getting better forever. As a society, we are capable of burning down the house much faster than we built it.

That is certainly true. Many nations that were once very wealthy and powerful, such as the British and Roman Empires, now enjoy only a small fraction of their former glory. If we are not vigilant, our nation could eventually lose its status as the most powerful in the world. However, the "failure" of former world powers is relative because the standard of living today in virtually every fallen empire far exceeds what it was at the height of their power.

Additionally, most if not all empires that fell did so because they were extracting too much wealth from the masses to boost elite classes, rather than expanding opportunity for everyone and encouraging innovation. Democratic forms of government strive to empower the masses and are far more conducive to economic growth, so they appear to be less vulnerable to those risks so far.

No one can predict the future, and many things could threaten our way of life as we know it today. However, while much is wrong in the world, the good still far outweighs the bad. We have more reason to believe things will continue to improve than that things will fall apart.

As we discussed earlier, there is no value in worrying about things we cannot control. One thing is certain—if you are determined to maintain a perpetually pessimistic view of the world, it will severely limit your personal growth and potential prosperity.

Do you feel like our nation is on the brink of tearing itself apart because of an unprecedented political divide? How do you think Americans felt about our nation's future during the Civil War? Look how far we've come since then. If someone could have lived from the Civil War until now, could they have had enough faith in the future to invest? If they hadn't, look at all the growth they would have missed out on.

As Hans Rosling writes in his book *Factfulness: Ten Reasons We're Wrong about the World—and Why Things Are Better Than You Think*, "I see all this progress, and it fills me with conviction and hope that further progress is possible. This is not optimistic. It is having a clear and reasonable idea about how things are. It is having a worldview that is constructive and useful."[20]

The future is bright, and you are entitled to participate in the tremendous wealth-building opportunities that lie ahead. While there is no single right way to invest, you now have powerful tools to help you avoid your greatest threats and improve your chances of success.

Remember that fear and greed are the root causes of almost every major investment failure because they lead to destructive behaviors. Don't give into the temptation to time the market, pick individual stocks, or chase the latest trends. You don't have to do any of that to be successful.

Don't be afraid to invest or fooled by a promise of high returns with no risk. Know your costs and read the disclosures.

Learn to embrace uncertainty, clarify your goals, and develop a sound financial plan. Determine your risk tolerance, set realistic expectations, and choose a disciplined, diversified investment strategy. Tune out the noise, and find an excellent coach who can help you make prudent decisions and stick to your plan through thick and thin.

Simple, right? I know, it's not easy, but you can do it if you improve your mindset and ask for help from the right people when you need it.

Most of all, remember what investing is really for. It's not just about the money. Happiness won't automatically come from having more and more of it. You must be clear about your goals and realize how much is enough so you can let go of what you cannot control.

No one should have to suffer the immense loss and heartache that too often result from taking the excessive, unnecessary chances we have discussed throughout this book. You have worked way too hard and sacrificed too much to allow unscrupulous or incompetent salespeople and organizations to confiscate your wealth through tantalizing promises they cannot keep.

If you have already been a victim of such losses, I am very sorry. I know how discouraging and overwhelming it can be to suffer such large losses and not know if you'll be able to recover.

If you have faith, you *will* recover! Yes, faith is an important principle of spiritual power, but I'm not just talking about that.

Faith is truly believing that if you do everything in your power to grow, improve, and overcome your challenges, even when you have no idea how things will work out, eventually things *will* get better. It doesn't work if you just sit around and hope things will get better on their own or blame others for your woes. It requires positive action on your part.

A brighter tomorrow starts with learning the right lessons from your losses so you can move forward with a better plan. Hopefully this book has helped you realize the true reasons why some of your former investments may have failed.

Don't give up on yourself and don't give up on investing. There is always hope for the future if you put prudent investing principles into practice.

You deserve to experience the same peace of mind and confidence that my clients who I mentioned in the introduction now enjoy. After we helped them clarify their goals, develop a solid plan, determine their risk tolerance, and implement a disciplined investment strategy, they are sleeping better at night now than ever before. They are confident they will have a wonderful retirement with the freedom to focus fully on their family and hobbies rather than constantly stressing about fluctuations in the market.

If you have questions about how to implement any of this, I'd love to hear from you. My team and I are here to help you simplify your life and enhance your peace of mind so you can attain a brighter future and more fully enjoy the journey along the way. Whatever you are chasing, now you have better tools to dramatically improve your chances of obtaining it.

The best is yet to come. If you are willing to trust in the power of the market and invest prudently rather than chasing that elusive easy street, you will likely be astonished at your ability to build substantial wealth, achieve your most important life goals, and make a significant difference for good in the lives of the people around you.

KEY POINTS OF CHAPTER 7

1. You don't have to time the market, pick stocks, or chase the hottest trends to be a successful investor.
2. The market can be a very effective tool for growing wealth if you learn how to harness its power prudently.
3. The market generally grows over time because it represents the continual improvement of products and services—millions of people working every day to make the world a better place.
4. Uncertainty can be good because it allows for higher potential returns and the possibility that life could turn out even better than you expected.
5. You can improve your chances of investing success by clarifying your goals, developing a plan, determining your risk tolerance, choosing your investment strategy, and focusing on what you can control.
6. Your goals should be SMART: Specific, Measurable, Ambitious, Realistic, and Time-bound.
7. Proper diversification and asset allocation are key to maximizing potential returns while minimizing risk.
8. Most people benefit from hiring an advisor to help manage their investments because they lack the time, ability, desire, or discipline to do it on their own, or they want to ensure their family will be okay after they're gone.
9. If you hire an advisor, be sure to find a qualified fee-based fiduciary advisor who you can understand and who is an honest coach with your best interests at heart.
10. While much is wrong in the world, the good still far outweighs the bad. You can grow substantial wealth if you trust in the power of the market, invest prudently, and have faith in the bright future that lies ahead.

ABOUT THE AUTHOR

For more than two decades Adam Dawson has helped hundreds of people simplify their life and enhance their peace of mind through sound financial guidance and a disciplined approach to investing. He loves teaching how to maximize gains and minimize losses because he learned the pains of not having enough money as a child in a broken home. He is the author of *Timeless Principles of Financial Security* and the CEO of Capstone Capital Wealth Advisors, an independent registered investment advisory firm based in Henderson, Nevada.

Dawson regularly appears as a guest lecturer throughout the community and especially enjoys teaching children and teens financial literacy. He holds a bachelor's degree from Brigham Young University and the CERTIFIED FINANCIAL PLAN-NER™ certification, which requires rigorous training in every area of personal finance, including investment management, retirement planning, insurance planning, tax planning, and estate planning.

Adam lives in Henderson with his wife, Andrea, and their four children. He loves hiking, running, and cycling, and has done one triathlon. He would do more if they let him swim with a life jacket. Adam is also an accomplished singer, pianist, and composer. Maybe that explains why he has never quite been able to dunk a basketball, even though he is six foot four.

ADAM DAWSON, CFP®
CEO | PARTNER
702.433.7588
CAPSTONECAP.COM

▲ CAPSTONE
▲▲ CAPITAL
WEALTH ADVISORS

GLOSSARY

401(k) – An employer-sponsored retirement savings account with tax benefits that allows employees to contribute a certain amount from each paycheck. Employers often contribute a portion on behalf of their employees, too.

Alternatives – Essentially any investment that cannot be classified as stocks, bonds, or cash. They often carry higher risk, higher costs, and lower liquidity. Examples include real estate, commodities, collectibles, cryptocurrency, hedge funds, venture capital, and private debt. (See definitions of these terms in this glossary.)

Annuity – An investment issued by an insurance company with guarantees and tax deferral (growth isn't taxed until you make a withdrawal). They usually have high internal costs and low liquidity, meaning you must hold them for a long time to reap the benefits.

Asset – Something with monetary value, such as a stock, bond, property, or other investment.

Asset allocation – The makeup of your total investment holdings, expressed as a percentage held in each type of asset. Understanding this ratio helps ensure your investments align with your financial goals and risk tolerance.

Average annual rate of return – Since most investments do not produce the same return each year, this is an important measurement because it shows the average percentage gain or loss per year over time.

Benchmark – A group of assets chosen by financial analysts to represent a particular segment of the market, such as the Dow

Jones Industrial Average or S&P 500 index. Benchmarks are used to compare the performance of other investments.

Bid-ask spread – The difference between the buy price and sell price of a stock, bond, or other security. It is a built-in, hidden fee you pay to those who facilitate the securities transactions you make.

Bitcoin – The largest and most popular cryptocurrency. See "cryptocurrency."

Bond – An investment that allows you to loan money to a government entity or corporation in exchange for a guaranteed interest rate and return of your deposit after a certain period. Due to the guarantees, bonds typically have lower risk and lower long-term returns than stocks, but higher risk and higher returns than cash.

Bond ladder – Owning many different bonds that mature at different times.

Broker – A person or company that buys and sells stocks, bonds, and other assets on behalf of investors, typically for a transaction-based commission or fee (different from an investment advisor, who does not typically receive transaction-based compensation).

Brokerage firm – A company that facilitates trades between buyers and sellers of assets, such as stocks, bonds, and real estate.

Broker-dealer – A company that buys and sells securities (stocks, bonds, etc.) not just on behalf of its clients, but also for its own account.

Capital – Another word for money or other assets.

Capital appreciation – An increase in the value of an asset.

Capital call – The legal requirement to contribute additional money to an investment deal when the general partner calls for it, typically in real estate and private equity limited partnerships.

Capital gain or loss – The amount an asset has grown or declined in value since you bought it. Selling it less than a year after you bought it results in a short-term capital gain or loss. Waiting more than a year to sell results in a long-term capital gain or loss, typically at a lower tax rate. Until sold, they are called unrealized capital gains or losses.

Caps and floors – The maximum amount you can gain (cap) or lose (floor) over a certain period in an indexed annuity or universal life insurance policy.

Cash – Safe money that is not at risk of investment losses and can be withdrawn anytime, such as checking or savings accounts.

Cash value – The amount that can be withdrawn from a life insurance policy.

Certificate of deposit (CD) – A type of bank deposit that you agree not to withdraw for a specific period in exchange for a higher guaranteed interest rate.

CERTIFIED FINANCIAL PLANNER™ professional – Also known as CFP®, a financial advisor who has committed to always put clients' best interests first and has completed rigorous training and testing in every area of personal finance, including investment management, retirement planning, insurance planning, tax planning, and estate planning.

Chasing yield – Taking more risk than you should in an effort to attain higher returns. High-yield (junk) bonds are one example, which pay higher interest rates than high-quality bonds, but are much less likely to pay you back.

Cohesive team – An advisory team that works together in unity and open communication to support each other and provide a consistent, excellent experience for all clients, rather than each advisor on the team only serving his or her own clients separately.

Collectibles – Art, antiques, baseball cards, and anything else of value that can be collected and traded for money.

Commission – A transaction-based fee paid to an investment broker or insurance agent for recommending a particular investment or insurance product, normally calculated as a percentage of the total amount purchased or invested.

Commodities – Tangible assets such as gold, silver, crude oil, natural gas, grain, and cattle. They tend to be raw materials that are used to produce other goods.

Compound interest – When you reinvest the interest you earn, that interest earns even more interest, creating an exponential growth effect over time.

Correlation – How closely two or more assets move in a similar direction and magnitude as market conditions change. Positive or high correlation means they behave very similar to each other regardless of market conditions. Low or zero correlation means they behave very differently. Negative correlation means they behave opposite of each other. Finding investments with low or negative correlation can help smooth out the returns in a portfolio.

Credit rating – A grade given to a company or government entity, indicating its financial strength and ability to meet its obligations. Institutions with high credit ratings are safer bets than those with low ratings or no ratings.

Credit rating agency – An organization that publishes credit ratings to help investors determine the risk of investing in a particular company or government entity. The main three are Standard & Poor's (S&P), Moody's, and Fitch.

Cryptocurrency – An unregulated form of digital money that allows people to make fast, secure payments directly to each other over the internet without using any banks or central banking systems.

Death benefit – The amount a life insurance company promises to pay the listed beneficiaries when the insured person dies.

Default rate – The percentage of bond interest and principal payments that were not made on time by a bond issuer.

Derivatives – Contracts that derive their value from another asset, such as a specific stock or an index like the S&P 500. Stock options and commodities futures are examples of derivatives. They can be used to offset risk or magnify potential gains through leverage.

Dimensional Fund Advisors (DFA) – A very large investment firm that provides low-cost mutual funds, ETFs, and SMAs with a disciplined, scientific approach.

Diversify/diversification – Owning a wide variety of assets to reduce the risk of total loss that could result from focusing too much on one investment.

Dividend – Income paid by a stock, at the company's discretion, representing your share of profits earned by the company.

DIY – Do it yourself rather than hiring a professional. Unfortunately, for some people this ends up meaning "damage it yourself."

Dow Jones Industrial Average (the Dow) – An index calculated from the prices of only 30 major U.S. stocks. This is the index quoted most often in the news when discussing stock market performance, although it cannot adequately represent the performance of the thousands of publicly traded U.S. companies.

Emerging markets – Developing economies with high growth potential, such as China, Taiwan, India, South Korea, Brazil, South Africa, Saudi Arabia, and Mexico.

ETF – Exchange-traded fund, which pools deposits from many investors to purchase a collection of professionally managed securities like a mutual fund, but often more tax efficient and trades like a stock.

Expense ratio – The percentage of total assets in an investment fund that are allocated to expenses for managing and marketing the fund. Most investors are not aware of these expenses.

FAANG – Acronym for Facebook, Apple, Amazon, Netflix, and Google, used for a while to reference the hyper-growth of these five technology leaders.

Fact sheet – A short summary of the investment objectives, past performance, holdings, and expenses of an investment fund.

FDIC-insured – Bank deposit amounts that are guaranteed up to a certain limit by the Federal Deposit Insurance Corporation, an agency of the U.S. government, when a bank fails.

Fear (when it comes to investing) – Unfounded anxiety over potential losses, vulnerability to peer pressure, and a desire to keep up with the Joneses, leading to poor investment decisions.

Fee-based – Advisors who derive their income primarily or exclusively from advisory fees, typically a small percentage of total assets managed, rather than transaction-based commissions.

Fiduciary – Advisors who are legally obligated to always put their clients' best interests ahead of their own. Registered investment advisors and CFP® professionals are examples of fiduciaries.

FINRA – Financial Industry Regulatory Authority, which works under the direction of the SEC to oversee broker-dealers and their investment professionals to help ensure fair dealings with investors.

Fixed income – An investment that provides an unchanging, guaranteed interest rate for a certain period, such as bonds, Treasury bills (T-bills), and certificates of deposit (CDs).

FOMO – Fear of missing out.

Force sell – A brokerage firm's right to automatically sell investments in an account to cover margin loan balance requirements when the value of the investments held as collateral decline by too much. See "margin call."

Futures contract – An agreement to buy or sell a certain amount of a commodity at a predetermined price and future date. This can minimize the risk of price fluctuations for both buyers and sellers when a commodity needs to be purchased in the future. It can also be used to speculate on future price movements for potential gain.

General partner – The manager of a limited partnership (a type of investment) who actively runs the business and accepts personal liability for its debts and other obligations.

Greed (when it comes to investing) – Our innate desire to acquire wealth as quickly and easily as possible, which can lead to irrational, imprudent choices that harm our financial and emotional well-being when taken to extremes.

Growth stock – Ownership in a publicly traded company that is focused on reinvesting profits to grow, rather than paying dividends to shareholders.

Guaranteed lifetime withdrawal benefit – Optional feature you can add to some annuities for an extra fee, providing a certain amount of guaranteed monthly income for the rest of your life without losing the ability to withdraw additional funds (although that could reduce or eliminate future guarantees).

Hedge – An investment in something that offsets the risk associated with another asset. Hedging can reduce potential losses, but it can also minimize potential gains. Diversification, options, futures, and even cash can be used to hedge risk.

Hedge fund – An alternative investment that focuses on non-traditional assets and uses leverage, short selling, or derivatives to enhance returns or minimize risk. They are generally much more expensive, more aggressive, and less regulated than regular mutual funds.

High yield – A fixed-income investment that pays a higher interest rate than normal, usually due to higher risk.

Holdings – The specific assets included in a fund or owned by an investor.

Holistic financial planning – A financial planning process that considers your whole financial picture rather than focusing only on a specific issue.

Illustration – The projected performance of a proposed life insurance or annuity policy based on certain assumptions. An "in-force" illustration shows how an existing policy has performed so far and how it is expected to perform from this point forward.

Index – A group of assets chosen by financial analysts to represent a particular segment of the market, such as the Dow Jones Industrial Average or S&P 500 index. Indexes are used for benchmarking (measuring relative investment performance) and for building many mutual funds and ETFs.

Index funds – Mutual funds or ETFs that invest in the stocks constituting an index, such as the S&P 500.

Indexed annuity – A type of annuity whose performance is tied to the S&P 500 or another index, but subject to the drag of hidden fees, rate caps, limited participation rates, and the lack of dividends.

Interest rate – The annual percentage of your investment value paid to you from a bank, bond issuer, insurance company, or private borrower.

International stock – Ownership in a publicly traded company based outside of the U.S.

Investment advisor representative – An investment professional who works for a registered investment advisor (RIA) and provides advice to its clients.

Investment-grade bonds – Bonds that are rated AAA to BBB by a credit rating agency, also called high-quality bonds. These are safer than bonds with lower ratings.

IPO – Initial Public Offering, when a company first "goes public" and its stock first becomes available for anyone to buy.

IRA – Individual Retirement Account, designed for personal retirement savings with tax benefits, subject to annual contribution limits and various withdrawal restrictions.

Junk bond – A bond that is rated below BBB, down to D, by a credit rating agency. These are riskier than investment-grade bonds.

Large-cap stock – Ownership in a publicly traded company with a market value of more than $10 billion (current stock price times the total number of stock shares outstanding).

Leverage – Accessing the returns on a large amount of assets with a small investment through borrowed funds or derivatives. This strategy is risky because it can significantly magnify gains or losses. Placing several small down payments to buy multiple rental properties and borrowing the rest, rather than paying cash for one property, is an example of leverage. Other examples include buying stocks on margin or accessing their returns through options.

Limited partnership (LP) – A business venture that allows "limited partners" to invest passively without any duties, restricting their potential loss to the amount of their investment in the partnership. The general partner runs the business and accepts personal liability for all of its obligations.

Liquidity – How quickly you can withdraw money from an investment without hefty penalties or other negative consequences.

Margin call – When your margin loan balance exceeds the maximum percentage allowed, normally due to investment losses in your account, the brokerage firm can force you to immediately deposit additional funds or sell some of your investments to pay the loan down to an acceptable level.

Margin loan – The ability to borrow a percentage of the value of your investment account from the brokerage firm holding it, with your account serving as collateral. It is a lot like a home equity line of credit, where you only have to pay interest when you carry a balance and it can be used for anything.

Market cap weighting – Many indexes and investment funds allocate a certain percentage to each company's stock based on its size relative to all other companies included. With market cap weighting, larger companies make up a higher percentage of the total value than smaller companies.

Market capitalization (cap) – The total market value of a company, based on its current stock price multiplied by the total number of stock shares outstanding.

Market makers – Intermediaries who facilitate the trading of stocks, bonds, and other securities among investors. They are paid through the bid-ask spread, which is the difference between the buy price and the sell price of a security.

Market value adjustment – A change to the amount you will receive if you pull money out of a fixed annuity early, in addition to any surrender penalties. If interest rates have risen since the annuity started, you will receive less than otherwise expected. If interest rates have fallen, you will receive more. This helps the insurance company offset interest rate risk.

Market-linked CD (certificate of deposit) – A banking product whose interest rate varies based on the performance of an underlying asset like the S&P 500 index. It is FDIC-insured but doesn't have a guaranteed fixed rate like a normal CD. It is riskier than a normal CD and could result in not earning any interest even after holding it for many years.

Maturity date – The date you are guaranteed to receive the full amount of your initial deposit back from a bond, CD, or other fixed income investment, as well as any unpaid interest.

Mid-cap stock – Ownership in a publicly traded company with a market value between $2 billion and $10 billion (current stock price times the total number of stock shares outstanding).

Mortality and expense (M&E) fees – Annual charges in various types of annuities to cover some of the guarantees and other expenses. Fee amounts vary, but the average is around 1.25 percent of the annuity value per year.

Mortgage recast – A recalculation of the monthly payment and amortization (repayment) schedule of a mortgage after a significant change to the loan balance has occurred, without refinancing. Examples include reducing the balance with large extra payments or increasing the balance beyond an acceptable level by not paying all interest charged, as with an option-ARM mortgage.

Municipal bond (muni) – A bond issued by a state, county, city, or other government entity. Interest paid on "muni" bonds is often tax-free.

Mutual fund – A professionally managed collection of securities purchased with deposits pooled from many different investors.

NASDAQ – National Association of Securities Dealers Automated Quotations, the second-largest stock exchange in the world, behind the New York Stock Exchange. The NASDAQ Composite index is one of the most widely followed indexes. It consists of more than 3,000 stocks and is heavily weighted in technology stocks.

New York Stock Exchange – The largest stock exchange in the world, based on total market values of the companies listed on it.

Option-ARM mortgage – An adjustable-rate mortgage allowing different payment options ranging from a 15-year fixed payment to a minimum payment that doesn't even cover the full monthly interest charges.

Options – Contracts that give an investor the right (not the requirement) to buy or sell an asset at a set price by a certain date.

Calls and puts are types of options, used to offset risk or enhance returns. A call gives you the right to buy a specific stock at a certain price until the expiration date. A put gives you the right to sell it at a certain price until the expiration date.

Outperformance – When a stock, mutual fund, or other security has produced a higher return than the general market.

Par value – The amount a bond issuer promises to pay the investor on the maturity date of the bond.

Participation rate – The percentage of an underlying asset's return that the investor is credited in a market-linked CD, structured note, indexed annuity, or indexed universal life insurance policy. For example, if the underlying asset's return is 10 percent for the year and your participation rate is 60 percent, you will receive a 6 percent return for the year.

Payment for order flow – A cut of the bid-ask spread paid to brokerage firms for routing orders to specific market makers to fulfill their stock, bond, and other securities trades.

Phantom tax – If your life insurance policy terminates before you die and you borrowed more from the policy than you paid into it, you will owe taxes on the difference even if you don't have the money anymore.

Ponzi scheme – A fraudulent plan in which early investors are paid fake returns from the funds of subsequent investors, rather than from actual investment returns.

Portfolio – An assortment of assets held by an investor.

Precious metals – Gold, silver, platinum, and other rare metals collected as a store of value.

Premium – Payment to an insurance company in exchange for insurance or annuity benefits.

Principal – The amount you originally invested.

Principal protection – The amount of your initial investment that is guaranteed to be returned to you, regardless of the outcome of the investment, mainly found in banking and insurance products.

Private debt – Loaning money to a private company that is not publicly traded. These typically pay higher interest than normal bonds because they're more risky and less liquid. Your investment cannot be sold on the open market like a traditional bond.

Private equity – Purchasing stock in an established private company with the plan to sell it to a larger company or take it public in the future. These can result in higher potential returns than normal stocks because they are more risky and less liquid. Your investment cannot be sold on the open market like a publicly traded stock.

Profit – Financial gain resulting from the difference between the amount you invested, including all expenses paid, and the ending value.

Prospectus – A disclosure document explaining the details of an investment, including the objectives, strategies, past performance, costs, and risks involved, to help prospective investors make an informed decision.

Rate of return – The percentage the value of an investment increases or decreases, normally measured on an annual basis.

Rating – See "credit rating."

Real estate – Land, anything built on it, and any natural resources associated with it.

Real estate investment trust (REIT) – An entity like a mutual fund that pools deposits from many investors to purchase and manage a number of properties–usually commercial income-producing real estate.

Rebalancing – Selling some assets that have outperformed to buy more assets that have underperformed, bringing your portfolio back to its original target allocation. For example, if your stocks consistently outperform your bonds and you never sell any stocks to buy more bonds, eventually you will end up with a much riskier asset allocation than you started with.

Recast loan – See "mortgage recast."

Registered investment advisor (RIA) – A company registered with the SEC or a state securities regulator to provide investment advice and manage investment portfolios.

Retirement account – A tax-advantaged investment account intended to eventually produce retirement income, such as a 401(k), 403(b), IRA, Roth IRA, SIMPLE, SEP, profit sharing plan, pension plan, etc.

Revenue sharing – Fee income collected by most mutual funds and ETFs that is shared with brokerage firms for the privilege of being listed on their platforms. This indirectly increases costs for investors through higher expense ratios for most funds (but not all).

Rider – An optional benefit or condition added to a life insurance or annuity policy for an additional fee.

Risk – The chance that something might not turn out as you expected. (See "Taming the Beast" section of Chapter 4, which defines various types of investment risk.)

Risk tolerance – The magnitude of deviation from your expected investment outcome that you're willing to accept.

Robo-advisor – An internet-based investment platform that uses computer programming to automatically manage people's investments with little to no human involvement.

Roth IRA – Roth Individual Retirement Account, designed for personal retirement savings with tax benefits, subject to annual contribution limits and various withdrawal restrictions. The main difference from a traditional IRA is that the growth in a Roth IRA can be withdrawn tax-free under certain conditions.

Russell 3000 – An index tracking 3,000 of the largest publicly traded U.S. stocks, seeking to gauge performance of the entire U.S. stock market.

S&P 500 – One of the most popular indexes cited to represent market returns, tracking 500 of the largest publicly traded U.S. stocks, constructed by Standard & Poor's.

SEC – Securities and Exchange Commission, an agency of the U.S. government responsible for protecting investors, facilitating access to capital to help companies grow, and maintaining fair, orderly, and efficient markets.

Sector – A group of stocks sorted by industry based on their primary business activity. For example, the S&P 500 is divided into 11 sectors: Information Technology, Health Care, Financials, Consumer Discretionary, Communication Services, Industrials, Consumer Staples, Energy, Utilities, Real Estate, and Materials.

Securities – Tradable financial assets such as stocks, bonds, and options.

Securities lending – Transferring shares of stock or another security temporarily to a borrower in exchange for a fee and collateral. This facilitates short selling and hedging strategies and generates additional income for brokerage firms, fund companies, insurance companies, and investors holding the securities borrowed.

Separately managed accounts (SMAs) – Professionally managed funds like mutual funds, but the investor personally owns each security in the fund, allowing for greater customization and control over tax implications of security sales.

Sharpe ratio – The return of an investment compared to its level of risk. A high Sharpe ratio signifies a higher return than expected for the amount of risk taken, and vice-versa.

Short selling – Selling a stock that you borrowed, hoping to buy it at a lower price later to pay off the loan and profit from the difference. You can make money if the stock price falls, but you can lose a lot if the price increases.

Short-term bonds – Bonds with short maturity dates, typically one to five years. They usually have lower yields and lower risk than long-term bonds.

Small-cap stock – Ownership in a publicly traded company with a market value between $250 million and $2 billion (current stock price times the total number of stock shares outstanding).

Spread – The difference between the buy price and the sell price of a stock, bond, or other security. It can also refer to the difference between the low interest rate banks pay on savings accounts and the higher interest rate they charge borrowers to earn a profit.

Standard deviation – A measurement of the variability of returns. In other words, how much above and below the average annual return you should expect an investment to perform, and how frequently extreme returns in either direction are likely to occur. For example, stocks tend to have higher standard deviations than bonds.

Stock – Ownership in a publicly traded company. Stocks are riskier than bonds or cash because they don't have any guarantees, but they also have higher potential returns through capital appreciation and dividend income.

Structured note – A banking product similar to a market-linked CD whose performance is tied to an underlying asset such as a specific stock or index. However, they are more risky because they are not FDIC-insured and tend not to have the same principal guarantees.

Suitability rule – When a financial advisor's recommendations must be reasonably suited to a client's needs, but not necessarily in the client's best interests. Broker-dealers and other commission-driven organizations tend to be held only to a suitability standard, which is not as stringent as a fiduciary standard.

Surrender charge – A penalty for taking a withdrawal from a life insurance policy or annuity during the surrender period. The penalty typically declines each year but could be as long as 15 years.

Target allocation – The original asset allocation (percentage of each type of asset to be held in the investment portfolio) chosen based on your goals, investment time horizon, and risk tolerance.

Time horizon – How soon you expect to withdraw funds from an investment.

Treasury bill (T-bill) – An investment with a fixed interest rate guaranteed by the U.S. government with a maturity date of one year or less.

Trust deed – When you loan money to a real estate developer or investor in exchange for high interest payments, a trust deed secures your investment against the value of the property until they repay you.

Turnover ratio – The percentage of holdings in a mutual fund or ETF that have changed over a one-year period, showing the frequency of securities trades within the fund. The higher the percentage, the higher the hidden internal costs due to bid-ask spreads.

Value stock – A company whose stock price is lower than it should be based on its earnings, dividends, sales, or value of its assets, usually due to some type of distress that causes concern among investors.

Vanguard – A very large investment company that is known for its low-cost, index-based mutual funds and ETFs.

Venture capital – A form of private equity investment focused on startups and early-stage small companies with high growth potential.

Volatility – The magnitude of variability in the performance of an investment. High volatility is more risky and can result in very large gains or very large losses.

Wealth advisor – An investment advisor who specializes in providing holistic planning and wealth management services to high-net-worth individuals and families.

Wealth management – Holistic, comprehensive financial advice addressing all aspects of affluent people's lives, including investment management, retirement planning, estate planning, tax planning, insurance planning, and even business succession planning.

Yield – Generally the income received from an investment, such as bond interest or stock dividends, expressed as a percentage of the amount invested.

NOTES

INTRODUCTION

[1] Jack Caporal, "Average Retirement Savings in the U.S.: $65,000," The Motley Fool, updated June 2, 2023, www.fool.com/research/average-retirement-savings.
[2] Bob McKenzie, *The Hockey News*, 1983.
[3] Michael Jackson, "They Don't Care about Us," *HIStory: Past, Present, and Future, Book I* (New York: Epic, 1995).

CHAPTER 1: TIMING THE MARKET

[1] "S&P 500 Index—90 Year Historical Chart," Macrotrends, accessed June 20, 2023, www.macrotrends.net/2324/sp-500-historical-chart-data.
[2] In U.S. dollars. For illustrative purposes. Best performance dates represent end of period (Nov. 28, 2008, for best week; April 22, 2020, for best month). The missed best consecutive days examples assume that the hypothetical portfolio fully divested its holdings at the end of the day before the missed best consecutive days, held cash for the missed best consecutive days, and reinvested the entire portfolio in the Russell 3000 Index at the end of the missed best consecutive days. Frank Russell Company is the source and owner of the trademarks, service marks, and copyrights related to the Russell Indexes. Past performance is not a guarantee of future results. Indices are not available for direct investment. Their performance does not reflect the expenses associated with the management of an actual portfolio. Study conducted by Dimensional Fund Advisors LP, an investment advisor registered with the Securities and Exchange Commission.
[3] Based on S&P 500 returns from 2007 to 2017 with dividends reinvested.
[4] Iddo Magen, "The Dangers of Zero Gravity," Weizmann Institute of Science, February 27, 2017, davidson.weizmann.ac.il/en/online/sciencepanorama/dangers-zero-gravity.
[5] "Why a Stock Peak Isn't a Cliff," Dimensional, December 21, 2021, www.dimensional.com/us-en/insights/why-a-stock-peak-isnt-a-cliff.
[6] Brian Dolan, "Santa Claus Rally Definition," Investopedia, updated December 21, 2022, www.investopedia.com/terms/s/santaclauseffect.asp.
[7] Amanda Reaume, "Santa Claus Rally: What Is It, When Can It Occur?" Seeking Alpha, updated November 8, 2022, seekingalpha.com/article/4474942-what-is-santa-claus-rally.
[8] James Chen, "Super Bowl Indicator Definition," Investopedia, updated February 7, 2023, www.investopedia.com/terms/s/superbowlindicator.asp.

[9] Larry Swedroe, "Harry Dent and the Chamber of Poor Returns," CBS News MarketWatch, August 19, 2013, www.cbsnews.com/news/harry-dent-and-the-chamber-of-poor-returns.

[10] Kevin Stankiewicz, "Here's Our Rapid-Fire Update on all 34 Stocks in Jim Cramer's Charitable Trust Portfolio," CNBC, October 13, 2022, www.cnbc.com/2022/10/13/october-rapid-fire-update-on-all-34-stocks-in-cramers-portfolio.html.

[11] Murray Coleman, "Jim Cramer vs. S&P 500: Chasing 'Mad Money,'" Index Fund Advisors, updated November 29, 2021, www.ifa.com/articles/cramer_chasing_mad_money.

[12] Steven Goldberg, "Jim Cramer's Stock Picks Stink," Kiplinger, updated May 18, 2016, www.kiplinger.com/article/investing/t052-c007-s001-jim-cramer-s-stock-picks-stink.html.

[13] "Loss Aversion," BehavoiralEconomics.com, accessed June 20, 2023, www.behavioraleconomics.com/resources/mini-encyclopedia-of-be/loss-aversion/.

[14] Adam Shell, "Dow Ends Wild Day Down 1,175 Points, Largest Point Drop In History," *USA Today*, February 5, 2018, www.usatoday.com/story/money/2018/02/05/dow-falls-300-points-open-extending-declines-last-week/306400002/.

[15] List of largest daily changes in the Dow Jones Industrial Average," Wikipedia, accessed June 19, 2023, en.wikipedia.org/wiki/List_of_largest_daily_changes_in_the_Dow_Jones_Industrial_Average.

[16] "Dot-com Bubble," Wikipedia, accessed June 22, 2023, https://en.wikipedia.org/wiki/Dot-com_bubble.

[17] "Great Recession, Great Recovery? Trends from the Current Population Survey," Monthly Labor Review, April, 2018, https://www.bls.gov/opub/mlr/2018/article/great-recession-great-recovery.htm.

[18] Ian Webster, "Stock Market Returns Between 2000 and 2022," S&P 500 Data, accessed June 22, 2023, www.officialdata.org/us/stocks/s-p-500/2000?amount=1000000&endYear=2022. Past performance is no guarantee of future results. Indices are not available for direct investment. Their performance does not reflect the expenses associated with the management of an actual portfolio. In U.S. dollars. For illustrative purposes only.

[19] Leslie Kramer, "What Caused the Stock Market Crash of 1929 and the Great Depression?" Investopedia, updated June 14, 2023, https://www.investopedia.com/ask/answers/042115/what-caused-stock-market-crash-1929-preceded-great-depression.asp.

[20] Lizzie Wade, "From Black Death to Fatal Flu, Past Pandemics Show Why People on the Margins Suffer Most," *Science*, May 14, 2020, www.science.org/content/article/black-death-fatal-flu-past-pandemics-show-why-people-margins-suffer-most.

[21] "How Much Impact Does the President Have on Stocks?" Dimensional, November 3, 2022, www.dimensional.com/us-en/insights/how-much-impact-does-the-president-have-on-stocks. Past performance is not a guarantee of future results. Indices are not available for direct investment. Their performance does not reflect the expenses associated with the management of an actual portfolio. In US dollars. Growth of wealth shows the growth of a hypothetical investment of

$1 in the securities in the S&P 500 Index. S&P data © 2022 S&P Dow Jones Indices LLC, a division of S&P Global. All rights reserved. Data presented in the growth of wealth chart is hypothetical and assumes reinvestment of income and no transaction costs or taxes. The chart is for illustrative purposes only and is not indicative of any investment. Dimensional Fund Advisors LP is an investment advisor registered with the Securities and Exchange Commission.

[22] "Do Markets Care Who Runs Congress?" Dimensional, October 25, 2022, www.dimensional.com/us-en/insights/do-markets-care-who-runs-congress.

CHAPTER 2: PICKING STOCKS

[1] Wes Crill, "Myth-Busting with Momentum: How to Pursue the Premium," Dimensional, November 5, 2021, www.dimensional.com/us-en/insights/myth-busting-with-momentum-how-to-pursue-the-premium.

[2] Adam Hayes, "Recency (Availability) Bias," Investopedia, November 29, 2022, www.investopedia.com/recency-availability-bias-5206686.

[3] Larry Swedroe, "The Impact of Recency Bias on Equity Markets," The Evidence-Based Investor, June 25, 2021, www.evidenceinvestor.com/the-impact-of-recency-bias-on-equity-markets/.

[4] Wes Crill, "Have the Tech Giants Been DeFAANGed?" Dimensional, June 10, 2022, www.dimensional.com/us-en/insights/have-the-tech-giants-been-defaanged.

[5] "Largest American Companies by Market Capitalization," CompaniesMarketCap.com, accessed June 19, 2023, companiesmarketcap.com/usa/largest-companies-in-the-usa-by-market-cap/.

[6] "Market Capitalization of General Electric (GE)," CompaniesMarketCap.com, accessed June 19, 2023, companiesmarketcap.com/general-electric/marketcap/; "Market Capitalization of Apple (AAPL)," accessed June 19, 2023, companiesmarketcap.com/apple/marketcap/.

[7] Wes Crill, "FAANGs Gone Value," Dimensional, August 25 2022, www.dimensional.com/us-en/insights/faangs-gone-value.

[8] Maggie McGrath, "Target Profit Falls 46% on Credit Card Breach and the Hits Could Keep on Coming," *Forbes*, February 26, 2014, www.forbes.com/sites/maggiemcgrath/2014/02/26/target-profit-falls-46-on-credit-card-breach-and-says-the-hits-could-keep-on-coming/?sh=12c664c97326.

[9] "The Post-Enron 401(k)," *Forbes*, October 20, 2003, www.forbes.com/2003/10/20/cx_aw_1020retirement.html?sh=51457c4b2824; "What Enron Employees Have Lost," NPR, January 22, 2002, legacy.npr.org/news/specials/enron/employees.html.

[10] "Tesla—Stock Split History," Macrotrends, accessed June 19, 2023, www.macrotrends.net/stocks/charts/TSLA/tesla/stock-splits.

[11] James Chen, "What Is Hindsight Bias?" Investopedia, September 29, 2022, www.investopedia.com/terms/h/hindsight-bias.asp.

[12] "Fear of Flying," Anxieties.com, accessed June 19, 2023, https://anxieties.com/self-help-resources/fear-of-flying.

[13] "The Data on Day Trading," CurrentMarketValuation.com, February 21, 2023, https://www.currentmarketvaluation.com/posts/the-data-on-day-trading.php.

[14] Michael Mayhew, "Buy-Side Spending on Investment Research Expected to Fall in 2021," Integrity Research Associates, July 5, 2021, www.integrity-research.com/buy-side-spending-on-investment-research-expected-to-fall-in-2021/.

[15] Scott Powell, "Equity Research Overview," CFI, updated May 31, 2023, corporatefinanceinstitute.com/resources/career/equity-research-overview/.

[16] "Entrepreneurship and the U.S. Economy," U.S. Bureau of Labor Statistics, updated April 28, 2016, www.bls.gov/bdm/entrepreneurship/entrepreneurship.htm.

[17] Vijay Govindarajan and Anup Srivastava, "The Scary Truth About Corporate Survival," *Harvard Business Review*, December 2016, hbr.org/2016/12/the-scary-truth-about-corporate-survival.

CHAPTER 3: CHASING WHAT'S HOT

[1] "NFL History—Super Bowl Winners," ESPN, accessed June 19, 2023, www.espn.com/nfl/superbowl/history/winners.

[2] "Morgan Stanley Inst Discovery," Morningstar.com, accessed June 19, 2023, www.morningstar.com/funds/xnas/mpegx/performance.

[3] John Coumarianos, "The Best and Worst Funds of 2020," Citywire, December 22, 2020, citywire.com/pro-buyer/news/the-best-and-worst-funds-of-2020/a1442624.

[4] "NexPoint Climate Tech Y," Morningstar.com, accessed June 19, 2023, www.morningstar.com/funds/xnas/hszyx/performance.

[5] "The Fund Landscape 2022," Dimensional, www.ifa.com/pdfs/the-fund-landscape-dfa.pdf.

[6] "Dimensional vs. the Industry" as of December 31, 2022. Performance data shown represents past performance and is no guarantee of future results. The sample includes funds at the beginning of each respective period. Survivors are funds that had returns for every month in the sample period. Outperformers (winner funds) are funds that survived the sample period and whose cumulative net return over the period exceeded that of their respective benchmark. Each fund is evaluated relative to its respective primary prospectus benchmark. Where the full series of primary prospectus benchmark returns is unavailable, funds are instead evaluated relative to their Morningstar category index. Dimensional fund data provided by the fund accountant. Dimensional funds or sub-advised funds whose access is or previously was limited to certain investors are excluded. US-domiciled, USD-denominated open-end and exchange-traded fund data is provided by Morningstar. Mutual fund investment values will fluctuate, and shares, when redeemed, may be worth more or less than original cost. Diversification neither assures a profit nor guarantees against a loss in a declining market. There is no guarantee investment strategies will be successful. Past performance is no guarantee of future results. ETFs trade like stocks, fluctuate in market value, and may trade either at a premium or a discount to their net asset value. ETF shares

trade at market price and are not individually redeemable with the issuing fund, other than in large share amounts called creation units. ETFs are subject to risks similar to those of stocks, including those regarding short-selling and margin account maintenance. Brokerage commissions and expenses will reduce returns.

[7] "A Tale of Two Decades: Lessons for Long-Term Investors," Dimensional, January 2020, chapters.onefpa.org/greaterindiana/wp-content/uploads/sites/17/2020/02/Dimensional-article-February-2020.pdf. There is no guarantee investment strategies will be successful. Investing involves risks, including possible loss of principal. Investors should talk to their financial advisor prior to making any investment decision. There is always the risk that an investor may lose money. A long-term investment approach cannot guarantee a profit. Indices are not available for direct investment. Their performance does not reflect the expenses associated with the management of an actual portfolio. Past performance is not a guarantee of future results. Diversification does not eliminate the risk of market loss.

[8] "Which Country Will Outperform? Here's Why It Shouldn't Matter," Dimensional, January 17, 2023, www.dimensional.com/us-en/insights/which-country-will-outperform-heres-why-it-shouldnt-matter. In U.S. dollars. MSCI country indices (net dividends) for each country listed. Does not include Israel, which MSCI classified as an emerging market prior to May 2010.

[9] "An unprecedented 168 mutual funds returned more than 100% in 1999," Pensions&Investments, January 13, 2000, www.pionline.com/article/20000113/ONLINE/1130707/an-unprecedented-168-mutual-funds-returned-more-than-100-in-1999.

[10] Aaron Lucchetti, "Nicholas-Applegate to Lay Off Some Staff, Close Tech Fund," *The Wall Street Journal*, October 3, 2002, www.wsj.com/articles/SB1033601019201729673.

[11] "Zoom Video Communications Inc (ZM)," YCharts, accessed June 19, 2023, ycharts.com/companies/ZM/performance/price; "Apple Inc (AAPL)," YCharts, accessed June 19, 2023, ycharts.com/companies/AAPL/performance/price; "Amazon.com Inc (AMZN)," YCharts, accessed June 19, 2023, ycharts.com/companies/AMZN/performance/price.

[12] "Annual S&P Sector Performance," Novel Investor, accessed June 19, 2023, novelinvestor.com/sector-performance/.

[13] "IPOs: Profiles Are High. What About Returns?" Dimensional, August 1, 2019, www.dimensional.com/us-en/insights/ipos-profiles-are-high-what-about-returns

[14] Dominic Rushe, "Facebook IPO: Five Things That Went Wrong With the Social Network's Debut," *The Guardian*, May 24, 3012, www.theguardian.com/technology/2012/may/24/facebook-ipo-mark-zuckerberg-nasdaq.

[15] Smita Nair, "Why did Facebook's Shares Fall After Its Initial Public Offering?" Yahoo!News, January 14, 2014, news.yahoo.com/why-did-facebook-shares-fall-225006922.html.

[16] Snap Inc.," Yahoo!Finance, accessed June 20, 2023, finance.ya-hoo.com/quote/SNAP/history?period1=1488412800&period2=1514678400&interval=1d&filter=history&frequency=1d&includeAdjustedClose=true.

[17] "Snap Inc.," YCharts, accessed June 20, 2023, https://ycharts.com/companies/SNAP/performance/price

[18] "Spotify Technology - Stock Split History | SPOT," Macrotrends, accessed June 20, 2023, www.macrotrends.net/stocks/charts/SPOT/spotify-technology/stock-splits; "Spotify Technology," Yahoo!Finance, accessed June 20, 2023, finance.yahoo.com/quote/SPOT/history?period1=1522713600&period2=1671753600&interval=1d&filter=history&frequency=1d&includeAdjustedClose=true.

[19] "GameStop - Stock Split History | GME," Macrotrends, accessed June 20, 2023, www.macrotrends.net/stocks/charts/GME/gamestop/stock-splits.

[20] Alexander Jones, "GameStop: One Year Since Retail Investors Took on Wall Street," International Banker, February 23, 2022, internationalbanker.com/brokerage/gamestop-one-year-since-retail-investors-took-on-wall-street/.

[21] Adam Hayes, "What Are Meme Stocks, and Are They Real Investments?" Investopedia, September 12, 2022, www.investopedia.com/meme-stock-5206762.

[22] Leslie Kramer, "The Stock Market Crash of 1929 and the Great Depression," June 4, 2023, www.investopedia.com/ask/answers/042115/what-caused-stock-market-crash-1929-preceded-great-depression.asp.

[23] Mark Hulbert, "25 Years to Bounce Back from the 1929 Crash? Try Four-and-a-Half," *New York Times*, April 26, 2009, www.live-mint.com/Money/Oww1BVK1roWvXRUCd0VjIJ/25-years-to-bounce-back-from-the-1929-crash-Try-fouranda.html.

[24] "Stock Market Crash of 1929," Federal Reserve History, November 22, 2013, www.federalreservehistory.org/essays/stock-market-crash-of-1929; "Stock Market Crash of 1929,"Britinnanica, updated March 27, 2023, www.britannica.com/event/stock-market-crash-of-1929; A Brief History of the 1929 Stock Market Crash, April 8, 2018, www.businessinsider.com/the-stock-market-crash-of-1929-what-you-need-to-know-2018-4.

[25] "Updated Investor Bulletin: Leveraged and Inverse ETFs," U.S. Securities and Exchange Commission, February 23, 2023, www.sec.gov/investor/pubs/leveragedetfs-alert.

[26] "Status of Washington Mutual Bank Receivership," FDIC, updated October 23, 2020, www.fdic.gov/resources/resolutions/bank-failures/failed-bank-list/wamu-settlement.html.

[27] Jason Zweig, "An Iowa Farmer Tried to Dodge Stock-Market Turmoil. It Cost Him $900,000," *The Wall Street Journal*, January 13, 2023, www.wsj.com/articles/regulation-d-private-offering-debt-equity-11673625595?st=1hc5230hccalfnn&reflink=desktopwebshare_permalink.

[28] Thomas Kenny, "Historical Performance Data of High-Yield Bonds," *The Balance*, October 24, 2022, www.thebalancemoney.com/high-yield-bonds-historical-performance-data-417116.

[29] Alex Crippin, "Transcript & Video: Ask Warren Buffett on CNBC's *Squawk Box*—Part 7," CNBC, updated September 13, 2013, www.cnbc.com/2009/03/09/transcript-video-ask-warren-buffett-on-cnbcs-squawk-box-part-7.html.

30 "Buffett on Gold," Gregg Turk Foundation, accessed June 21, 2023, www.gturk.org/buffet-on-gold.

31 Matt DiLallo, "Why Warren Buffett Hates Gold," *USA Today*, September 21, 2014, www.usatoday.com/story/money/2014/09/21/why-warren-buffett-hates-gold/15909821/.

32 "Gold Prices 1792-1973," Maguire Refining, accessed June 21, 2023, www.maguireref.com/wp-content/uploads/2012/03/GoldPricesChart.pdf.

33 Mark Hulbert, "25 Years to Bounce Back from the 1929 Crash? Try Four-and-a-Half," *New York Times,* April 26 2009, www.livemint.com/Money/Oww1BVK1roWvXRUCd0VjIJ/25-years-to-bounce-back-from-the-1929-crash-Try-fouranda.html.

34 "Gold Prices—100 Year Historical Chart," Macrotrends, accessed June 21, 2023, www.macrotrends.net/1333/historical-gold-prices-100-year-chart.

35 "Price of Gold 2011," SD Bullion, accessed June 21, 2023, sdbullion.com/gold-prices-2011.

36 "Price of Gold in 2015," SD Bullion, accessed June 21, 2023, sdbullion.com/gold-prices-2015.

37 "Price of Gold in 2020," SD Bullion, accessed June 21, 2023, sdbullion.com/gold-prices-2020.

38 "Stock Market Returns Between 1980 and 2022," S&P 500 Data, accessed June 21, 2023, www.officialdata.org/us/stocks/s-p-500/1980?amount=1000000&endYear=2022.

39 "What Is the History of the S&P 500 Stock Index?" Investopedia, updated April 13, 2023, www.investopedia.com/ask/answers/041015/what-history-sp-500.asp.

40 The Royal Mint, accessed June 21, 2023, www.royalmint.com/invest/discover-more/storage-fees/.

41 Jeff Reeves, "Beware Gold's Hidden Costs," The Street, September 25, 2010, www.thestreet.com/opinion/beware-golds-hidden-costs-10871461;
Bob Frick, "7 Ways Not to Buy Gold," Kiplinger, March 2, 2011, www.kiplinger.com/article/spending/t026-c011-s001-7-ways-not-to-buy-gold.html

42 "Customer Advisory: Beware of Gold and Silver Schemes Designed to Drain Your Retirement Savings," Commodity Futures Trading Commission, accessed June 21, 2023, www.cftc.gov/LearnAndProtect/AdvisoriesAndArticles/CustomerAdvisory_COVID19PreciousMetals.htm.

43 "Silver Prices—100 Year Historical Chart," Macrotrends, accessed June 21, 2023, www.macrotrends.net/1470/historical-silver-prices-100-year-chart; "Platinum Prices—Interactive Historical Chart," Macrotrends, accessed June 21, 2023, www.macrotrends.net/2540/platinum-prices-historical-chart-data.

44 Napoleon Hill, *Think and Grow Rich* (New York: Random House, 1996), 22.

45 Les Christie, "Foreclosures up 75 percent in 2007," CNN Money, January 29, 2008, money.cnn.com/2008/01/29/real_estate/foreclosure_filings_2007/.

46 Joel Kurth and Christine MacDonald, *The Detroit News,* June 24, 2015, www.detroitnews.com/story/news/special-reports/2015/05/14/detroit-abandoned-homes-volume-terrifying/27237787/.

[47] Louis Aguilar, "Detroit's Housing Market Has Been Broken Since 2006, Study Says," BridgeDetroit, April 15, 2021, www.bridgedetroit.com/detroits-housing-market-has-been-broken-since-2006-study-says/.

[48] Adam Millsap, "What The Boom And Bust Of Williston, North Dakota Teaches Us About The Future Of Cities," *Forbes*, June 7, 2016, www.forbes.com/sites/adammillsap/2016/06/07/williston-nd-and-the-rise-and-fall-of-american-cities/?sh=3893e9c23cf3.

[49] Hannah Sparks, "Infamous Bitcoin Pizza Guy Who Squandered $365M Haul Has No Regrets," *New York Post*, May 2021, 24, ny-post.com/2021/05/24/bitcoin-pizza-guy-who-squandered-365m-has-no-regrets/;
"Bitcoin USD," Yahoo!Finance, accessed June 21, 2023, finance.ya-hoo.com/quote/BTC-USD/history/.

[50] Wayne Duggan, "The History of Bitcoin, the First Cryptocurrency," *US News & World Report*, May 10, 2023, money.usnews.com/investing/articles/the-his-tory-of-bitcoin.

[51] "What is Bitcoin?" Coinbase, accessed June 21, 2023, www.coin-base.com/learn/crypto-basics/what-is-bitcoin.

[52] Samyuktha Sriram, "Bitcoin Becomes Best Performing Asset of The Decade, Returning Ten Times More Than Nasdaq 100," Yahoo!, March 16, 2021, www.yahoo.com/video/bitcoin-becomes-best-performing-asset-132208120.html.

[53] "Bitcoin," CoinMarketCap, accessed June 21, 2023, coinmarketcap.com/cur-rencies/bitcoin/.

[54] "Bitcoin," CoinDesk, accessed June 21, 2023, www.coindesk.com/price/bitcoin/.

[55] "What Really Happened to LUNA Crypto?" Forbes Digital Assets, September 20, 2022, www.forbes.com/sites/qai/2022/09/20/what-really-happened-to-luna-crypto/?sh=1261d2a74ff1.

[56] Bill Chappell, David Gura, Lisa Lambert, "Bankman-Fried is Arrested as Feds Charge Massive Fraud at FTX Crypto Exchange," December 13, 2022, www.npr.org/2022/12/12/1142361088/bankman-fried-ceo-ftx-crypto-ex-change-arrested-bahamas-charges-sdny.

[57] Brian Nibley, "Tracking Down Lost Bitcoins and Other Cryptos," SoFi Learn, September 13, 2022, www.sofi.com/learn/content/how-to-find-lost-bitcoin/.

[58] "Securities and Exchange Commission v. Matthew Wade Beasley et al.," United States District Court, District of Nevada, accessed June 21, 2023, www.sec.gov/litigation/complaints/2022/comp25434.pdf.

[59] "J&J Purchasing: When It Sounds Too Good to Be True," Hindenburg Re-search, March 24, 2022, hindenburgresearch.com/jj-purchasing/.

[60] "Affinity Fraud: How to Avoid Investment Scams That Target Group," U.S. Securities and Exchange Commission, October 9, 2013, www.sec.gov/inves-tor/pubs/affinity.

[61] "Bernie Madoff," Britannica, updated April 25, 2023; Adam Hayes, Bernie Madoff: Who He Was, How His Ponzi Scheme Worked," Investopedia, up-dated March 29, 2023, www.investopedia.com/terms/b/bernard-madoff.asp;

Marty Steinberg and Scott Cohn, "Bernie Madoff, Mastermind of the Nation's Biggest Investment Fraud, Dies at 82," April 14, 2021, www.cnbc.com/2021/04/14/bernie-madoff-dies-mastermind-of-the-nations-biggest-investment-fraud-was-82.html

CHAPTER 4: GOING BROKE SAFELY

[1] Hilary Parker, "Physical Side Effects of Oversleeping," WebMD, January 15, 2022, www.webmd.com/sleep-disorders/physical-side-effects-oversleeping; Andrea Schmitz and Shira Polan, "What Would Happen If You Never Got Out of Bed," Business Insider, November 4, 2020, www.businessinsider.com/bed-rest-what-would-happen-body-never-got-up-2019-9.

[2] Beth Mallory, "Horse Riding Accident Statistics in 2023 (Latest U.S. Data)," HorsesOnly, updated May 17, 2023, horsesonly.com/horse-riding-accidents/.

[3] Maryalene LaPonsie, "How Living Longer Will Impact Your Retirement," *US News & World Report*, April, 22 2020, money.usnews.com/money/retirement/articles/how-living-longer-will-impact-your-retirement.

[4] Jean Eaglesham, "Wall Street Re-Engineers the CD—and Returns Suffer," *The Wall Street Journal*, September 6, 2016, www.wsj.com/articles/wall-street-re-engineers-the-cdand-returns-suffer-1473180591?reflink=desktopwebshare_permalink.

[5] www.cantella.com/regbidocs/Investors%20Guide%20to%20Structured%20Products.pdf

[6] Jim Probasco, "6 Reasons to Beware of Market-Linked CDs," Investopedia, August 21, 2021, www.investopedia.com/articles/investing/092316/6-reasons-beware-marketlinked-cds.asp; "Equity Linked CDs," U.S. Securities and Exchange Commission, updated October 12, 2006, www.sec.gov/answers/equitylinkedcds.htm.

[7] Aye Soe, "S&P 500 Dividend Aristocrats: The Importance of Stable Dividend Income," S&P Dow Jones Indices, September 23, 2021, www.spglobal.com/spdji/en/research/article/a-fundamental-look-at-sp-500-dividend-aristocrats/.

[8] Jean Eaglesham, "Wall Street Re-Engineers the CD—and Returns Suffer," *The Wall Street Journal*, September 6, 2016, www.wsj.com/articles/wall-street-re-engineers-the-cdand-returns-suffer-1473180591.

[9] "SEC, FINRA Warn Retail Investors About Investing in Structured Notes with Principal Protection," U.S. Securities and Exchange Commission, updated June 2, 2011, www.sec.gov/news/press/2011/2011-118.htm

[10] "The Complicated Risks and Rewards of Indexed Annuities," FINRA, July 14, 2022, www.finra.org/investors/insights/complicated-risks-and-rewards-indexed-annuities; "Updated Investor Bulletin: Indexed Annuities," Investor.gov, July 31, 2020, www.investor.gov/introduction-investing/general-resources/news-alerts/alerts-bulletins/investor-bulletins/updated-13.

CHAPTER 5: IGNORING COSTS

[1] "The House Edge and Its Effect," GamblingSites.com, updated April 2023, www.gamblingsites.org/casino/beginners-guide/house-edge/

[2] Mark Maremont and Alexandra Berzon, "How Often Do Gamblers Really Win?" *The Wall Street Journal*, October 11, 2013, www.wsj.com/articles/how-often-do-gamblers-really-win-1381514164.

[3] Rob Wile, "Back in The Day, Brokers Got Away with Murder In Trading Commissions," Business Insider, March 31, 2014, www.businessinsider.com/historical-trading-commissions-2014-3.

[4] John Divine, "How Robinhood Changed an Industry," *US News & World Report*, October 17, 2019, money.usnews.com/investing/investing-101/articles/how-robinhood-changed-an-industry.

[5] John Detrixhe, "Charles Schwab is cutting brokerage fees to zero, but that doesn't mean it's free," Quartz, October 1, 2019, qz.com/1719659/charles-schwabs-zero-fee-commissions-still-have-costs.

[6] Ken Little, "Understanding Bid and Ask Prices in Trading," The Balance, June 30, 2021, www.thebalancemoney.com/understanding-bid-and-ask-prices-3141317.; Akhilesh Ganti, "What Is a Bid-Ask Spread, and How Does It Work in Trading?" Investopedia, May 31, 2022, www.investopedia.com/terms/b/bid-askspread.asp.

[7] "Ally Invest," Ally, accessed June 20, 2023, www.ally.com/invest/robo-automated-investing/.

[8] Alexandra Twin, "There Ain't No Such Thing as a Free Lunch: Meaning and Examples," Investopedia, December 23, 2022, www.investopedia.com/terms/t/tanstaafl.asp.

[9] Mansoor Iqbal, "Fortnite Usage and Revenue Statistics (2023)," Business of Apps, January 9, 2023, www.businessofapps.com/data/fortnite-statistics/.

[10] Suzette Gomez, "Signs Of Gambling Addiction In Robinhood App," Addiction Center, February 2, 2021, www.addictioncenter.com/news/2021/02/gambling-addiction-robinhood-app/.

[11] "Robinhood's Slow Demise," SeekingAlpha.com, May 2, 2022, seekingalpha.com/article/4505714-robinhoods-hood-stock-slow-demise.

[12] "SEC Charges Robinhood Financial With Misleading Customers About Revenue Sources and Failing to Satisfy Duty of Best Execution," U.S. Securities and Exchange Commission, December 17, 2020, www.sec.gov/news/press-release/2020-321.

[13] Matt Egan, "Robinhood Settles Lawsuit Over 20-Year-Old Trader Who Died by Suicide," CNN Business, July 1, 2021, abc7news.com/robinhood-settles-lawsuit-alex-kearns-stocks-settlement/10851075/.

[14] George Glover, "Fewer Retail Investors Are Trading Stocks and Cryptocurrencies on Robinhood as Markets Suffer a Sell-off," Business Insider, August 3, 2022, markets.businessinsider.com/news/stocks/job-cuts-resignation-robinhood-retail-investing-stocks-cryptocurrencies-vlad-tenev-2022-8#; Annie Massa and Mathieu Benhamou, "Robinhood Gave Its Customers Access to IPOs That All Flopped," *Bloomberg*, November 8, 2022,

www.bloomberg.com/news/articles/2022-11-08/robinhood-gave-its-customers-access-to-ipos-that-all-flopped?leadSource=uverify percent20wall.

[15] Oscar Gonzalez, "Robinhood Sued for Wrongful Death After Young Trader's Suicide," CNET, February 8, 2021, www.cnet.com/tech/mobile/robinhood-sued-for-wrongful-death-after-young-traders-suicide/.

[16] "Mutual Fund and ETF Turnover Ratio," Personal Fund, accessed June 20, 2023, personalfund.com/mutual-fund-and-etf-turnover-ratio/.

[17] "Stock market returns between 2003 and 2022,"S&P 500 Data, accessed June 20, 2023, www.officialdata.org/us/stocks/s-p-500/2003?amount=1000000&endYear=2022.

[18] Pacome Breton, "Harnessing the Power of Long-Term Investing," Nutmeg, August 18, 2022, www.nutmeg.com/nutmegonomics/increasing-your-chances-of-positive-portfolio-returns-the-facts-about-long-term-investing/.

[19] "Time, Not Timing, Is What Matters," Capital Group, accessed June 20, 2023, www.capitalgroup.com/individual/planning/investing-fundamentals/time-not-timing-is-what-matters.html.

[20] Anna-Louise Jackson, "This Chart Shows the Secret to Never Losing Money in the Stock Market," May 5, 2021, money.com/stock-market-chart-rolling-returns/; "U.S. Stock Market Returns—a History from the 1870s to 2022," January 5, 2023, themeasureofaplan.com/us-stock-market-returns-1870s-to-present/.

CHAPTER 6: DISREGARDING DISCLOSURES

[1] "Securities and Exchange Commission vs. Matthew Wade Beasley et al., United States District Court, District of Nevada," June 29, 2022, www.sec.gov/litigation/complaints/2022/comp25434.pdf.

[2] "Consumer Handbook on Adjustable-Rate Mortgages," The Federal Reserve Board, accessed June 20, 2023, files.consumerfinance.gov/f/201204_CFPB_ARMs-brochure.pdf.

[3] "Countrywide Financial: The Subprime Meltdown," Center for Ethical Organizational Cultures Auburn University, accessed June 20, 2023, harbert.auburn.edu/binaries/documents/center-for-ethical-organizational-cultures/cases/countrywide.pdf.

[4] Julia Kagan, "Option Adjustable-Rate Mortgage (Option ARM)," Investopedia, October 12, 2021, www.investopedia.com/terms/o/option_arm.asp.

CHAPTER 7: HARNESSING THE POWER OF THE MARKET

[1] "Wind," Center for Science for Education, "Wind," accessed June 20, 2023, scied.ucar.edu/learning-zone/how-weather-works/wind.

[2] Ethan Shaw, "List Three Factors That Affect Wind Direction," Sciencing, November 22, 2019, sciencing.com/list-factors-affect-wind-direction-7420202.html

[3] Pacome Breton, "Harnessing the Power of Long-Term Investing," Nutmeg, August 18, 2022 www.nutmeg.com/nutmegonomics/increasing-your-chances-of-positive-portfolio-returns-the-facts-about-long-term-investing/

[4] "Largest Companies by Market Cap," accessed June 20, 2023, companies-marketcap.com/.

[5] Sean Williams, "If You Invested $10,000 In Apple for Its IPO In 1980, Here's How Much You'd Have Now," The Motley Fool, October 12, 2022, www.fool.com/investing/2022/10/12/invested-10000-in-apple-ipo-in-1980-how-much-now/;."Apple, Inc. (AAPL) Yearly Returns, 1Stock1.com, accessed June 20, 2023, www.1stock1.com/1stock1_148.htm.

[6] "The Future of Investing," Dimensional, accessed June 20, 2023, static1.squarespace.com/static/5a29de13e5dd5b5fb7021e6c/t/62870fac4a7f90402dc03313/1653018551921/us_matrix-book-2022.pdf.

[7] "Stephen R. Covey," GoodReads, accessed June 20, 2023, www.good-reads.com/quotes/7378445-think-about-taking-a-trip-on-an-airplane-before-taking.

[8] "Do Skyscrapers Sway?" Skydeck, accessed June 20, 2023, theskydeck.com/do-skyscrapers-sway/.

[9] Terry Gross, interview with Kate Ascher, "How the World's Tallest Skyscrapers Work," Fresh Air, NPR, November 7, 2011, podcast, www.npr.org/transcripts/141858484.

[10] Steven Beslic, "LeBron Has Never Posted His Career Average in a Single Regular-Season Game," Basketball Network, February 8, 2021, www.basketballnetwork.net/latest-news/lebron-has-never-posted-his-career-average-in-a-single-regular-season-game; "LeBron James," Statmuse, accessed June 20, 2023, www.stat-muse.com/nba/player/lebron-james-1780.

[11] "Stock Market Returns Between 1993 and 2022," S&P 500 Data, accessed June 20, 2023, www.officialdata.org/us/stocks/s-p-500/1993?amount=100&en-dYear=2022.

[12] "S&P 500 Total Returns," Slickcharts, accessed June 20, 2023, www.slick-charts.com/sp500/returns.

[13] Past performance is not a guarantee of future results. Indices are not available for direct investment. Their performance does not reflect the expenses associated with the management of an actual portfolio. In U.S. dollars. S&P data ©2022 S&P Dow Jones Indices LLC, a division of S&P Global. All rights reserved. Data presented is hypothetical and assumes reinvestment of income and no transaction costs or taxes.

[14] Percent of world market capitalization as of December 31, 2021. Information provided by Dimensional Fund Advisors LP. Market cap data is free-float adjusted and meets minimum liquidity and listing requirements. Dimensional makes case-by-case determinations about the suitability of investing in each emerging market, making considerations that include local market accessibility, government stability, and property rights before making investments. China A-shares that are available for foreign investors through the Hong Kong Stock Connect program are included in China. 30 percent foreign ownership limit and 25 percent inclusion factor are applied to China A-shares. For educational purposes; should not be used as investment advice. Data provided by Bloomberg.

Diversification neither assures a profit nor guarantees against loss in a declining market.

[15] "Dimensional vs. the Industry" as of December 31, 2022. Performance data shown represents past performance and is no guarantee of future results. The sample includes funds at the beginning of each respective period. Survivors are funds that had returns for every month in the sample period. Outperformers (winner funds) are funds that survived the sample period and whose cumulative net return over the period exceeded that of their respective benchmark. Each fund is evaluated relative to its respective primary prospectus benchmark. Where the full series of primary prospectus benchmark returns is unavailable, funds are instead evaluated relative to their Morningstar category index. Dimensional fund data provided by the fund accountant. Dimensional funds or sub-advised funds whose access is or previously was limited to certain investors are excluded. US-domiciled, USD-denominated open-end and exchange-traded fund data is provided by Morningstar. Mutual fund investment values will fluctuate, and shares, when redeemed, may be worth more or less than original cost. Diversification neither assures a profit nor guarantees against a loss in a declining market. There is no guarantee investment strategies will be successful. Past performance is no guarantee of future results. ETFs trade like stocks, fluctuate in market value, and may trade either at a premium or a discount to their net asset value. ETF shares trade at market price and are not individually redeemable with the issuing fund, other than in large share amounts called creation units. ETFs are subject to risks similar to those of stocks, including those regarding short-selling and margin account maintenance. Brokerage commissions and expenses will reduce returns.

[16] Aditya Rayaprolu, "How Much Data Is Created Every Day in 2023?" Techjury, updated February 27, 2023, techjury.net/blog/how-much-data-is-created-every-day/#gref.

[17] Review of *Simple Wealth, Inevitable Wealth*, Novel Investor, accessed June 20, 2023, novelinvestor.com/notes/simple-wealth-inevitable-wealth-by-nick-murray/.

[18] Ronald Bailey and Marian L. Tupy, *Ten Global Trends Every Smart Person Should Know, And Many Others You Will Find Interesting* (Washington, D.C.: Cato Institute, 2020).

[19] Avinash, "Everything Is Amazing and Nobody is Happy: Louis C.K.," The Educationist, July 14, 2014, www.theeducationist.info/everything-amazing-nobody-happy/.

[20] Hans Rosling, *Factfulness: Ten Reasons We're Wrong About the World—and Why Things Are Better Than You Think* (New York: Flatiron Books, 2018), 69.

CAPSTONE
CAPITAL
WEALTH ADVISORS

702.433.7588
capstonecap.com

SCAN ME

www.ingramcontent.com/pod-product-compliance
Lightning Source LLC
Chambersburg PA
CBHW071535200326

41519CB00021BB/6495